THE
CHILTERN
RAILWAYS
STORY

Birmingham-bound Chiltern Clubman passing King's Sutton. (Chiltern Railways)

THE
CHILTERN
RAILWAYS
STORY

HUGH JONES

The
History
Press

Chiltern Railways

For my grandchildren

First published 2010

The History Press
The Mill, Brimscombe Port
Stroud, Gloucestershire, GL5 2QG
www.thehistorypress.co.uk

British Library Cataloguing in Publication Data.
A catalogue record for this book is available from the British Library.

ISBN 978 0 7524 5454 2

Typesetting and origination by The History Press
Printed in Great Britain
Manufacturing managed by Jellyfish Print Solutions Ltd

CONTENTS

FOREWORD

John Nelson, former Managing Director, British Railways, Network SouthEast

Chiltern Railways have played an important part in my life. I was chairman of the company when it was being prepared for privatisation and served as a non-executive director of the holding company for nearly ten years from 1998. Much earlier than that, as a young child growing up in the 1950s, I was a frequent traveller from my home town of Wendover, a family connection with the railway that was to continue when my parents later moved to Gerrards Cross. I was myself a Marylebone commuter at a time when the line's very existence was threatened. How long ago that seems now.

Chiltern Railways has become a symbol of all that has been good about privatisation. Innovative in just about every aspect of its activity, the company has enjoyed more or less continuous double-digit annual growth since its inception. In the early days of privatisation, when other companies were unwilling to risk investment without guarantees of an extended franchise, Adrian Shooter and his team took the opposite view. The confidence they showed in the business and in their own ability to make things happen was not misplaced. With it came the award of a twenty-year franchise, done with the promise of further substantial investment, a role model for what could and should be more widely applied.

Above all Chiltern's success has been built on an overriding belief in the importance of meeting the needs of its customers and on the ability of a generally young and energetic management team, wisely led, that knows how to get things done. They value all of the people who work within the company and in turn the company's staff have enormous pride in what they do. There is an identification with passengers that extends way beyond the company's platforms and car parks to the community as a whole.

That Chiltern Railways has succeeded is beyond doubt. The company has regularly topped the popularity poll amongst the franchised train companies and shows every sign of being able to keep up the same impetus in the more uncertain days heralded by the current recession.

This book tells the story of Chiltern Railways. It is a story that deserves to be told and is one from which many can learn.

John Nelson, October 2009

INTRODUCTION

This is a heartening story about a team of ordinary people who were prepared to take a risk in pursuit of a vision they all shared. They faced many serious challenges from all directions and there were times when only sheer determination kept them going, but in the end they succeeded in doing something quite extraordinary.

Because this is a team story, early in writing it I felt it essential for the team to have the chance to tell their own stories (and good stories they are too), hence Part 2 'Other Voices'.

In writing and editing this story I have done my best to avoid the obvious twin dangers of allowing it to become either a polemical argument for or against rail privatisation, or an Adrian Shooter hagiography. I have done my best to simply tell the story as it is and I am content for the readers to draw their own conclusions. Of course there are important lessons with national relevance, but many are so obvious no intelligent person needs me to re-emphasise them. One thing that endears Chiltern to their passengers is their honesty when they get things wrong, and this has carried through into the freedom Adrian Shooter and his team have given me to write a 'warts and all' narrative. I believe this to be a strength.

The Chiltern story goes back some years before rail privatisation and Adrian Shooter is the first to acknowledge his debt to the likes of Chris Green, Richard Fearn and John Nelson. Happily, they are still around and their own voices are heard in Part 2.

Writing the story has been a fascinating challenge. The start of Chiltern coincided with my retirement and it was doing one or two minor pieces of work for Chiltern that made me realise there was a fascinating human-interest story here well worth the telling. Apart from anything else the interest and enthusiasm of the Chiltern people themselves was infectious. Because it has been such a team effort, I felt it appropriate that 50 per cent of all royalties should go to the Railway Children charity.

Hugh Jones, May 2010

ACKNOWLEDGEMENTS

The principal acknowledgement must go to Adrian Shooter and all the staff of Chiltern Railways; it is their story and they have allowed me to record it as it happened. Moreover, many of them have given generously of their time to help me get an accurate record of the story, even when they had more pressing things on their minds! Particular thanks go to Lesley Knight for facilitating so many meetings, and Mark Beckett and his successor Graham Cross for their assistance with archive material. Also Allan Dare for his maps; Engineering Director Kate Marjoribanks for arranging access to the Aylesbury depot; Paul McCarthy, manager of Wembley depot, and his colleague Lionel Smith both for showing me around as well as their memories of the old Marylebone depot; Ian Baxter for his help with photographs and Richard Harper for his assistance in proofreading and digging out archive material.

Sincere thanks as well to all those who allowed me to interview them; most of their voices can be heard in Part 2. Editing the book was very difficult and I have done my best not to spoil their contributions.

For technical help with photography as well as learning to love my computer, I must express my gratitude to Katheryn West and Mike Carwithen of Photo Finish, Banbury; James Blake of Hub Computers, Banbury; Mike Mensing of Fareham, Hampshire, for his help with photos of the Chiltern line in steam days; friends John Leslie and George Ware for help with my computer; Cyril Ayden for advice with techniques of indexing and former journalist Peter Braithwaite for advice on editing my material when bringing the story up to date. Also to my friend Alan Donaldson who has read the book in proof.

There are two people, however, whose constant encouragement, support and practical advice over the years, from the very start when we all recognised that it was a story worth the telling, has kept me going. They are retired Birmingham journalist and first chairman of Solihull and Leamington Spa Rail Users Association, Keith Gascoigne, and Alex Turner, Chiltern's first director of marketing and sales.

I am also very indebted to Amy Rigg and the staff at The History Press for their advice, guidance and encouragement, as well as all the extra work my sudden serious illness created for them during the final stages of preparation.

I must also acknowledge the contribution from my wife Rosemary for her incisive advice on my writing, her patience with all those boxes of papers cluttering the landing, and above all for her generous hospitality to all those hapless interviewees who have been persuaded over the years to beat a path to our front door!

To all these and many others, a very big thank you!

Hugh Jones

STATUE OF THE UNKNOWN NAVVY AT GERRARDS CROSS STATION

Can you hear me,
can you see
Don't you hear me
don't you see

We worked, how we worked like
the devil for our pay
through the wind, through the snow,
through the rain

Blasting, cutting through God's country like a knife
sweat stinging my eyes, there has to be a better life

Ah but I can hear my children's cry

Original lyrics by Phil Collins and Genesis, reproduced here by kind permission of Music Sales Ltd, London. Genesis was one of the contributing sponsors for the statue.

50 per cent of royalties from sales of this book will be donated to the Railway Children Charity.

Railway Children

Railway Children is a charity that exists to help vulnerable children in grave circumstances and in particular those living on the streets. Since 1995, Railway Children has helped thousands of children and young people living alone and at risk on the streets in the UK, India and East Africa.

For these children, the streets are often the only means of support available but also where they suffer abuse and exploitation. We believe that early intervention is crucial to preventing children living on the streets coming to harm. Our aim is to reach children on the streets before an abuser does.

PART I

The Victorian Navvy.

CHAPTER 1

'ANY REASON FOR DELAY?'

For Chiltern Railways, Thursday 30 June 2005 started much like any other day. Rain showers were forecast, unusually for what had been a drier than average month. Nevertheless, trains ran with their accustomed reliability and punctuality which over the previous decade had endeared this relatively small company to its customers.

Rob Brighouse and his family had a barbecue planned that evening for friends and family. Rob, a civil engineer by profession with overseas experience in Hong Kong, was at that time a project director with Chiltern Railways. Brighouse's particular responsibilities at that time included monitoring a number of projects that were part of Chiltern's 'Evergreen 2' development, including the new maintenance depot at Wembley as well as a 'watching brief' on behalf of Chiltern for the new joint Tesco–Network Rail project to construct a tunnel over the main running lines at Gerrards Cross. The concept was that, by building a concrete tunnel first and then filling in the surrounding cutting, a base would be created upon which Tesco planned to build a superstore and car park.

Brighouse managed to get home on time and, despite the threat of showers, friends had gathered, meat sizzled, corks popped and conversation was warming up. A delightful summer evening promised, until the telephone rang.

A few miles away, train driver Dan Gregory was bringing the 17:40 service from Stratford on Avon to Marylebone into Gerrards Cross. The time was about 19:30. Gregory had relieved another Banbury driver, Paul Wright, at Banbury and although the Class 168 Clubman was running well by High Wycombe he was just a couple of minutes down on the schedule. On a semi-fast service such as this with many stops, keeping time was always going to be difficult, but with a non-stop run ahead after Gerrards Cross an 'on time' arrival at Marylebone was still achievable.

Gregory noticed it had started to rain as the train slowed for the platform. Looking ahead through the new tunnel under construction he saw what appeared to be dust. This was not unusual as it was a building site. The fluorescent tube lighting inside the tunnel was on; Gregory stopped the train, released the doors and carried out his normal platform duties.

Keen to make a brisk departure, Gregory checked the 'up starter' signal at the platform end, closed the doors and peered back along the length of the train to check that the orange lights along the roof-edge cantrail were out, indicating that all the doors were secure. Gregory then re-checked the signal and applied power to all the under-floor engines. As he sat down he saw a large cloud of dust coming out of the tunnel, lights flickering and disappearing. As the train accelerated into the artificial gloom Gregory suddenly realised that the tunnel was collapsing in front of him and he immediately applied the emergency brake to try and prevent hitting the falling debris. Luckily, the train had not moved very far down the track and still managed to stop just short of the signal, still showing green, indicating that despite the debris ahead, the track circuits were still intact. Gregory's immediate thought was 'what is coming the other way?' He knew a train from Marylebone would be due shortly, heading into the tunnel from the opposite direction.

Gregory pressed the emergency button on the Cab Secure radio and spoke instantly to the duty signaller at Marylebone, sharply getting across the message that the tunnel had collapsed.

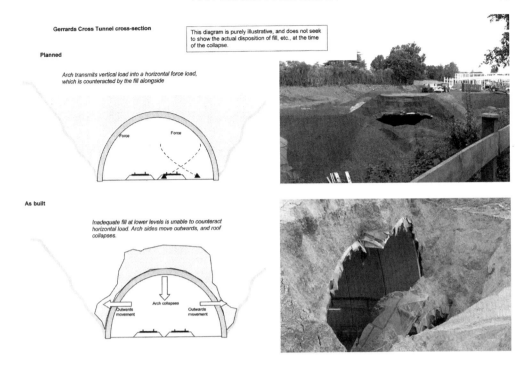

Gerrards Cross Tunnel cross-section

This diagram is purely illustrative, and does not seek to show the actual disposition of fill, etc., at the time of the collapse.

Planned

Arch transmits vertical load into a horizontal force load, which is counteracted by the fill alongside

Force   Force

As built

Inadequate fill at lower levels is unable to counteract horizontal load. Arch sides move outwards, and roof collapses.

Outwards movement   Arch collapses   Outwards movement

The signaller repeated it back to Gregory then hung up. Gregory's next reaction was to protect the adjoining 'down' (northbound) line by placing on it track-circuit clips. This action put the protecting signal to red on the other line. The next emergency procedure would have been to reinforce the protection on the 'down' line by placing emergency detonators but clearly this was no longer an option as it would have meant going through the collapsing tunnel. Gregory went forward on the platform and spoke to the signalman again on signal post telephone ME116, informing the latter that track-circuit clips had been placed and asking if detonators would also be required? If so, how was he supposed to get through the tunnel? The signalman assured him detonators would not be required in the circumstances as – thanks to Gregory's previous prompt message – he had placed a stop order on all trains. Relieved, Gregory then made an announcement to the passengers alerting them that they would not be proceeding as there was a problem with the tunnel ahead. Remembering there was a revenue protection inspector in the rear cab he called him to come forward, 'You won't see this every day!' Then he spoke to the signalman again requesting permission to reverse back into the platform so that passengers could leave and await the now required alternative transport, many taking photographs as they headed for the exit.

Simultaneously with the events taking place in the tunnel, at 19:35 a security guard in the site office complex heard a loud rumble and went out to investigate. To his horror he saw a section of the tunnel had collapsed and telephoned Project Manager Stephan Christian. Christian immediately came on site; he noted Driver Gregory at that moment telephoning from signal ME116.

The emergency services responded very quickly and were on the scene within about five minutes and were able to establish that, fortunately, no one was trapped inside the tunnel.

Back at the Brighouse barbecue at Haddenham the telephone rang and was promptly answered by Alice, Rob Brighouse's twelve-year-old daughter, who brought it to her father. 'Tell them I'll call back later', was Rob's natural response. Alice looked thoughtful for a moment. 'Dad, it sounded urgent', she observed presciently.

Once Brighouse got the message he dashed for the car and made for the site as quickly as possible. As he drove his mind was obsessed by the worry that a train with passengers may have been trapped under the debris. On arrival and greeted by the news that no one had been hurt, he quickly communicated his relief and an initial appraisal of the situation to Company Chairman Adrian Shooter. Brighouse then walked up onto the top of the tunnel and was shocked at what he saw. Clearly, the prompt action taken by Driver Gregory had averted a major disaster. Shooter then mobilised the operational train planning team who worked overnight to construct an emergency timetable for services the following day.

Many of the citizens of Gerrards Cross had long opposed Tesco's plans to build a superstore in their town. Their local press had undertaken surveys of local opinion that showed up to 80 per cent of those asked opposed the plans. Early on Friday morning, Brighouse made his way to survey the collapse in daylight. As he returned from the site he was accosted by an elderly lady waving a walking stick and exclaiming 'best thing that could have happened!' Fortunately, the following day being a Friday and with a weekend ahead, Brighouse, Shooter and colleagues were able to contact Beatrice Paul at nearby Denham airfield whose generous co-operation allowed them to construct a temporary 400-space Park and Ride car park in time for Monday morning. A shuttle service then operated between Denham and Marylebone while a through service between Birmingham and Marylebone operated at hourly intervals, reversing at Princes Risborough and Aylesbury and reaching the capital along the original Great Central main line via Aylesbury.

One week later, on 7 July, London was in a state of emergency following the bombings and Chiltern's shuttle from Marylebone to Denham was the only train service operating in the immediate aftermath. The following week, on 14 July, there was a major chemical fire adjacent to the railway at Wembley that again temporarily closed the line.

Subsequent investigations and the official report by White Young Green Rail for Jackson Civil Engineering Ltd, commissioned to address the issues required to seek formal approval for the re-opening of the tunnel for rail traffic, showed that the basic design for the tunnel was sound, but that errors had occurred in the tipping of the spoil and rubble in-fill around the concrete tunnel structure. The TechSpan construction manual states that 'under no circumstances shall the differential level of backfill between opposite sides exceed 0.5m'. Unfortunately, to meet a requirement to maintain access to the east (i.e. London end) portal, the fill material had not been built up to the level specified, while at the same time fill continued to be placed and compacted over the tunnel arch leading to an overload of material on the arch units (see photograph).

The tunnel was built using the TechSpan segmental pre-cast arch system. The three-pin arch system consists of two half units per span, with a specially shaped crown joint including a stainless steel facing to facilitate construction. The units are staggered such that they butt together at the crown and are self-supporting once erected; each unit will support the opposite half of the next unit to be placed. This was not a tunnel in the conventional sense of a small clearance to the train profile, but rather a 'covered way' with a clear span of 20m and a typical clearance to the tracks of 8.5m in order to accommodate future electrification, four tracking, gauge enhancement and speed improvement.

Post-collapse, after careful safety investigation, the damaged sections were carefully removed. Seven weeks and two days after the collapse, several technical reports and much local interest later, the tunnel re-opened and normal services resumed.

In retrospect, how did Chiltern's customers feel they had coped? Afterwards, passenger surveys were carried out both by Chiltern Railways themselves and also Passenger Focus (the Government replacement for the old Rail Passenger Committees) in partnership with Transport for London.

Both recorded the highest praise for the Chiltern staff, who were commended for their politeness and availability, and the level of information given by them. The three areas of lowest satisfaction were the journey times in the replacement timetable, the frequency of trains in the replacement timetable and the levels of information available from radio and television. Passengers were also critical of the compensation scheme offered by Chiltern and the availability of alternative car parking. Overall, 49 per cent of responders expressed themselves as very or fairly satisfied, 19 per cent impartial and 17 per cent fairly or very dissatisfied; 15 per cent did not answer.

At the time of the tunnel collapse, Graham Cross was Chiltern's business development manager. His memories of that period remain very vivid. He first heard that there had been an incident on national television at home that evening, but it was not until he arrived at Marylebone next morning for work that he learned the full extent of the tunnel collapse and the implications for services. He spent virtually the whole of that day on the concourse along with other senior managers handing out the hastily put together information, diverting passengers and helping organise replacement bus services. He remembers one young woman in tears because she was not going to be able to reach Bicester before the end of visiting time at the local prison where she had arranged to meet her boyfriend. The only plus side was that no one had been killed or injured.

It quickly became apparent that many passengers were avoiding the replacement buses and choosing instead to drive to an alternative railway station. Acting as quickly as possible, Chiltern had arranged the emergency car park at Denham airfield and also produced an 'improved' temporary timetable which was due to be launched a week later on 7 July, the day of the London bombings. Cross found that particular day very disturbing. All Underground services were suspended and Marylebone was the only main-line station in London that remained open, and that was only for the shuttle service to Denham. The Amersham line was closed most of the day. Cross again spent most of that day on the concourse and remembers well how edgy it felt. He wondered if this was how people had felt in 1940. He and his colleagues also felt they had let down their passengers. The whole atmosphere was quite scary and the weather was very hot.

The effect on Chiltern's business was profound. Cash flow plummeted as regular commuters found alternative – and in some cases cheaper – options. Some switched to Silverlink services on the West Coast Main Line (WCML) while others chose First Great Western.

When Chiltern claimed compensation from Tesco the 7/7 London bombings made the case more difficult, the defendant's lawyers claiming that that, and not their tunnel, was the prime cause of Chiltern's financial loss. The legal process was long and difficult and dragged on well into 2006.

The effects on Chiltern's finances were catastrophic. In many cases ticket sales continued to decline after the tunnel was re-opened and eleven months later, by May 2006, had dropped back to the levels of 2002. This was especially the case with sales at the stations between Denham and Princes Risborough that traditionally provide much of the core of Chiltern's business (High Wycombe being Chiltern's busiest station outside London) and are known as the Heartlands.

At this time Chiltern's managing director was Cath Proctor. Apart from being one of the youngest managing directors of any railway company, Cath was now faced with the biggest challenge in Chiltern's history. Very quickly she had to put together and implement an effective recovery plan before costs permanently outran income. Already her regular briefings to passengers during the time of the tunnel shut down had earned plaudits from both passengers and those subsequently running the inquiry. Having carefully analysed all the factors, Proctor put a briefing paper together for all staff which was delivered in May 2006. One of Proctor's opening paragraphs put the situation starkly and succinctly:

When the line re-opened on 20 August after 7 weeks of closure, passenger numbers initially built back at a fair rate. But around Christmas time, we began to notice that the recovery in passenger numbers had ground to a halt. Since then we have seen several periods of very disappointing passenger revenue results; some periods have been flat, relative to the same period last year, and others have actually shown shrinkage. This is very serious, because the business relies upon growing passenger numbers to increase the amount of farebox revenue we take which helps pay for our investments and compensate for the reducing level of subsidy we receive each year from the Government. Put simply, if our revenues fall below our costs, we will stop making profits. Without profits, we cannot invest and improve, and our business will become unsustainable… We cannot afford to carry on as we are. What is certain is that there will be change ahead. In developing plans to modernise and regain advantage over our competitors, some job functions will change size and shape, and for some of you, that may be hard. But I, Adrian [Shooter], and our [then] owners John Laing plc, are certain that the wrong thing to do is to sit back and do nothing but watch the company decline. What we have to do – all of us – is to focus our efforts behind recovery plans, to ensure that in a year or two from now, we are back where we should be, amongst the very best of the UK's train operators.

Where had all the passengers gone, and why? Proctor's analysis of ticket sales by other neighbour-ing operators showed that full fare and season ticket sales from, for example, Maidenhead on the Great Western line into Paddington, close to Beaconsfield, and both Coventry and Birmingham International on the WCML, both of which compete with Warwick Parkway for London traffic, had increased very steeply following the tunnel collapse. There were two main reasons for this: Chiltern passengers, forced to seek other routes, found that the alternatives were in many cases now offering a product as attractive if not better than Chiltern, thanks to new rolling stock and infra-structure improvements such as the WCML upgrade. Remember, when Chiltern started in 1995 it had had a flying start thanks to BR's Total Route Modernisation with new track, trains and signal-ling, conceived and orchestrated by Chris Green and Richard Fearn. Now, some of those forced to use the lines of Chiltern's competitors found – certainly in the case of the WCML – a vastly improved service with brand new, comfortable rolling stock and punctuality averages that were steadily closing the gap on Chiltern's record. By contrast, Chiltern's rolling stock was, in many cases, now the oldest and starting to look decidedly dated and worn. In all previous years, the annual year on year increases in Chiltern's ticket sales had grown more quickly than the industry average; now the situation was reversed. Recovery was going to be tough.

In considering the overall finances of railway companies, it is important to bear in mind that it is an industry where approximately two thirds of the costs are fixed, in the form of track charges, roll-ing stock charges, fuel and the costs of staff. The essence of Proctor's recovery plan was to restore the company to a profitable basis by recovering previous levels of passenger growth while at the same time maintaining a safe, reliable and welcoming railway and containing costs. In order to achieve that, Chiltern set about simplifying its fare structure and using smart cards, Chiltern being the first National Rail TOC to routinely accept Oyster cards. With the autumn 2006 timetable, which coincided with the completion of infrastructure works known as Evergreen 2, the opportunity was taken to improve competitiveness by speeding up some of the West Midlands services. Also, it was acknowledged that the long-vaunted Chiltern Class 168 Clubmans were starting to look tired. They were now to be gradually put through total refurbishment. Finally, Proctor reminded all her colleagues of one of the key things that Chiltern's passengers had long appreciated which was the company's attention to detail with regard to such matters as train cleanliness, rectifying things that didn't work properly and passenger information.

The results? Team Chiltern responded very positively and by the autumn of 2006 sales figures were starting to achieve their pre-tunnel gradient. However, the management team by now was feeling somewhat exhausted, not least because many were also involved in the legal battles with Tesco over compensation. One of them said it showed that it was possible to recover from a sticky situation even if at the time the task had looked impossible, provided one constantly concentrated on all aspects of the product.

The compensation case was eventually settled out of court for an undisclosed sum, and in February 2009 it was announced that Network Rail had given design approval for the rebuilding of the tunnel.

And Driver Gregory? He remembered feeling physically nauseous in the immediate aftermath of the tunnel collapse. He was very conscious that had his train been running two minutes earlier, according to schedule, he and his passengers could well have been in the tunnel when it came down. The next morning he drove to Banbury to sign on. Although he would not be driving, he knew there would be reports to write. As he entered the offices he found it jammed full of his colleagues who presented him with a hard hat with 'TESCO' taped to it, a large tube of industrial strength glue and a copy of the official delay form which asked 'Can you recall any reason for the loss of time departing Gerrards Cross yesterday?'

CHAPTER 2

THE BEGINNINGS

For the twelve months leading up to midnight on 31 March 1995, Chiltern Railways had been operating in a hybrid state as a separate train operating unit (TOU) owned by British Railways. From 1 April, it became a distinct train operating company (TOC), a separate legal entity, though still owned by British Railways. This new company was led by Adrian Shooter who, with his team, was in the anomalous position of having to build up and run 'their' new railway company sufficiently successfully to attract a new private owner in twelve months' time, while directly competing with their own bid for a management buy-out (MBO).

The new Chiltern 'network' was relatively small and mostly made up of bits and pieces of outer London commuter routes north of the Thames, including the Aylesbury to London Marylebone line which was the only surviving passenger-carrying section of the original Great Central main line opened in 1899 to Manchester and the north, sharing tracks with London Transport's Metropolitan line out as far as Amersham.

Even when originally opened, Marylebone station itself had always been a calm, quiet place by comparison with other London main-line termini. The clergyman Ronald Knox once described it as the only London station where one could hear birdsong and there is the story of the London GP who, when advising one of his patients to go somewhere quiet to convalesce, added 'you might try Marylebone station!' Opposite is the impressive Great Central Hotel, back in 1995 the the headquarters of British Rail. It is still remembered by some who served in the Second World War as the London District Assembly Centre – a temporary billet and last look at a blitzed London for many young officers awaiting transport to an overseas posting.

Chiltern's other route reached Banbury by swinging west at Neasden and then swinging north again at Northolt Junction joining the former Great Western main line from Paddington to the West Midlands and Merseyside. It was part of the thinking behind rail privatisation that the Chiltern route should once again provide an alternative route to the Euston line between London and Birmingham, restoring the situation to that of before the 1960s when the Great Western had competed extremely successfully with London, Midland and Scottish (successor to the London and North Western) for the traffic between England's two largest centres of population. This was echoed in a thoughtful Bow Group paper examining overall railway strategy by David Campbell Bannerman in March 1993.

The Great Western Railway had reached Birmingham in 1852 and Wolverhampton in 1854 via an extension to their Oxford branch which had turned northwards from the main line to Bristol and South Wales at Didcot, headed to Oxford then still further northwards following the Cherwell Valley, reaching Banbury by 1850, then onwards via a gap shared with the Oxford canal through the ironstone escarpment that stretches from Edge Hill into the Northampton Uplands and so on to Leamington Spa, Warwick and Birmingham Snow Hill. At an earlier point in the story the Great Western had even considered reaching Birmingham over London and North Western Railway (LNWR) metals, presumably running into that company's Curzon Street station, via a link from Banbury to Rugby; long abandoned earthworks north of Banbury being still

visible today. Not for nothing was the mid-Victorian GWR known as the 'Great Way Round.'
The fascinating but very litigious and complex story of the Great Western's struggle with its rival
to reach Birmingham is described in detail in both McDermott's classic *History of the Great Western
Railway*; Rex Christiansen's Vol. 7 in the *Regional History of the Railways of Great Britain* series,
David and Charles, 1973; and John R. Kellett's *The Impact of Railways on Victorian Cities*, Routledge
and Kegan Paul, 1969.

If the Great Western's original (broad gauge) line almost described two sides of a right-angled
triangle to reach the West Midlands, the route of their chief rival, the LNWR, described the
hypotenuse to that triangle thanks to the shorter and more direct route from London Euston to
Birmingham New Street chosen by its original builder, Robert Stephenson. Despite this, by 1870
the broad gauge GWR had achieved a creditable two-hour and twenty-minute timing between
London and Birmingham (by comparison, in 1984 British Rail Inter-City allowed two hours and
thirty-eight minutes over the same route with diesel traction).

By the end of the nineteenth century, inter-company rivalry was even more intense and the
GW was seeking further ways to shorten journey times. At the same time the Great Central
Railway, which reached the capital somewhat late in the day (1899), was also meeting strong competition from long-established rivals, and found that the increasingly congested tracks they shared
with the Metropolitan Railway between Quainton Road some miles north of Aylesbury and their
new terminus at Marylebone inhibited further development. In addition to any technical factors,
personal animosity between the general managers of both companies culminated on 25 July 1898
in the Metropolitan's John Bell personally setting the signal at Quainton Road to danger to prevent the passage of a southbound Great Central coal train.

This outburst of petulant behaviour, far from resolving any problems, simply provoked the Great
Central into joining forces with the Great Western to construct a new line from Marylebone that
avoided the Metropolitan line altogether. From the perspective of John Bell and the Metropolitan,
it was a classic case of shooting oneself in the foot!

A few weeks after the above incident, the Great Western and Great Central joined forces to
build what is referred to still as the 'Joint Line'. This correctly describes the line between Northolt
Junction/South Ruislip to Ashendon Junction a few miles north of the present-day Haddenham
and Thame station. The line was built in three sections, although not always in chronological
sequence. In 1903 the Great Western built a new line from Old Oak Common to Northolt/South
Ruislip. This was the first stage of their Acton to Wycombe link authorised by a Parliamentary Bill
in 1897. At Northolt it connected with the new Great Central link from that company's main line
at Neasden. This line, opened for goods traffic in November 1905 and passengers in April 1906,
ran via Wembley and Sudbury and Harrow Road and is now part of Chiltern's main line from
Birmingham to Marylebone. At Wembley, in a fit of Edwardian eccentricity, approximately on
the same spot where now stands the stadium, the Great Central chairman, Sir Edward Watkin had
begun to build something approaching a replica of the Eiffel Tower. The project ran out of money
and never rose above its first stage.

Starting in 1901 the two companies built the second section, a new jointly owned double-
track main line from Northolt Junction to High Wycombe, where it met the existing single-track
Maidenhead, Wycombe, Thame and Oxford branch, and on to Princes Risborough following the
route of the existing single-track Wycombe Railway to Princes Risborough. Double track was
created by building a new 'up' line and improving the alignment of the original single line. The
building of the line between Northolt to Wycombe was marred by a roof fall in the White House
Farm tunnel north of Beaconsfield that killed six workmen in 1902. Their names are commemo-
rated on a memorial in High Wycombe cemetery.

At High Wycombe the joint company built a new station with staggered platforms, four through
lines and a massive retaining wall requiring 1.5 million Staffordshire blue engineering bricks.
Princes Risborough station was also rebuilt with four through lines, plus bays for the Watlington
and Aylesbury branches, and on to Ashendon Junction where the Joint Line officially ended and
the Great Central built the five and three-quarter miles from there to re-join their existing main
line at Grendon Underwood about two and three-quarter miles north of Quainton Road.

From Ashendon Junction, where the earthworks of the original flyover are still visible, the Great Western carried straight on for Bicester and a junction with their original 1850 route from Didcot and Oxford at Aynho Junction just south of Banbury. En route the Great Western also built a long-vanished station at Blackthorn, just a few miles south of Bicester, where today the line passes over the A41. This was in anticipation of the area having massive housing developments, a sort of Oxfordshire 'Metroland'. This never happened and the station eventually closed during the 1950s.

Thus, by 1910 the Great Western at last enjoyed the ability to compete on equal terms. Their new line from Birmingham to the West Midlands was both shorter than that of their LNWR rival and considerably shorter than their own previous route via Oxford. It was not only engineered for high speed but also enjoyed a more generous loading gauge that allowed more spacious rolling stock. This was in part thanks to the Great Western having laid some of its original lines to accommodate its 7ft broad gauge and the Great Central having from the beginning adopted the wider Continental loading gauge[1] in anticipation of the completion of Edward Watkin's dream for a Channel Tunnel and through services from Manchester to Paris, finally realised about ninety years later. However, it is a sad comment on Government grasp of basics and strategic transport planning that the Great Central, the only main line in Britain built to accommodate the width and height of Continental rolling stock, both passenger and freight, was mostly abandoned and ripped up in the 1960s.

The Great Western lost no time in exploiting their new asset and Friday 1 July 1910 saw one of Mr Churchward's 'Saint' class 4-6-0 locomotives no.2902 *Lady of the Lake*[2], depart Birmingham Snow Hill and, despite being delayed by a late running train, reach Paddington exactly two hours later, thus inaugurating the famous GWR 'two-hour expresses' that in speed and comfort now rivalled the LNWR. These two-hour schedules, leaving Paddington every two hours at ten minutes past the hour, were maintained (except during the First World War) until the outbreak of war in September 1939. Now the Great Way Round had become God's Wonderful Railway!

Following nationalisation of Britain's railways in 1948, services initially continued much as before throughout the 1950s, though the two-hour London–Birmingham timing was not achieved again until the introduction of the diesel electric Blue Pullmans in the 1960s, themselves merely a stop-gap measure pending completion of the Euston line electrification. Once the new services started from March 1967 with a best journey timing of only one hour forty minutes between Birmingham New Street and Euston, the Blue Pullmans ceased and the line was allowed to slide into a long slow decay, despite a final brief one-hour fifty-minute schedule using diesel locomotives.

Symbolising that decline, Snow Hill itself was demolished in 1977 and following post-Beeching rationalisation the former GWR line itself – reached now from New Street via Bordesley Junction – was steadily downgraded with longer journey times, fewer through trains and line singling south of Aynho Junction. Moreover, this once great main line beyond Birmingham through the Black Country to Shropshire, mid-Wales and the Mersey docks at Birkenhead, was seriously downgraded. For many communities without access to the newly electrified WCML, the paltry remaining services were a poor substitute. By the early 1980s the new services included a few through Inter-City trains from Birmingham New Street to London Paddington via the old Oxford route.

From Marylebone a service now ran to Banbury via the Joint Line and Bicester every two hours and took, on a good day, one hour and forty minutes for the seventy-three-mile journey, with a maximum line speed of 60mph along the now largely singled line. The trains were four-car units of first generation diesel multiple units (DMUs) that lacked corridor connections and possessed only one toilet. These noisy, draughty and very uncomfortable trains were increasingly aged and powered by diesel engines no longer manufactured, so fitters frequently had to cannibalise spare parts at night to provide for the next day's service (see Chapter 5 for more on this 'make do and mend' culture). That they went at all is probably a tribute to the rugged quality of their original build. Only those who used the appalling service, prior to the Total Route Modernisation that began the line's renaissance in the late 1980s, can appreciate the depth of anger, frustration and general despair among those brave souls who struggled on by train. Regular hefty hikes in peak-time fares were greeted with the kind of derision one would expect. In 2003, in a move designed to enable more modern trains to be refurbished without reducing peak-time capacity, Chiltern reintroduced a refurbished single-car version of this original design to operate the peak-time shuttle between Aylesbury and Princes Risborough!

The lowest point was reached in the early 1980s, when a scheme was tabled to close Marylebone altogether and turn it into a coach terminal. A busway north from the station through the tunnels would have affected access north. Trains from High Wycombe would have been diverted to Paddington, and the Aylesbury route replaced by Underground trains to Baker Street. That this misguided project foundered owes much to a combined effort of user groups, enlightened British Rail managers and the fortuitous climb out of the early 1980s recession which produced considerable traffic growth (see Chapter 9 – The Line that Nearly Died).

By the late 1980s even the stoical travelling public was getting restive. So fed up was he with the rising stream of complaints from his constituents that, by 1989, Banbury MP Tony Baldry called a public meeting in Banbury's Town Hall to which Brian Johnson, a senior manager for BR Inter-City, was invited to answer questions. As luck would have it, that particular evening the trains suffered worse delays than usual and instead of the expected fairly quiet occasion with a few commuters and the occasional railway enthusiast, quite dramatically a tidal wave of very angry commuters suddenly forced its way into the modest-sized council committee room determined to give vent to their long frustration.

Brian Johnson bravely bore the brunt, rather unfairly as it happened. Like many BR managers he was a committed professional who had for years been doing his level best to provide a half-decent public service in the face of ongoing severe cost constraints (compounded by all those inconsistencies of Government transport planning that have sadly characterised the history of Britain's railways since 1948). Furthermore, his particular responsibility was the Inter-City division which was actually not at all bad, in contrast to the dismal DMU service from Marylebone to Banbury. From personal recollection on that particular September evening when the meeting became heated, Baldry deftly proposed that a local rail users action group be established. This met officially for the first time on 7 October 1989 and adopted the title of Cherwell Rail Users Group, the acronym hinting at the dismal service. The members comprised a fascinating mixture of accountants, academics, textile designers, scientists, teachers, civil servants, bankers, local Government officers and City business people. The author had the privilege of being elected the first chairman and well remembers acrimonious initial meetings with BR managers until gradual improvements began under the influence of Network SouthEast's new director, Chris Green (see Part 2, Chris Green, 'The Line that Nearly Died'). At the same time, similar action groups of regular travellers sprang up at Haddenham and Thame and further north at Solihull and Leamington Spa, soon combining their activities to good effect.

By 1991 the nearly completed M40 was already bringing tangible economic and social benefits to the era.

For rail travellers, although the first of the new turbo diesel trains was about to be delivered, overall not much had yet changed. At a rail users meeting in north Oxfordshire, two retired former railwaymen, Don Holmes (former station master at Banbury and one of Chris Green's original mentors) and his colleague Jack Cowperthwaite, pointed out that there would be no overall improvement without a cost/benefit study of the whole route. Part of the problem was that under BR, since the 1960s, no one department or division had had an overall strategic responsibility for this whole alternative trunk route between London and Birmingham. Network SouthEast stopped at Banbury. The Central division of BR's Regional Railways had responsibility from Birmingham as far as Leamington Spa; in between was a 'no-man's land' traversed by a few Inter-City Cross-Country services and the occasional freight train.

Consequently, in the hope that it might be a catalyst, rail users compiled a brief ten-page discussion paper, 'The M40 Corridor and its Rail Services', which was sent to Tony Baldry and all the other MPs whose constituencies lay along the route. It drew heavily on published documents making the point that the 'corridor' effects of the M40 would materially alter the economic base and pattern of both business and commuter travel along the Corridor. For example, based on experience elsewhere, the arrival of newer more advanced industries will effect changes to the skill base as workers re-train and necessarily become more mobile as they seek out new job opportunities. Turning to local train services, the Cambridge-based publication *The M40 Review* echoed local concerns when it commented:

> However, the big question is whether BR is wise to go on regarding Banbury as an outer-commuter terminus. With the growth of the M40 Corridor, demand is certain to move north to locations like Leamington Spa.
>
> The Chiltern line is in Network SouthEast which is essentially London based. There could be a case for going back to the days of the Great Western, and making Banbury, and the cities beyond it, Inter-City.
>
> The Rail Users Group paper itemised nine very specific problems and concluded: 'the particular requests, complaints and suggestions of Banbury rail users scarcely need re-iterating. We do feel we are engaged in the dialogue of the deaf and wonder sometimes if there is any point in continuing. The service continues to stumble along, though we appreciate that with the age of much of the rolling stock combined with the ludicrously high staff turnover of 30 per cent in Network SouthEast, it's probably little short of a miracle that we get any sort of service at all!
>
> We have ceased regular monitoring of services because of despair, not lethargy, having noted that things have now deteriorated to the extent that no two rail journeys on any one day are likely to be trouble free.
>
> We cannot help feeling that there is still a big blank in the minds of BR Management when it comes to the routes servicing the M40 Corridor. Can we get together to do something about it?

This was sent off to all the parties mentioned in the second half of 1992. At that time, by a happy coincidence, Banbury MP Tony Baldry was also Under Secretary of State for the Environment and quickly set up a meeting between the rail users and the appropriate senior manager from Network SouthEast. This took place on Wednesday 28 October 1992 at the somewhat forbidding-looking Department of the Environment building in Marsham Street, London, and was chaired by Baldry. Others present included Wing Commander Rowlands, who worked at the MOD, representing the North Chiltern Rail Users (Nick Walker, their Secretary being unable to attend himself), Austen Kopley and Hugh Jones representing Cherwell Rail Users, and Richard Fearn, then director of the Thames and Chiltern Division of Network SouthEast. The agenda, agreed with all parties beforehand, consisted of two broad strategic items, 'The M40 Corridor and its Rail Services' and 'Crossrail, and opportunity for second thoughts', this latter being of particular concern to the North Chiltern Group. Sadly, on this occasion no one from the newly formed Leamington Spa group could attend.

In the forefront of the minds of those present was the concept of a professional study of the rail services along the entire length of the M40 Corridor and ways to get the enthusiastic support of all the parties including BR, local authorities and perhaps also the Department of Environment itself. It was felt by rail user groups that much of the data on the daily travel patterns within the Corridor was readily available from both county and district councils as well as various universities' economics departments. In addition, it was suggested that a survey be done of the travel patterns and requirements of companies either already – in or re-locating to places within – the Corridor. All this, it was put to Dick Fearn, would draw out the business opportunities BR could exploit for developing rail travel in imaginative and relevant ways. It was further suggested that with the Channel Tunnel then nearing completion, this would also create a developing need for better rail links (a few years later, a future chairman of Cherwell Rail Users Group was regularly travelling from King's Sutton to Brussels).

The concerns about Crossrail were simply that the planned inclusion of the Aylesbury via Amersham route would suck away a very high proportion of the daily commuters from the Chiltern lines, thus undermining the modernisation scheme and the future viability of Marylebone. Instead, additional electrification and inclusion within the overall Crossrail scheme of the route from Paddington to High Wycombe was suggested. This would create the potential for eventually extending right through to Birmingham, opening up the tantalising prospect thus of linking Birmingham directly into London's business heart.

Fearn responded by saying he was supportive of the idea of a rail study for the Corridor, but he also reminded the rail users that the Chiltern lines were receiving a great deal of public money for route modernisation and were unlikely to get another bite at the cherry for some time. Moreover, BR was indeed already using data from local authority sources for forward planning and this, combined with their own computer models was predicting exciting possibilities for the Snow Hill to Marylebone route. Indeed, he revealed that a through service north of Banbury to a new (though much smaller) Snow Hill would be restored from the start of the May 1993 timetable, but he asked those present to keep that information from the press for the time being. He envisaged the new service complementing rather than competing directly with the Inter-City route from New Street to Euston. He also said that the strategic link between Paddington and Northolt, once part of the Paddington-Banbury-Birminghan Snow Hill main line, would indeed be retained in case it may be needed for future development of Crossrail.

However, not long after this meeting took place, the Government again put Crossrail on hold. By 2010 things had moved on considerably, and a preliminary works area underway for a revised Crossrail scheme from Maidenhead and Heathrow in the west, through to Shenfield in the east. Plans for an expansion to the corresponding north–south 'Thameslink' route scheme are also well underway.

A further meeting took place at Marsham Street in March 1993 at which Graham Handley, Chief Executive of Cherwell District Council, along with Head of Planning Alan Jones, generously offered the services of their council to co-ordinate a consortium of the local authorities along the Corridor. This was the start of the M40 Rail Forum, that for a while at this formative stage played a useful and constructive role by facilitating the exploration and exchange of ideas between local authority transport planners, railway managers and passenger representatives on a regular but informal basis. Work began with a seminar at Bodicote House, Banbury, in September 1993, at which all parties pledged support and financial contribution towards a study of rail services within the Corridor. This was undertaken by Peter Headicar from the planning department of Oxford Brookes University. This was published as Working Paper No.152, 'Promoting Rail Use in the M40 Corridor' in June 1994 by the Oxford Brookes University School of Planning (copies may still be available from Oxford Brookes University School of Planning, Gipsy Lane, Headington, Oxford, OX3 0BP).

The report's eight sections plus technical appendices covered: introduction; demographic, social and economic characteristics of the Corridor; current development and transport policies both regional and national; rail services in the Corridor including a cost comparison between road and rail; characteristics of rail use in the Corridor; the future context for rail in the Corridor including future travel conditions, implications of rail privatisation for both freight and passenger business; the future role of rail in the Corridor, outlining ways of promoting rail use; and finally an agenda for action, outlining various cost-effective ways for converting rhetoric into reality and continuing the initiative.

By the time it was published, the benefits of the Total Route Modernisation had begun to feed through, and commuter numbers from Banbury to London were growing. As far as the longer distance Cross-Country services were concerned, the report showed that business travel comprised only 10 per cent on Cross-Country services, the vast majority of passengers were only travelling about once a year to visit family and friends, or were students travelling to and from college.

Re-reading the report fifteen years after it was first published, although the numbers may have changed, one is impressed by how much of the original thinking is still valid. Certainly, at the time and throughout the early stages of Chiltern Railways, Alex Turner, the first director of sales and marketing, and his team followed the report's philosophy closely producing results that now speak for themselves.

Prior to his assuming the directorship of Network SouthEast in 1986, Chris Green was enjoying his role as managing director of ScotRail where many improvements had happened. It was therefore with some reluctance that he obeyed the official summons and headed south. Where Scotland was aggressively positive, London culture was still based upon slow decline and a belief that businesses were continuing to move out of London. This was odd, since in fact Mrs Thatcher's economic revolution was in full swing with tremendous growth in financial services in the City well under way. Green could see that, far from decline, commuter numbers to and from London were increasing. Moreover, across the Channel, the French were already leading the world with their network of high-speed TGV lines and had already built four 'Crossrail-type' RER systems underneath Paris.

By contrast, Green was told his first big task was to close Marylebone so that it could be converted into a coach station (for Green's own story, see Part 2, 'The Line That Nearly Died'). Happily, he found on close inspection that the numbers in the plans for compensatory alternative services using Paddington and Baker Street did not stack up. Moreover, in his battle to retain Marylebone, Green had very positive support from many of the newly forming rail user groups up and down the line, as well as – possibly more importantly – very positive support from MPs of all political colours whose constituents would be directly affected.

Accordingly, Green was able to recommend to the BR Board that the closure plans be withdrawn and his deputy at that time, John Oxley, described what he later called the best day in his long railway career when he attended the Marylebone closure public enquiry for the purpose of informing the panel that BR was withdrawing its plans for the closure.

Having stopped the closure, Green next had to do something positive about the appalling and extremely worrying state of the line. On reflection he said the line's only claim to fame was that it regularly earned income as a set for nineteenth-century films: nothing had to be changed! The Total Route Modernisation in the early 1990s, led by Green, meant that by the time Adrian Shooter was appointed in 1993, he and his team benefited from a modern and well-equipped railway; enabling them to reach new levels of excellence.

In August 1993, when rail privatisation had been going through Parliament, Adrian Shooter had been the director of engineering performance for British Rail. The then BR Board Chairman Sir Bob Reid invited all his senior managers to tell him where they would like to go in the soon to be privatised railway, whether it be the Office of the Passenger Rail Franchising (OPRAF); the Office of the Rail Regulator (ORR); Railtrack (RTK), the company that would own the track; signals and stations; the train leasing companies that would actually own all the trains (ROSCOs); infrastructure maintenance; or Train Operating Companies (TOCs) who would actually run the trains.

Shooter had no doubts; he had wanted to run a railway company since the age of six! For some months he had been turning over in his mind the idea of a management buy-out, and when handed a list of twenty-five new Train Operating Companies (TOCs) to choose from, he picked two or three, including Chiltern; very soon afterwards he was invited to go and run it as a Train Operating Unit within BR. He was told: 'It is for you to set it up', which delighted him as he knew the area well, having worked there twenty years previously, and at the time was living nearby in Bedford.

Chiltern was going to be a relatively small company created by splitting the old Thames and Chiltern division of BR's Network SouthEast, in line with Conservative thinking designed to create customer choice along the London–Birmingham route. Of the twenty-five new TOCs created from the old BR management divisions, most of the MDs had been the previous BR Divisional Managers with responsibility for everything in a vertically integrated organisation, including train operating, track, signalling and stations. During the run up to privatisation they had had the depressing task of dissecting their organisations, arguing with trade unions about which staff would be going where and generally disposing of their empires. The psychological effect of all this was to prove quite significant.

By contrast, Shooter did not fit this mould. He had time from August 1993 until 1 April 1994 to think strategically and build his new team. He also knew that the proposed Chiltern route from Birmingham to London via High Wycombe, opened by the Great Western Railway and Great Central in July 1910, had thereafter competed very successfully for the London to Birmingham traffic.

Through services were resumed along the route by the Chiltern Line's division of British Rail in May 1993, between Marylebone and the new (much smaller) Birmingham Snow Hill station, with a journey time of two hours and twenty minutes – considerably slower than the GWR services in the early twentieth century, but with many more stops. Because Chiltern was to be a small private company, Shooter used the time now available to him to take some advice on how one would structure such a company (it would come from some surprising directions) and to set about looking for the right people to lead it.

As a professional railwayman, Shooter already knew that above all else he needed an operations director experienced in organisation and train crew management. He had in mind Owen Edgington, Train Crew Manager for Trainload Freight and previously chief inspector at St Pancras, when Shooter had been area manager there in 1984. They had discussed the idea of a management buy-out even before Adrian knew Chiltern would be his destiny. Thus, immediately upon his return from annual leave he called Edgington: 'Right, I've got a job for you Owen', and just before Christmas 1993 Edgington became Chiltern's first employee (for Edgington's own story, see Part 2, 'The Operations Director's Story').

But even before that there had been many basic strategic decisions. Railway timetable planning, a complex business, demands, decisions at least a year ahead: did Shooter want to go beyond Banbury to Stratford-upon-Avon or Birmingham? His answer was clear: he intended to run an hourly service to Birmingham from September 1994. Did he want to manage Banbury station? The answer was 'yes'. Shooter had to wait until 2004 before also taking on Leamington Spa, Warwick and two smaller stations to the north, by which time Chiltern had also decided on Birmingham Moor Street as their 'gateway' station to the Midlands city.

The two men got down to talking about the type of organisation they wanted – for operations and engineering good people from within BR but for marketing and finance, people from outside the railway industry. Subsequent history suggests they chose well.

One of the first was a young man from Essex, Steve Murphy, who had worked previously for Shooter in the Red Star parcels service and was now their assistant manager at Euston. Realising it was a time of change and opportunity to try something very different, he applied to join Chiltern. After having survived the Shooter interview techniques involving a number of tests and interesting challenges designed to demonstrate flair and imagination, enthusiasm for the challenges of privatisation, a thoroughly professional approach to the railway industry as well as an ability to eat cold fish and chips (see Murphy's version in Part 2), Murphy joined as specifications manager and rose rapidly to become managing director in 2003. He was seconded to Dublin as managing director, south and west, Iarnrod Eireann (Irish Railways) in 2004/5, working under former BR managing director of Thames and Chiltern and Railtrack Midland Zone Director Richard Fearn and by 2007 he was back as managing director of Chiltern's associated company London Overground.

Shooter was clear in his own mind that he wanted someone with the right track record in outside industry to fill the key position of director of sales and marketing. In the end the post went to Alex Turner. Turner, a Classics graduate with an impressive CV in private industry was at the time enjoying running his own consultancy having been made redundant six months previously by WH Smith. He had spotted an advertisement in the *Sunday Times* in September 1993: 'Commercial Directors required for Rail Privatisation' and decided to investigate further. Looking back, he admits that when the interview day with Shooter and Edgington arrived his heart was not altogether in it as he was also exploring work in the television industry.

Shooter felt this silver-haired, somewhat crumpled, blue pinstripe sitting in front of him was the man for the job, though suspected Turner's keen intellect and original turn of mind would also cause a few bumps along the way. However, Shooter could see that Turner was not convinced it was for him.

As it happened, Shooter's next interviewee was also a BR graduate trainee, an enthusiastic young woman with a striking personality and hairstyle to match who was extremely keen to come and work for Chiltern as area manager, south, with responsibility for Marylebone and all stations as far as Beaconsfield. This was the first time Cath Proctor met the two people who were to have the greatest influence on her subsequent railway career, Adrian Shooter and Alex Turner.

At the end of Proctor's interview, Shooter turned to her and said, 'I am seriously considering appointing you but that will depend upon your ability to go out from here and persuade that silver-haired man you saw leaving here before you to accept a post with us. I want him but he is having doubts. If you can persuade him in the next half hour, I shall appoint you.'

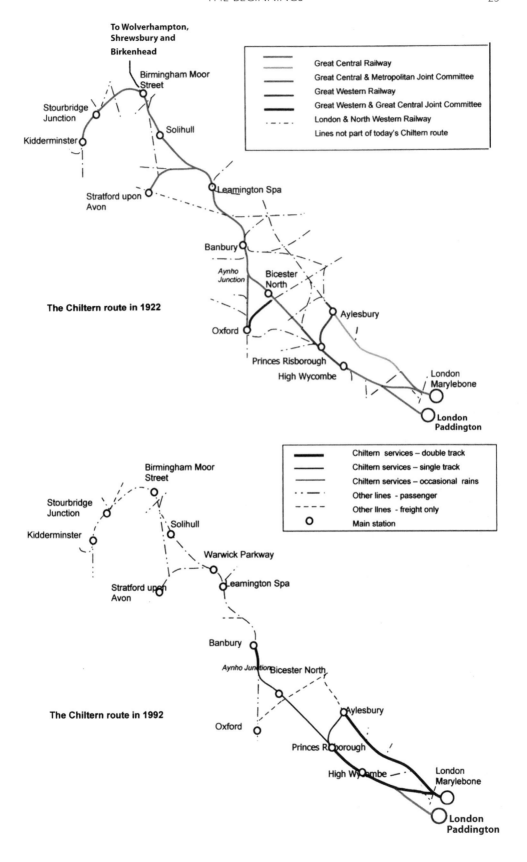

The Chiltern route in 1922

The Chiltern route in 1992

So, Proctor's first task was to help appoint her boss (for Proctor's version, see Part 2, 'My Ten Years as a Railwayman'). Subsequently, Proctor has never been sure whether Turner ever quite forgave her!

Shooter chose well: what became the senior marketing team of Turner, Murphy and Proctor went on to drive Chiltern's very strong financial success, way beyond what had been projected. After Turner left Chiltern, Proctor succeeded him as head of marketing and both she and Murphy later went on to become, in succession, managing directors of Chiltern. During Proctor's watch she had to face the extra stresses created by the Gerrards Cross tunnel collapse, the 7/7 bombings and the Wembley fire. That she was able to rally the staff into getting Chiltern's financial position back on track says much about both her and her mentor, Alex Turner.

The most difficult position to fill was that of finance director. Shooter had discarded piles of CVs and interviewed thirty-two candidates before finding Tony Allen, now one of the longest serving and most respected financial directors in the railway industry. Allen is a Londoner, with a passion for Tottenham Hotspur, and a chartered accountant with a sound record of improving the profitability of manufacturing and consumer distribution businesses as diverse as Courage Brewery and Mary Quant. Allen, who had never worked in the public sector before, found the initial culture shock startling, but once Chiltern started on its own private sector journey Allen and Turner together proved a dynamic team (for his own account, see Part 2, 'The Finance Director's Story').

Finally, just before Chiltern 'went live' as a separate Train Operating Unit on 1 April 1994, the senior management team was completed with the arrival as personnel manager of Caroline James from British Aerospace.

During all the interviews for his team, Shooter had made clear his intention to try for a management buy-out, causing some candidates to drop out, but through the spring of 1994 other posts were gradually filled, some by people asking to join, others came across simply to continue the jobs they were already doing such as drivers, station managers and staff, booking office sales staff and other on-train personnel. Signallers went to Railtrack and track maintenance staff to one or the other of Railtrack's many sub-contractors.

One slightly later but very significant member of the team was Mark Beckett, who joined as business manager in August 1995 and played key roles in the successful franchising processes, becoming development director for Laing Rail, before moving on. He was succeeded by Graham Cross, who had previously been the franchise manager for Chiltern at the Office of Passenger Rail Franchising (OPRAF) before joining Chiltern in January 2004.

However, as every senior manager would agree, very high in the list of key personnel is their PA. Shooter is no exception, having had three of what he calls his 'rottweilers', a thoroughly misleading description to anyone who has ever had the pleasure of meeting them! Shooter makes the same startling demands on these remarkable and indispensable people as on everyone else at Chiltern, including speaking Japanese, introducing him to the latest in communication technology and designing locomotive wheel sets! Their own story in Part 2, 'The PA's Story', is most entertaining.

It was decided very early on by Shooter that the management structure of Chiltern would be kept deliberately 'flat' while the headquarters, rather than the imposing Victorian edifice of Marylebone, would be based on the second floor of the offices of a firm of solicitors in Aylesbury.

NOTES

1   Continental loading gauge, or Berne gauge, means that while the track gauge now used on the majority of lines on mainland Europe is the same as the British 4ft 8½in (now 1,432mm), the rolling stock is somewhat wider and higher. This has obvious implications for the ease of through running of both freight and passenger stock between mainland Europe and the UK via the Channel Tunnel because of clearances under bridges and through tunnels.

2   The name of the locomotive that hauled the special train from Birmingham Snow Hill to Paddington on Friday 1 July 1910 came from Keith Farr's article in *Backtrack* April 2002. Farr quotes the delightful story of the well wisher who threw a horseshoe into the cab for good luck. When Churchward heard of this, he had the horseshoe mounted in 2902's cab where it remained until the locomotive was withdrawn in 1949. (Where is that horshoe today?) Stanley C. Jenkins in his very thoroughly researched book states it was 2910 *Lady of Shalott*.

The first Great Central Railway express leaving Marylebone on 9 March 1899. (Chiltern Railways)

Marylebone station in 1899. (Chiltern Railways)

Left: The first London to Birmingham two-hour express, via the Ashendon and Aynho line, leaving Paddington station at 9.10 a.m., 1 July 1910. (*Great Western Railway Magazine,* 1910)

Left: Scene from *Metroland*; a Metropolitan Railway train calls at Amersham. (Chiltern Railways)

Below: A crowded platform 1 at the original Victorian Banbury station, probably taken about 1949/50, showing a fascinating wealth of historic detail. (John Leslie)

Above: GWR No.6000 *King George V* heading the 07:25 Wolverhampton–Paddington between Solihull and Widney Manor, 12 August 1960. (Michael Mensing)

Below: The first train over the route from Aynho Junction–Bicester on 1 July 1910 waits to leave Banbury. (Chiltern Railways)

Above: Banbury station, 31 December 1956, showing the original Victorian station in the process of being demolished as the new station building rises under the scaffolding. (Alan Donaldson)

Below: Ripping it up! It is 1968 and the former GWR main line is being singled between Aynho Junction and Bicester. (Alan Donaldson)

CHAPTER 3

THE CHILTERN STRATEGY

At midnight on 31 March 1994, Chiltern Lines became a separate Train Operating Unit (TOU), still legally under the British Railways Board until 1 April 1995 when it would become a separate legal entity trading under the present name of Chiltern Railways. Shooter's team's first task was to prove they could run and develop Chiltern Lines as a viable unit on its own and start on their second requirement to produce a British Railways business plan to enable BR to sell the Chiltern franchise two years hence, by April 1996. Their third priority was to begin to work on their own management buy-out business plan. The work on the BR plan alone would involve hundreds of hours with lawyers and merchant bankers, while all the while, and strictly in their own time, also very discreetly putting together their own MBO bid documents.

The team's first priority was to run the railway and for this they needed to get to know their customers. One of Shooter's first actions was to distribute a news sheet, *Welcome to Chiltern Lines*, to all their staff and customers. It has always been a characteristic of Chiltern Railways that all staff, no matter what their position, have been acknowledged as an essential part of the team, and he decided to try very hard to establish a personal relationship with each one. At that time this totalled about 250 in number. This was not so easy by 2007 when Chiltern employed some 725 people. The leaflet front-paged, quite deliberately, the modest and economical company head-quarters on the second floor of the Aylesbury solicitor's office, with a picture of Shooter. Its text read in part:

> Everyone working for Chiltern Lines TOU can look to the future with confidence. You have made tremendous strides over the last couple of years and I am entirely confident that we can build on these achievements and provide an even better service for our customers in the future.
>
> As you will know, the key to this success is the Total Route Modernisation. The £85 million investment, completed in 1992, has taken the line from the brink of closure to being judged the best in Britain by the *Evening Standard*.
>
> People have seen and appreciated the innovations: customer numbers have increased by no less than 25 per cent since the investment was completed. But we need to continue this increase, which means we must put the customer at the centre of everything we do. That is why we located Chiltern Lines headquarters at Aylesbury, taking us closer to our people using our services.
>
> An example of our continuing improvement is the summer 1994 timetable: we are providing more through trains to Birmingham, enhancing the High Wycombe to Marylebone service and improving our Sunday services. We are also taking over Banbury and King's Sutton stations and we will be looking at enhancing others.
>
> I hope you will enjoy working with our new organisation, and join with me in striving to provide the best possible service for our customers. I look forward to working with you.

Very rapidly the accompanying rather uninspiring mission statement was changed, as a result of staff comments, to read:

Our mission is to be the best passenger railway in the UK. All day, every day we aim to offer a
safe, reliable, welcoming and value for money service. Our business will prosper because customers use us repeatedly and recommend the service to others.

Most people tend to be slightly cynical about mission statements, regular rail users not excepted,
but this statement has endured and, by 2003, Chiltern had in fact been voted the best UK railway
company three years running.

On the leaflet's inside pages were photographs of all the new senior management team along
with, very bravely, their direct line telephone numbers.

Meanwhile, negotiations to turn the TOU into a TOC continued; some issues were handed
down from the BR Board, others such as track-access agreements had to be negotiated twice,
once with Railtrack and again with London Underground for the Aylesbury via Amersham route.

Chiltern's finance manager Tony Allen (he and his senior management team became directors
once Chiltern became a private company) now had to introduce his BR colleagues to the way
finance worked in private business. BR, in its half century of existence, had become very good at
understanding and controlling costs related to infrastructure and train utilisation. It had not been
good at understanding where its revenue came from; this was where Allen's experience was vital.

By spring 1995 Shooter and Turner were concerned that the growing business was leading to
unacceptable overcrowding at peak periods as well as needing extra trains to provide the planned
hourly Birmingham services. If their franchise bid was successful, they aspired to an altogether more
superior type of new train suited to that market; in the meantime they needed something quickly.

They turned to the BR Board to acquire a few more Class 165 Turbos, designed specifically for
London commuter work but popular with staff and customers (despite having no air conditioning or tables and inadequate toilet and luggage provision). In its business case Chiltern used its
own figures on revenue growth, based on actual results. These were significantly above BR's own
forecasts, reflecting traditionally cautious BR thinking. In its reply, BR refused Shooter's request,
doubted Chiltern's growth figures and in effect suggested driving the extra passengers off by
raising fares or making them stand for long periods. In the event, Chiltern arrived at a stop-gap
solution by being able to sub-lease a few additional Class 165 vehicles from Thames Trains, largely
thanks to the intervention of John Nelson, BR Managing Director for Network SouthEast.

The episode highlights the fundamental difference between the Governmental responsibility
to contain costs and safeguard the public purse and the entrepreneur who was prepared to take
risks to grow the business (it also makes BR's 1988 decision to invest £85 million for the Total
Route Modernisation of Marylebone–Banbury all the more remarkable). This issue of investment
in rolling stock and infrastructure was to re-surface several times over the next twelve months as
Shooter and his team negotiated with OPRAF over the terms of their own bid for the franchise.

Exactly one year after becoming a TOU under BR, Chiltern became a stand-alone Train
Operating Company (TOC), though still nominally within BR, on 1 April 1995. Now the
Chiltern team had to help the Government to sell the franchise for the railway. There was a lot of
encouragement within BR for management buy-outs, even to the extent of organising a seminar
by Price Waterhouse. Shooter recollects that what they were told bore no resemblance whatsoever
to what actually happened!

Shooter felt strongly that Chiltern should be one of the first franchises to be sold, having
noted from the bus industry that he who was first got the best deal. Unfortunately London
Underground, whose line to Amersham Chiltern shared, persuaded OPRAF that the deal would
be terribly complicated and that the planned Crossrail project would fairly soon kill off Chiltern
anyway. Chiltern was put back from No.1 to No.25.

The Chiltern team were alarmed: an election might lead to a change of Government and scrap-
ping of privatisation, and in any case deals at the end of the line would not be as commercially
attractive. As it turned out, several of the final batch of franchisees had to be bailed out of financial
difficulty or otherwise supported through ownership changes, by the Government. The biggest
example of this in the late 1990s was Prism, whose rail business, based on four aggressively won
franchises, was eventually bought by National Express.

By contrast, it had already been impressed on the Chiltern team at the start that if they got into financial trouble, there would be no rescue package. By 2003, Chiltern, despite tight margins, was still solvent though in the final run up – in 2002 – to the award of their second twenty-year franchise, there were times when it had been very much a 'skin of their teeth' job (by 2009, they were managing without Government subsidy). The Chiltern team had a hard fight to move their bid up the batting order from No.25 while at the same time the Government was knocking franchise bids off from the top down. The two processes met at No.8.

By May 1995 the senior management team had finished the BR business plan and set about their second task of selling the company franchise. At this stage it is important to bear in mind that it was obvious to all those involved that the Government and BR were making up the procedures as they went along. Shooter well remembers facing rows of grey suits from the City who clearly had not a clue about the realities of railway finance or operation.

BR firstly required Chiltern's senior management to collaborate with accountants to produce a document called a 'Long Form Report' which took months. In retrospect, Shooter feels it was rather a pointless exercise and a dreadful waste of time. Then, a glossy booklet was published with the aid of merchant bankers Kleinwort Benson for the benefit of those bidding. Again, months and many long nights were spent going over every line with both them and Linklaters, the lawyers acting for BR.

In retrospect, those who were the leading protagonists at the time found it difficult to convey to others just how exhausting and often downright exasperating the demands of all this were on them and their families. Whole days and evenings were spent in offices with usually two nights a week spent until 9 or 10 p.m. It was at this time, in 1995, that Mark Beckett joined Chiltern and was almost immediately involved in this painstaking and often tedious exercise. In particular, Beckett had a close involvement with the key 'Invitation To Tender' document which he recalls as a nightmare, though of course necessary to protect against any possible future litigation on the grounds of being mis-sold. For example, it even took forever to agree on the definition of a station! Answers had to be provided for seemingly obvious statements such as: 'Chiltern operates between London and Birmingham; please prove'. Even worse was dealing with statements of opinion, for example: 'The area served by Chiltern is relatively affluent; please prove'!

Even Beckett found his naturally equable temperament severely tested. The process eventually resulted in six volumes stacking nearly 3ft high.

In its final eighty-two-page form, the 'Invitation to Tender' document, published at the end of January 1996, was sent to all pre-qualifying bidders. Its sections covered:

1) Key information, including the company's key strengths, the key financial and operational statistics, current year budget and longer term outlook.
2) Description of the business, including the historical background, the Total Route Modernisation programme, service characteristics, stations, the Chiltern telephone enquiry bureau (a positive lifeline of sanity for Chiltern passengers in the chaotic early days of the National Rail enquiry service), rolling stock and trade marks.
3) The markets, competition and historical passenger revenue. This covered the passenger market, both rail and non-rail competition, influences on demand patterns, historical passenger revenue, the complications both operational and commercial, of the interface with London Transport and the ORCATS system of ticket revenue sharing that applied to all National Rail operators.
4) The operating environment. This dealt with the level of train services, the timetable that would be in force at the commencement of the franchise and which would form the basis for the Passenger Service Requirement (PSR), the detailed mandatory service requirements decreed by OPRAF.

The setting 'in stone' of this latter point by OPRAF was to create a few headaches for future Chiltern timetablers by denying them flexibility to meet customer demand. One or two bits of mild eccentricity dating from way back in the BR days were also unearthed, such as one particular

late night service that usually ran virtually empty. Diligent investigation revealed that it had originally been scheduled for the personal convenience of a certain highly placed BR official!

This section also dealt with load factors including PIXC. PIXC stands for 'Passengers In eXcess
of Capacity', i.e., how many standing passengers are permitted, because in practice it is not always
possible to ensure that no more passengers are carried than these capacities allow. Under the terms
of the franchising agreement, the franchise director (now the DFT) will allow these capacities to
be exceeded by PIXC. This is calculated thus:

$$\text{PIXC} = \frac{\underline{\text{Aggregate of passengers in excess of capacity on peak train}}}{\text{Total number of passengers on peak train}} \times 100 \text{ per cent}$$

Under the franchise agreement, Chiltern must plan peak services to keep PIXC at or below
3 per cent averaged over morning and evening peaks and 4.5 per cent in either peak. Crowding
within these limits may not be unduly concentrated on any particular route or service.

4) (continued) Section 4 also dealt with the contractual framework of performance regimes. These
   dealt with Chiltern's obligations to passengers (via the Passenger's Charter), Railtrack, LUL
   and the Franchising Director (OPRAF) and provide an agreed set of incentive and penalty
   payments between each party. The system is complicated and based on comparisons of actual
   performance against agreed benchmarks. In the twelve months to 16 September 1995, Chiltern
   performed in excess of all Passenger's Charter punctuality and reliability standards.
        Section 4 also covered leaf fall, engineering works, safety and fare regulations.
5) This dealt with the directors, management in general and employees. It covered (in the case
   of the directors) their previous backgrounds and all areas of responsibility, remuneration and
   working conditions. The total number of Chiltern staff at this time (on 30 January 1996)
   was 366.
6) Section 6 gave the financial results for the year ending 31 March 1995 which showed, before
   interest and financial support (i.e. Government subsidy) was factored in, an overall operating
   loss of £17.4 million.
7) This covered the budget and trading in the current year projected to 31 March 1996. These
   figures indicated a volume growth of 10.2 per cent peak and 14.2 per cent off-peak. When
   translated into estimated revenue, this would have reduced the level of subsidy needed down
   to £15.3 million.
        Section 7 also dealt most comprehensively with those factors that could affect future passen-
   ger revenue, both peak and off-peak. It also included a very detailed breakdown of the running
   costs of each individual department and the formula for calculating drivers' hours.
8) Instructions and procedural issues relating to the invitation to tender.

Mark Beckett's arrival in the company earlier in 1995 had been occasioned by pressure from John
Nelson, at that time Shooter's boss as the last director of BR's Network SouthEast, advising him to
apply for a Charter Mark for Chiltern. At the time, Shooter had felt it a rather irritating distraction
from his other tasks, but when further pressed he asked if BR could release someone to help sort
it out. At this time Beckett was at Euston House as part of the privatisation team, experience that
was to prove very useful for Chiltern.

Duly seconded to Chiltern to work on their application for a Charter Mark, Beckett vividly
remembers his arrival at Aylesbury. Shooter, busy as always, asked him to join him on the train to
Marylebone and spoke while Mark made notes. Three days later Adrian Shooter read his report,
was very impressed and offered him the temporary job.

The Charter Mark application in July 1995 duly earned Chiltern the coveted award, which was
presented on 4 December 1995 by the Prime Minister. This was important as it put a marker on
the ground demonstrating that Chiltern was a train operator able to deliver the type of service
quality that the Government was looking for. It may well have helped Chiltern to work up the
pecking order in the bidding process.

Shooter, on the look out still for promising talent, persuaded Beckett to accept a permanent position. Although not a member of the MBO team, he rapidly came to play a central role with Alex Turner in formulating the business plan and subsequent later bids.

By now, having completed the business plan required by British Rail, the Chiltern team rolled their sleeves up and got stuck into their own bid. Allen and Shooter acted quickly to get some financial advisers on board. They eventually chose the Milton Keynes office of Grant Thornton; although not the largest accountancy firm, they felt an instant rapport with these people led by their managing partner Bill Lyth. The Chiltern team could understand what they were saying and they remained the Chiltern auditors for some years until after the later buy-out by John Laing.

Finance was a major worry for the Chiltern directors. The MBO team were not wealthy business people; they had little money to pay accountancy fees. Fortunately Shooter was able to persuade Grant Thornton to work on a contingent fee basis, i.e. if Chiltern did not win the franchise, they would pay nothing. If they did win, they would pay a mark up of 50 per cent.

Next came the search for legal advisers. As Shooter pointed out, in this particular contest there were absolutely no prizes for coming second, therefore he knew they had to obtain the best and so Grant Thornton came up with McKenna & Co. who agreed to work on the same basis as Grant Thornton.

Finance was also a priority and Grant Thornton advised finding a venture capitalist. Shooter initially was cautious. He and the team knew they required expertise in financial engineering but Shooter, as a mechanical engineer, also knew there were many projects included in the Chiltern MBO bid that would require first-rate project management skills. Furthermore, he and the team were acutely aware that none of them had any experience in actually bidding for anything.

Consequently, rather than going out to find a venture capitalist, the Chiltern team, having clarified the kinds of expertise they needed, did an 'industry sector' study, outlining the skills they wanted and what type of industry might contain them, right on down to which individual companies could provide them. Among the memories of the participants at the time, Allen was quite taken aback by the arrogance displayed by some in the City who assumed the Chiltern people just wanted to buy and sell to make a quick profit; he found them incapable of grasping that the Chiltern people really were committed to just wanting to run an excellent railway and generate a good profit by growing the business. Allen was also impressed by the lack of a process for privatisation; everyone seemed to be making it up as they went along. At times he felt he would have got better advice from the passengers on the Marylebone concourse! (Author's note: not such a daft idea, see emergence of user groups in Chapter 2.)

The upshot of this process was the discovery of John Laing who had diversified from civil engineering into support services and, having missed out on the bidding for rail infrastructure companies, were now looking for opportunities with train operating companies. They had just done an equal and opposite thinking excise to Chiltern whom they had identified as one they wanted to talk to. Shooter met with John Laing and it turned out they were quite keen to do a deal. By now Shooter and his team had a clear idea of the financial structure they wanted for their potential company: 51 per cent management and 49 per cent between John Laing and venture capitalists.

Helped by Grant Thornton the team arranged a 'beauty parade' of four or five venture capitalists in November 1995. It was very much a two-way affair, as clearly Chiltern had to convince them that they were worth backing in the first place. As luck would have it, just before the scheduled meeting all bar two pulled out. The cause was that a leading (then in opposition) politician, Clare Short MP, had indicated during a radio/television interview that if the Tories privatised the railways, an incoming Labour Government would re-nationalise without compensation. While in fact there is no precedent for this, it is simply not something that Governments do; nevertheless several of the venture capitalists believed it. With a shortlist of two, Adrian Shooter opted for 3i who agreed but said before confirming they would want to meet the rest of the management team. This was done over breakfast a few days later in Aylesbury (all these activities had to be done out of normal office hours, which were spent trying to sell the franchise to someone else). The meeting went well and 3i proved to be supportive from then on.

With most of his ducks in a row, Shooter now looked around for a suitable chairman. He had a pretty good idea of the kind of person he was looking for and went off to discuss it with an old friend at Imperial College London, Professor Sir Hugh Ford, who at the time was also president of the Institute of Mechanical Engineers. Shooter had in mind someone, probably in their sixties, with an engineering background and experienced in running companies where safety was axiomatic. Also, if possible, knowledge of a business where customer service was important so the candidate could therefore understand the tension between these last two requirements.

Sir Hugh discussed a fairly long list with Shooter and together they also interviewed some senior people from the City. Shooter recalls that he found short-listing and interviewing candidates to be his own boss a fascinating exercise! Eventually, Sir Hugh said, 'I think you ought to meet Dick Morris'. He was referring to Sir Richard Morris, a chemical engineer who, among many other interesting posts, had formerly been chief executive of the North Sea oil engineering company Brown and Roote UK (Haliburton), and had held directorships with Courtaulds Limited and British Nuclear Fuels, industrial adviser to the Barclays Bank Group, president of the Institution of Chemical Engineers, vice-president of the Society of Chemical Industry, member, and for a time deputy chairman of the Advisory Board to the Research Council, a governor of the Royal Post-Graduate Medical School, Hammersmith, pro-chancellor of Loughborough University and also chairman of the University Council, visiting professor of Chemical Engineering at Strathclyde University, vice-president of the Fellowship of Engineering. He was president of the association for Science Education for 1990. He was also chairman of Devonport Management Ltd and Devonport Royal Dockyard 1987–91; the Howard Humphreys Group from 1987–90 and United Kingdom NIREX Ltd since 1989. He held Honorary Doctor of Science Degrees from Bath, Birmingham, Leeds and Loughborough Universities. Sir Richard was at the time aged seventy-one.

To Shooter he sounded extremely interesting, and so it was arranged that he should go and take lunch with Sir Richard at his club. Shooter encountered an energetic personality with an obviously lively mind. About halfway through his description of the task, Shooter was slightly taken aback when Sir Richard interjected 'Right, I'll do it!' Up to that point Shooter couldn't remember actually having offered him the post! Anyway, he did, subject to Sir Richard having the approval of the other directors. Shooter duly reported back to his team. 'What!' exclaimed a startled Turner, 'you can't have an old blighter like that!'

'You'd better meet him,' replied Shooter and lunch was arranged for the following week at The Bell at Aston Clinton, after which Sir Richard was unanimously given a warm welcome aboard as the chairman of what by then was named 'M40 Trains', the umbrella company formed by the Chiltern Directors, John Laing Ltd and 3i. By now it was the late autumn of 1995.

In January 1996 M40 Trains was invited to tender for the franchise and, much to their delight, in March 1996 the MBO team were informed that they had been shortlisted, along with Stagecoach and Connex.

CHAPTER 4

'NO PRIZES FOR COMING SECOND'

No Italian football team could have demonstrated more passion at this time than 'Shooter's little army', as they came to be known within some sections of the industry. To win, the team had to come up with something special. They could only make a shrewd guess at what particular innovations the other two bidders would offer, and while they had plenty of ideas of their own they would require significant investment. Given the tight financial environment and the personal as well as corporate financial risks involved, the financial projections were checked over by various teams of consultants.

The team knew they were bidding from a strong base; over four years passenger numbers had increased by 60 per cent with revenue in proportion. They had the advantage of recent Total Route Modernisation with modern rolling stock and infrastructure and all the managers and staff were highly motivated. But how far could the business be developed? Would their own calculations on costings and revenue growth be confirmed, what options did they have and how should they prioritise?

The 1991 Census returns used by the London-based LEK Partnership noted the striking population increases in the Chiltern market area, particularly in Aylesbury Vale and North Oxfordshire. The study also showed that in 1994 most of Chiltern's revenue came from stations around London and that this was unlikely to change. Furthermore, while the proportion of Chiltern's customers using the train as a means of getting to work exceeded the national average, the further analysis showing flow by flow penetration comparisons with the former Southern Region electric lines into London shows clearly that Chiltern has an enormous market potential that had yet to be realised.

If the top ten revenue-earning stations on Chiltern were all in the London area, very little Chiltern revenue came from elsewhere. In 1994 Chiltern had very little of the through London to Birmingham market. Most of its revenue was from commuting at both ends of the line and the revenue at the Birmingham end was modest. The virtual ending of through trains from Birmingham to London along the old Great Western route under BR after 1968 had destroyed that customer base, leaving merely a romantic folk memory. It was going to be a tough battle to start the recovery.

Both the London and Birmingham commuter markets offered great opportunities. The lost Birmingham–London market would have to be rebuilt from scratch. A simple comparison with the London, Tilbury and Southend (LTS) TOC, which had a similar population base to Chiltern, illustrated the opportunities in the London market. LTS already had a much greater market penetration with 23 million annual journeys, averaging out at 24.3 journeys per inhabitant, compared to Chiltern's 7 million annual journeys and an average of 7.8 journeys per inhabitant.

Each market needed a different strategy, and prompted discussion between the directors. For example, Turner had doubts about the Birmingham–London market per se, believing that Chiltern's greatest opportunity here lay in tapping the travel needs of the affluent south Birmingham hinterlands around Dorridge, Solihull, Lapworth and Warwick rather than the city centre itself. This led eventually to the building of the very successful Warwick Parkway station.

In the BR version of the Chiltern business plan published in February 1995, the projected growth in passenger revenue had been given as:

94/95	95/96	96/97	97/98	98/99	99/00	2001	2002	2003
£22.8m	£25.5m	£26.6m	£27.7m	£28.2m	£28.5m			

Chiltern's own MBO business plan gave a more cautiously optimistic projection with passenger revenue increasing at around 5 per cent per annum over the seven-year period:

£22.5m (actual)	£25.3m	£27m	£28.7m	£30.3m	31.7m	£32.6m	£33.4m	£34.1m

For comparison, the actual revenue achieved over the same years was:

£22.5m	£25.3m	£28.6m	£33.4m	£38.8m	£44.5m	£53.1m	£55m	£60.2 m

In the spring of 1996, Chiltern's principal equity partner in M40 Trains, John Laing Plc, as part of their due diligence, commissioned the consultants Steer Davies Gleave to review the passenger forecasts for the Compliant bid and for the main variant options. These latter included: 1) do nothing; 2) compliant bid; 3) the option of introducing new trains on the Birmingham–London through services, with modest line speeds and journey time enhancements; 4) variant option, that is, new trains but with line speed increases up to 100mph and an overall journey time running very close to the Euston–New Street timings achieved by the WCML.

The 'do nothing' option was the basis of the compliant bid and implied Chiltern continuing to benefit from the Route Modernisation for the duration of the initial seven-year term of the franchise, but with management taking little further initiative to develop and build on customer demand. Services would still be run entirely with the Class 165 commuter trains. Based upon the example of the Bedford–St Pancras modernisation (which also included electrification), the initial advantage of Total Route Modernisation would gradually tail away, including the increase in the commercially crucial peak loadings, because of such factors as overcrowding on trains and in car parks (already by 1996, car parks at six of Chiltern's most profitable stations were close to capacity). Thus, perceptions of Chiltern's service quality would suffer in the eyes of the customers.

Nevertheless, there would still be growth overall, particularly from the West Midlands to London traffic (+212 per cent) and other such factors as employment in Central London growing proportionally with growth in GDP, increasing congestion on the M40, particularly at the London end and the general increase in population along the M40 Corridor. The study projected no significant inroad into the WCML Birmingham–London Inter-City market because under this option only a very limited reduction in overall timings would be possible. The only line speed improvement envisaged was limited to permitting the Class 165s to run more generally at their modest maximum of 75mph.

The Compliant bid was a simple variation of the 'do nothing' scenario with the acquisition of two new trains of superior accommodation and 100mph potential (though under this scenario they would still not be able to run faster than 75mph) and their employment on a morning and evening limited stop London–Birmingham service. The rest of the day they would operate a London–Banbury shuttle. Overall, it was calculated these new trains would create an additional 4 per cent demand. This would also allow the Class 165 trains so displaced to strengthen existing commuter services and thus reduce peak overcrowding. This scenario would earn an extra £4.8 million during the seven-year franchise.

Exploring options 3 and 4, the consultants concluded that combining the introduction of between three and nine new trains together with line speed improvements to allow running at 100mph, along with elimination of the single line between Princes Risborough and Aynho Junction and with the introduction of a half-hourly service between Birmingham and London on a one-hour forty-nine-minute timing overall would, given aggressive marketing, make serious inroads (50 per cent) into the existing WCML Euston services. The consultants also endorsed Shooter's belief in the South West Airlines concept of one-class value-for-money accommodation, proffering that Chiltern would thus capture a significant share of the Birmingham City market. The Evergreen 3 main line investment, to be completed in 2011, will deliver the capacity and capability to offer these services – although the competitive position with the West Coast route has of course also changed since the mid-1990s.

The Chiltern team endorsed this latter expansive vision. Shooter had always maintained his belief in the importance of going to Birmingham. However, given the level of investment that could sensibly be expected within the limits of a seven-year franchise, the realistic way forward was to set out what was practical in the Chiltern business plan. This would project annual revenue growth of 5 per cent, and simply hinted at Chiltern's future vision by stating that:

> In addition to the actions outlined in 1.5 (i.e. Continuing to provide a safe, reliable and civilised service to passengers, investing in additional and improved car parking and increased marketing activity focussed on identified priority catchment areas, improving ticketing systems and customer services), M40 Trains intends to pursue further opportunities for profitable growth. Dependent upon timing and detailed feasibility studies these opportunities include:
> - working with Railtrack to upgrade the infrastructure to allow speeds up to 100mph and introduce a dedicated London to Birmingham high-speed service
> - bidding for a second franchise – Thames Trains
> - operating light transit systems as part of DBFO schemes (Design, Build, Finance, Operate)
> - working with developers to open new stations and/or park and ride schemes
> - working with developers and/or retailers to improve station environments

The Chiltern team calculated that around £4.75 million was required to fulfil the minimum capital requirements of OPRAF and to provide the capital for the investments outlined above.

At the same time, the MBO team estimated that they should be able to generate a £24 million operating profit over the seven-year franchise. They believed there would be strong cash generation capable of financing further investment and giving internal rates of return in excess of 25 per cent pa to investors. This latter was based upon 30 per cent of revenue being guaranteed (OPRAF subsidy), subject to the final bid, and took into account approximately 60 per cent of operating costs fixed and contracted.

Acknowledging lessons learned from previous rail modernisation schemes highlighted in the consultants report, the MBO business plan tackled the issue of the overcrowding that was already an issue on peak-hour Chiltern services:

> Continued growth in passenger numbers is now beginning to impact on passenger perceptions of service quality, primarily because increasing numbers of regular peak travellers are finding it difficult to get a seat. If this is not to become a serious constraint on growth the business needs to lease additional coaches. The projections prepared by the management team foresee the leasing of additional vehicles in line with demand.

The part of the MBO business plan headed 'MBO Team Philosophy' gives in unequivocal terms the strength of their belief in their case. It restated their focus on revenue growth to deliver profits, stressed their lean management structure, reminded potential equity partners of the high fixed costs associated with operating a railway and put into bold type the maxim of their strategy to **stretch the business and its revenues** quite literally by increasing the average train length and the average journey distance. The MBO plan outlined the commitment to strengthen the existing 2 and 3-car sets to formations of 4 and 5-cars. They also referred to their preliminary discussions with rolling stock manufacturers about the supply of new air-conditioned higher specification trains.

The team continued to expound their forward-looking vision outlining plans to upgrade the track to permit speeds of 100mph and thereby reducing the overall journey time from 137 to a

Blue Pullman arrived Birmingham Snow Hill platform 5 with 10:10 ex-Paddington. This train will return to Paddington at 13:00 as the 'Birmingham Pullman'. (Michael Mensing)

maximum of 108 minutes, thus at last making Chiltern a serious competitor with the WCML for the London to Birmingham market. The essence of this infrastructure improvement, at this time, was the concept of a long dynamic passing loop north of Haddenham station and a 70mph cross-over south of Princes Risborough.

The vision continued by stating their intention to bid for the Thames Train franchise, part of the LUL Metropolitan line and opportunities for light rail schemes in various large urban areas through-out the United Kingdom. Further sections on cost control were a reminder that the team's vision for infrastructure development was indeed firmly grounded on the ballast of fiscal prudence.

Additional sections dealt with proposals for the radical development of marketing, including a rather flattering outline of the typical Chiltern customer, proposed new ticketing systems, planned improvements to car parking security, opportunities for additional revenue through payment by the train leasing company for Chiltern to undertake the heavy maintenance of its rolling stock, a thoughtful analysis of the competition from both the car as well as other rail companies and the strengths of the Chiltern MBO team in terms of qualifications and experience.

In short, the MBO business plan gave a convincing picture of a highly competent, thoroughly professional, but nevertheless progressively customer-focussed business.

On top of this very inspirational basis, Beckett and Turner also attached a separate extra docu-ment entitled 'Section 14, Non-Compliant Options; Delivering Chiltern's Full Potential'. This set out what the Chiltern team believed they could deliver, given a longer-term franchise, building on those proposals outlined previously.

If further evidence were needed that the Chiltern team were light years removed from the money-grabbing, quick in-and-out opportunists they were assumed to be by some in the City, this document hammered home the point beyond any doubt. As well as stressing how a longer franchise would deliver a substantially reduced requirement for financial support (i.e. Government subsidy), it pointed out the opportunity for major investment in infrastructure to eliminate capacity problems and dramatically improve journey times, thus giving the basis for major service enhancements, for new trains that would be fully paid for over the life of the franchise, real competition for West Coast, major redevelopment of car parking at selected stations and investment in sophisticated new ticketing facilities.

The document delved into history to remind the powers that be of how the route had previously been an an effective competitor to the West Coast line when the latter was being dug up last time around in the 1960s to install electrification. At that point, the Blue Pullmans had offered a very popular two-hour schedule between Birmingham and London. In bold type it was now stated:

M40 Trains intends to reintroduce fast express services between Birmingham and London with times faster than the Blue Pullman.

This supplementary document continued by outlining the marketing opportunities along the route in the areas of the West Midlands, Warwickshire, Oxfordshire and the south, negotiating with Railtrack to undertake significant investment in the track and an initial order for three new high-specification 100mph trains (nine vehicles). These would have reservable, one-class 'club'-style seating with more space, privacy and tables to work on, air conditioning and an at-seat trolley service.

The Chiltern team had already started work on their concept for a new type of train. While Shooter and his engineering director David Masson worked on the technical specifications, Turner and his team, following the example of South West Airlines in the US, started exploring with customers their ideas for one-class trains, albeit with the standard class accommodation enhanced to offer the new concept of 'club' class.

While some of the long time London commuters viewed the abolition of first class seating as further evidence of the decline and fall of western civilisation, the majority felt that given the relatively short journey time between London and Birmingham, one-class accommodation, provided it was of a sufficient standard to encourage business persons to leave their company BMWs and Ford Mondeos at one of the parkway stations and take the train, was acceptable. This was a very courageous decision by Shooter and Turner. In the event, had they got this bit wrong, the ensuing financial consequences would clearly have been serious.

It did also have an associated element of humour when Turner approached some of the manufacturers of railway seats with a request that Chiltern be supplied with a range of samples of various designs to gauge customer reaction. This rocked the industry — the idea that anyone should actually ask the passengers what they would like was an entirely novel concept. Chiltern went even further and passenger representatives were also invited later on to view and comment on the prototype of the new trains at the ABB works in Derby (see also Part 2, 'The Train Designer's Story').

Tragedy of a more personal kind then intervened. David Masson, Shooter's engineering director, was killed in a car crash while holidaying in East Africa during Christmas 1995. Masson's deputy Andy Hamilton took over, and during Christmas and the New Year Hamilton and Shooter between them wrote their specification for what became known as the Chiltern Clubman, the Class 168.

Chiltern's subsequent successes have been, in part, down to the willingness of Shooter and his team to look at new ideas from outside the railway industry, i.e. to think 'outside the box'. A clear example of this was to adopt some of the thinking behind the success of the US South West Airlines. *Nuts!* is the catchy title of Kevin and Jackie Freiburg's book chronicling the remarkable story of Rollin King, a San Antonio entrepreneur, John Parker, his banker, and Herb Kelleher who had a law practice in the same town, and how they conceived and started, against all the odds, South West Airlines.

South West Airlines is the only US airline that has consistently made a profit every year since it was started in 1971. Their success is down to a number of factors but the main ingredients are that, above all, they keep things simple, and this was the business model Shooter and his team adopted. South West Airlines has relatively new planes; Chiltern has relatively new trains. South West runs from secondary airfields (which incidentally are also frequently closer and hence more conveniently placed in relation to city centres and their business areas) and Chiltern runs between secondary stations in London and Birmingham. South West Airlines have a high utilisation of planes, Chiltern has a high utilisation of trains and, like South West, turns them around very quickly. This is because South West from the start created a flexible work ethic where pilots and flight attendants help with cleaning and stowing baggage. Chiltern's staff are encouraged to have similar attitudes. Like South West, Chiltern aims to offer good value for money and will be reliable, consistent and uncomplicated. For example, in its fare structure, Chiltern, in contrast to companies, keeps it simple and offers one-class accommodation.

When looking for a potential manufacturer for the new trains, Shooter was dismayed to find very little on offer in the UK. BR had not placed any orders for new trains since 1993, and during the pre-privatisation period several of the former BR train-building workshops, erstwhile household names, had closed. The experience of generations of highly skilled crafts persons was lost as the workers were made redundant.

Shooter knew what Chiltern needed was a superior type of DMU. No one appeared to be building, or even at that stage planning, any. His dilemma was that if he broadcast too loudly his wish to purchase new trains, one of the other bidders might pick it up and include it in their bid, thus nullifying what was probably the Chiltern team's strongest card. It was central to their ability to bid for a lower subsidy, and therefore they needed to be able to include a definite commitment to order as part of the final Chiltern bid.

Accordingly, Shooter put a notice in the *European Official Journal*, feeling reasonably safe that the British press would not be looking there. A couple of days later across the front page of the *Financial Times* was 'Management team from Chiltern, who are expecting to bid for the Chiltern franchise, are touting for new trains'. The management team in question naturally felt pretty sick when they read this. Fortunately their fears proved unfounded and neither of the other bidders appeared to have grasped the significance.

Over a dozen European companies replied. It was a requirement that the company must have experience of building DMUs. One reply was from a Berlin company called EWA who had built the *Flying Hamburger* in 1934. Shooter went first to Fiat and received a pretty dusty answer from their chief executive: 'Mr Shooter, do you own this company? No? Well, when you do, we can talk again.'

Next, ABB and Alsthom were approached. Alsthom's response was not very detailed and was based upon designs for trains they were building in Spain for Ireland. They were unable to answer Shooter's specific questions when he tried to perceive how they matched Chiltern's requirements. ABB at Derby had, meanwhile, used the order famine to analyse what kind of trains might be needed in the brave new world of privatisation. Product Development Manager Allan Dare (later to join Chiltern) had drawn up a 'business output specification' for a 100mph DMU, suitable for both inter-regional and commuter services. This closely matched the detailed specification drawn up by Shooter and Hamilton, so discussions got underway. At the time, convention dictated that all the design and tooling costs for a new build of trains would be recouped on the first sale. This was clearly impractical for the small build of only twelve vehicles required by Chiltern. ABB therefore bravely decided to set the price on the expectation that eventually seventy-five vehicles would be sold nationwide, and made an offer to Chiltern on this basis. Over the next few years ABB (later Adtranz, now Bombardier) would sell over 400 of these 'Turbostar' DMUs to train operators across the country, so the decision was well vindicated.

ABB's would be straight off the drawing board; not ideal but there was little choice. Shooter duly agreed the deal with John Harris, sales director for ABB at a hotel in Crick. Beckett was busy finalising Chiltern's final bid for the deadline of 23 May 1996 and by the 22nd there had still not been a formally signed contract from ABB. Shooter therefore took the draft contract to the railway exhibition running at the NEC, cornered Stig Svärd, ABB Chief Executive, on the ABB stand and got his signature. This proved to be the first deal for new trains made by a privatised rail company. After 1,064 days, the order famine was over.

On 10 June 1996, at 1 p.m. during the course of a regular management meeting, Shooter received a telephone call from Gary Backler at the Strategic Rail Authority: 'You'd better sit down. Congratulations, you've won the franchise!'

Not a lot was done at the meeting after that. Regrettably, Beckett, who had done so much work in the all important drafting of all the various documents, was not present. He was actually in a pub in Dartmouth on holiday when he received a pager message to 'call Adrian Shooter's PA. Urgent. About bid' (this was in the days before mobile phones). Beckett recalls that he started shaking like a leaf and recalls it took him a very tense twenty minutes to get sight of a public call box, call and hear the good news.

For the main players in the MBO it had been an exhausting twelve months. The pressures on them had been considerable, and in some instances almost too much for partners and families.

CHAPTER 5

LOCATION, LOCATION, LOCATION! THE MAINTENANCE PROBLEM

The Chiltern Railways story is essentially a people story; engage staff about their work and inevitably the conversation turns to people. Nevertheless trains, like any other machine, need regular and systematic maintenance, much of it nowadays undertaken by a few professionals during the night while the rest of us sleep. This chapter is, at least, in part a tribute and recognition to all those who do this essential nocturnal work to ensure our trains are ready for us, in the right place, clean, reliable, on time and above all, safe to ride in.

When the line to Marylebone was originally opened in 1899, the steam locomotive depot was at Neasden, with carriage sidings and a turntable provided at Marylebone itself. When British Rail made the switch from steam to diesel in the 1960s, the first generation Class 115 DMUs were routinely maintained at Marylebone in a depot converted from the original Victorian carriage shed. For heavier maintenance they were sent to Bletchley where, at the time, the area maintenance engineer was one Adrian Shooter. In general, the former GC lines in later years had been run down and were in a very dilapidated state (for a fuller description of what he found when he arrived as managing director, Network SouthEast in 1986, see Chris Green's 'The Line that Nearly Died' in Part 2). Writing of the then diesel depot, Green observed 'Marylebone diesel depot looked as though it had just emerged from the Blitz... I remember standing in the horror of Marylebone depot – more 1956 than 1986 – and feeling the deepest shame for what we had done to this forgotten group of staff... It was time to put some pride back into the line.'

An outline of the transformation of the Chiltern line during BR days, initiated by Green and implemented in turn by Chris Tibbitts and Richard Fearn, was included in Chapter 2. By 1991 it was obvious that some radical innovation was needed to provide for the proper maintenance of the eagerly awaited and imminently expected new Turbo Diesel Class 165 units.

Consequently, Green persuaded the BR Board to invest £3.5 million in a completely new state of the art maintenance depot on a green-field site at Aylesbury, just north of the station. Initially it had three roads, A, B and C and staff morale was transformed when the squalor of the old Marylebone depot was exchanged for this beautiful new, brightly lit and clean working environment.

Aylesbury was a wonderful improvement at a time when services were concentrated on that 'Aylesbury via Amersham' route, partly shared with London Transport. However, even in the latter days of BR and prior to privatisation, things on the Chiltern line were now moving fast, with the revival of services via Banbury to Birmingham's new Snow Hill station from May 1993, as well as the steady increase in numbers of the new Class 165 Turbo diesels followed soon after privatisation by the new Class 168 Clubmans. Thus, operations were increasingly focussed thereafter on services to Birmingham and the West Midlands. For comparison, when Chris Green arrived at NSE, the Chiltern line was operated by a seventy-five-strong fleet of Class 115 vehicles. By 2009, Chiltern Railways was operating a combined fleet of 167 vehicles consisting of Classes 165 and 168, plus the Class 121 operating the Aylesbury to Princess Risborough shuttle, plus some railhead treatment vehicles (Chiltern is the only Train Operating Company that carries out its own railhead treatment programme), as well as the Mark 3 passenger coaching stock and Class 67 locomotives operating the Wrexham and Shropshire services.

An even more dramatic comparison is illustrated by comparing the 1984 total of approximately sixty trains a day on all routes with over 300 trains operated each weekday by Chiltern Railways in 2009. This meant that, by the millennium, Chiltern Railways had a serious capacity problem at its new Aylesbury depot. To alleviate this firstly road D, which contained the underframe cleaning equipment, was extended to a four-car length and a further road – E – with wheel-turning lathe was added. In addition to daily cleaning and refuelling, the vehicles of the Chiltern fleet have 'A' maintenance schedules carried out every 5,000 miles and 'B' heavy maintenance every 20,000 miles. The Class 168 'Clubman' units cover 20,000 miles roughly every six weeks.

Thus, Aylesbury was no longer adequate. In addition to capacity issues, with the focus of Chiltern's operations spread more widely, including the West Midlands, the company was now incurring heavy additional costs both in fuel, staff and mileage charges imposed by Railtrack/NetworkRail for the increasing number of trains forced to run empty to and from Aylesbury, for example all those that started the next day from Banbury.

If Aylesbury was no longer the only spot, where then? In all, twenty-two possible sites were investigated by the Chiltern Board. In terms of geography, Marylebone was ideal and one of the options investigated was the sealed up second tunnel there, only to discover that someone had been allowed to build right down through it after purchasing the freehold from the British Rail Property Board.

Eventually, Wembley was identified, the nearest site to Marylebone and adjacent to Wembley Stadium station. The plans formed part of Chiltern's 'Evergreen 2' development and the completed complex is owned by M40 Trains under financial arrangements similar to those for Warwick Parkway.

Now most of the routine carriage washing, fuelling, 'A' maintenance exams (including those for the Class 67 locomotives and Mark 3 coaching stock for Wrexham and Shropshire trains) and light repairs are carried out at Wembley, freeing up Aylesbury for heavier work. Routine overnight cleaning and fuelling is also done now at Birmingham Tyseley and Stourbridge Junction. Heavy hand cleaning of the lower body sides of the Class 168 fleet is carried out at Stourbridge Junction, necessitated partly by the brake block dust from London Midland's Class 150s that hangs around inside Snow Hill tunnel.

Unlike Aylesbury, the bulk of the work at Wembley is carried out during daytime. From about 9:30 a.m. after the morning peak, trains start arriving with increasing frequency until between 12 p.m. and 1 p.m., after which the work and pressure on accommodation falls away steadily until 5 p.m., by which time most of the units have left to cover the evening peak.

In 2009, overall responsibility for all Chiltern's maintenance was with Engineering Director Kate Majoribanks. Kate, a chartered engineer, started her railway career as a graduate trainee during the final days of British Rail, followed a variety of postings including the Angel Trains ROSCO and South West Trains, before joining Chiltern in February 2009.

To assist the engineering director is Fleet Engineer Carl Harvey. Harvey has day-to-day management of the Aylesbury and Wembley depots and all their staff and stores including those at Stourbridge Junction. There is also Engineering Manager Simon Jarrett and Project Manager John Hartland, who has specific responsibility for the project for new and refurbished trains for both Chiltern and its associate company, London Overground.

In 2009, the depot manager at Wembley was Paul McCarthy. Paul started with London Transport, transferring to British Rail in 1979, working at both the old Marylebone and new Aylesbury depots. Although Paul clearly enjoys the daily challenges presented to him at his new state of the art Wembley depot, not least that of ensuring the standards of excellence required to maintain the depot to ISO 9002, his memories of the working environment at the old Marylebone diesel depot are every bit as graphic as Green's. Added to the general air of nineteenth-century squalor were the extra delights of cockroach infestations and frequent falls of glass roofing.

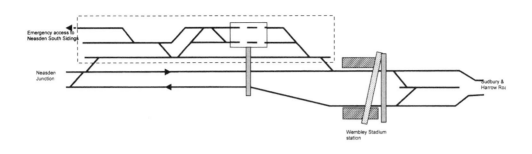

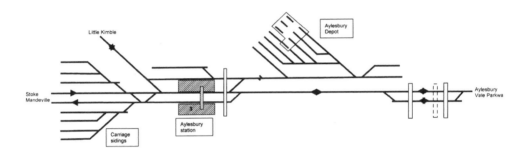

Below: Fitter Noel Scarry (Scaz) at work in Aylesbury depot. (Chiltern Railways)

Above: Charley Patel refuelling Class 165 unit. (Hugh Jones)

Below: The First of the Clubmans. Prototype No.168001 resting at Aylesbury. (Hugh Jones)

Above: Abi cleaning the underframe of Class 165 unit. (Hugh Jones)

Left: Preparing for work. (Mark Carwithen)

Below: Middle of the night and still arriving. (Mike Carwithen)

Lift for removing engines and gear boxes, Aylesbury. (Mike Carwithen)

McCarthy and his erstwhile colleague Lionel Smith described to me how the wire-reinforced glass-roof windows installed after the Second World War to replace those destroyed in the Blitz would regularly fracture with the thin wire reinforcement in the glass precariously holding broken shards suspended above the heads of the workers below. Work would have to then be suspended while an agile fitter climbed up a ladder, walked along the roof gutter and put his boot through the broken window pane to send it crashing down on the depot floor. The consequences for the working comfort of the staff in the depths of winter can only be imagined. It had the original pits designed for working on the old Gresley-designed Quad-Art articulated steam-hauled stock, which staff avoided entering if at all possible. There was even an ancient vacuum pump for testing the brakes of steam carriages along with a stock of replacement oval windows and lists of all the running numbers for the same.

It was a dump, but paradoxically the appalling working conditions created a strong bond among those working there, now remembered with some affection and a little nostalgia. There was leg pulling and practical jokes which would not be allowed in our more politically correct times. For instance, the driver who used a three-wheel Reliant Robin to come to work would occasionally find the apprentices had mounted the rear wheels on brake blocks so it would not drive away. One day it was even found placed on a flat truck at the end of the carriage sidings, but it was all taken in good part. This was further encouraged by the relative neglect by the senior management of the various regions who were nominally in charge of this sad remnant of the once proud Great Central.

Although prior to nationalisation in 1948 Marylebone had been part of the old London and North Eastern Railway with headquarters at King's Cross, Marylebone and the Chiltern lines later became attached to the London Midland and Western Regions. Intially, the Aylesbury route passed to the London Midland with the remainder of the Chiltern route remaining in Western Region. However, in the early 1960s the whole route became absorbed into the London Midland – before passing back to the Western in the 1980s. During this era, Marylebone and the Chiltern lines became a somewhat forgotten part of the network, developing its own traditions and practices, with priority given to bravely maintaining a public service come what may. A number of anecdotes illustrate this increasingly idiosyncratic little world of its own. All staff, drivers, fitters, cleaners and so on regularly adjourned to the supervisor's office for a cup of tea together. The traditional railway rules of craft demarcation were subordinated to the objective of pulling together to get the job in hand done, in the interest of serving the public with the obsolescent trains and equipment available. For example, the day the hurricane struck southern England in 1987, after all the London stations had been closed for reasons of safety, an elderly disabled lady turned up needing to return home to Princes Risborough. By this time the station had been officially closed, however, she was brought to the diesel depot by taxi where the staff clipped over all the points to access the main line, organised a special train which rushed her to Princes Risborough. Other stories from those days tell of drivers holding their trains for a few minutes for the benefit of regular passengers seen running late from station car parks.

Similarly, although Marylebone was essentially for refuelling, cleaning and only light maintenance, gradually the staff there took on more and more of the maintenance themselves, way beyond what they were officially required to do, for instance exchanging gearboxes. There was a practical reason for this because when units were sent away either to Bletchley or later, under the Western Region, to Old Oak Common, those places having carried out whatever heavy repairs were required would then find reasons to hang on to them to augment their own operational fleets for prolonged periods.

In this manner, Marylebone became even more self-contained with fitters drawing upon ever-increasing reserves of initiative to keep the old Class 115 units running, despite the rugged quality of their initial construction, especially the Leyland-Albion diesel engines and the sturdy final drive. For example, one day a vertically positioned exhaust pipe between the carriages rusted through and fell off. As the vehicle in question was needed later that day a convenient plastic-covered steel road signpost quickly 'disappeared' from the vicinity of Marylebone. It was sawn off at ground level, a flange rapidly welded on and the new 'exhaust pipe' bolted on as a replacement. The unit ran with this in place for several years until finally withdrawn for scrap, although there were occasional complaints from passengers about the smell of burning plastic!

On another occasion, a driver brought a train into Marylebone saying he would have to fail it as the riding was so rough it felt as if it was coming off the road. When the unit was brought into the depot for examination it was found the train had been operating for some time with a tyre missing from number eight wheel which was right under the cab. It was amazing that it had stayed on the track at all. Staff had to use sledge hammers to force a skate under the wheel to enable the vehicle to be dragged to Bletchley for repair.

Nothing could be a greater contrast from the old 'make do and mend' culture required twenty or more years ago than the situation today at Wembley and Aylesbury. This was very clearly illustrated in the press interview given by Jenny Crook, the Aylesbury depot operations manager during National Science and Engineering Week in 2009 to explain what it takes to keep the trains running. This is reproduced (courtesy of Chiltern Railways) below:

'In essence we worry about safety so that our passengers don't have to' says Depot Operations Manager Jenny Crook at Aylesbury depot.

Jenny has been with Chiltern since her graduation in 2004 and is responsible for making sure that the trains which pass through the depot on a daily basis are fully and rigorously checked and that every single part of the train is working properly and safely. 'It's five past midnight and one of our Class 168s (the trains which run from London to the West Midlands) comes onto the depot for refuelling,' she explains. 'They hold 1,500 miles worth of fuel and when there is about 100 miles of fuel left, we'll bring it in to refuel and do a fuel point check.'

'Prior to coming inside the depot, we empty the toilet tanks, never a popular job. After this, the train comes into the depot where we top up the fresh water for the toilets and refuel it. Refuelling a train isn't as simple as refuelling your car at the pump. We need to keep track of the level of fuel in each train so prior to filling it up, we electronically log the train number so we always know for sure how much fuel it has in it. We don't want to run the risk of our trains grinding to a halt because the tank is empty.'

'Whilst this is going on another member of staff will carry out a number of routine checks; engine oil, coolant levels, the toilets, checking the tripcock which is a safety system we use on the London to Aylesbury line where we share tracks with London Underground, and checking the cab and passenger areas to ensure there is no damage and that the unit is safe and ready for traffic. We will also carry out any checks for faults that drivers may have reported during the train's previous duties. The whole thing takes one and a half hours. Once this is done, cleaners go on board to give the interior of the train a thorough clean.'

This is, of course, a fairly routine exam but there are more rigorous exams that take place on a less frequent basis as Jenny continues, 'There is the A2 exam, where we carry out additional checks, including brake pads, after each 10,000 miles and then B exam which takes place every 20,000 miles (that's about every six weeks for a Class 168 unit).'

'The B exam covers just about everything. We remove all the dirt and debris from underneath the train; this removes potential fire risks and allows us to examine component parts in more detail. We check the wheels, the dampers and suspension which ensure our passengers have a smooth ride throughout their journey; we check the engine and change the oil and the filters and we simulate movement to ensure our safety systems are working correctly. Then there's the doors, the smoke detectors, the CCTV, air conditioning, toilets, fire extinguishers… just about everything is covered!'

Train safety is of paramount importance and Chiltern use a number of different safety features, as Jenny explains, 'On the line from Marylebone to Aylesbury Vale Parkway, we share some of the route with the London Underground and so share their safety systems. But on the London to Birmingham line we have nationwide systems: Automatic Warning System, and Train Protection and Warning System. In addition to this we also have our own additional safety system Automatic Train Protection.'

'The AWS is fitted throughout our route and on-track magnets 'speak' to the train about signals ahead. If the signal is not green then a horn sounds to alert the driver. If he doesn't respond to the warning then the brakes come on automatically to bring the train to a halt. We then have TPWS which is also standard throughout the UK. This system is always running in the background and applies the brakes if the driver was to speed or go past a red signal on a critical part of the network.'

'Finally, on both our lines south of Banbury we have ATP fitted. This feeds more information directly to the driver's cab informing him of speed changes and signal aspects coming up. If the driver fails to react to these the train will automatically intervene to reduce the speed. Unlike cars, trains have solid steel wheels. These can still get damaged and so the engineering team have to keep a close eye on them. Wheels are regularly checked at the depot but they have a bit of extra help with an on track system at Banbury called "Gotcha" which automatically checks for wheel damage every time a train passes over it.

'That's the everyday routine that trains go through to ensure they stay safe. Of course, there are times when trains will report particular faults and they get sent to the depot for repair. But Chiltern's trains are pretty reliable and major faults are few and far between.'

'We work to get the big things right,' says Jenny. 'We do listen to comments from passengers and drivers about problems with trains and try to sort them out as quickly as possible.'

So next time you've had a smooth and safe journey on one of our trains, do not forget to thank Jenny and her colleagues.

Early construction work on building Wembley depot. (Chiltern Railways)

Construction work at Wembley.
(Chiltern Railways)

Building the new Wembley Stadium station. (Chiltern Railways)

Construction work at Wembley.
(Chiltern Railways)

Wembley depot. (Chiltern Railways)

Above right: Completed Wembley depot with the new stadium in the background. (Chiltern Railways)

Above left: Wembley depot.   *Below:* Wembley Carriage Wash. (Chiltern Railways)

Construction work at Wembley.
(Chiltern Railways)

Below: Wembley. (Chiltern Railways)

Above, right and below: Wembley. (Chiltern Railways)

Carriage cleaning at Wembley. (Chiltern Railways)

Wrexham and Shropshire train stabling at Wembley
Class 67 locomotive and Mark 3 Coaches.

Wembley official opening by Transport
Minister Alastair Darling, with *(top)*
Company Chairman Adrian Shooter.
(Chiltern Railways)

Wembley staff 2005. (Chiltern Railways)

Wembley depot control room. (Chiltern Railways)

Above: Midday and Wembley is nearly full to capacity.

Below: Wembley depot manager Paul McCarthy and the maintenance workshop.

CHAPTER 6

GROWING THE BUSINESS

(Or one rat, the first track doubling and several metaphorical fat cats.)

At 2 a.m. on 21 July 1996, Chiltern Railways legally became a private company, with a franchise to run trains for the next seven years. Some days before, each member of staff had received a six-page briefing paper from their managing director. The overriding message to staff was shared involvement. In outlining the challenges and opportunities ahead, reference was made to the superior speed and enhanced comfort of the new trains for the Birmingham–London services, together with details of proposed improved services. Options were included for increasing track capacity on the single line section from Princes Risborough to Bicester, with shorter journey times, station improvements, new ticket products and train safety improvements. Shooter explained the need to generate an annual increase in passenger revenue to cover both the reductions in Government subsidy as well as the increased track access, train leasing and maintenance costs. The final section outlined details of the new Profit Sharing Scheme for all staff.

Almost immediately the order for the new trains was confirmed. This was the first order for new rolling stock by a privately owned main-line railway company in Britain since 1948, the first by any of the new train operating companies and the first new order for passenger trains in the UK for almost three years – 1,064 days in fact.

Simultaneously, planning started to deal with the twenty-seven-mile stretch of single track between Aynho Junction, just south of Banbury and Princes Risborough. Trains could pass at Bicester, but between there and Princes Risborough some eighteen miles away there was no passing loop. It was a major obstruction to Chiltern's need to grow their business. Consultants examining the financial and operating implications came up with four options. Firstly, do nothing: leaving the single line in place would still allow Chiltern to run an hourly service between Birmingham and London and the superior speed of the new trains would permit some slight reduction in overall timing. One or two additional trains could be run in the peaks, which would meet Chiltern's franchise commitment but only by making the line effectively a 'one-way street' during the peaks with the extra services southbound only in the morning and northbound in the evening. There was no possibility of running both simultaneously in the peaks and seriously competing with the West Coast route for London to Birmingham traffic.

Another option included a turnback siding at Haddenham and Thame, permitting a more intensive service between there and Marylebone. Option three was doubling the track between Princes Risborough and Haddenham, while Option four was doubling all the way between Princes Risborough and Bicester.

Shooter preferred the fourth option from the start. Chiltern needed to grow the business. The 'virtuous circle' of step by step growth would provide the extra revenue to pay for the leasing and running of the new trains as well as covering the gradual reduction in Government subsidy. It would also, hopefully, make more profit for the company.

Adtranz workers greeting news of the first order for 1,064 days! Chiltern Company Chairman Sir Richard Morris is fourth from the right. (Raymonds Photographers, Derby)

Shooter also knew that this route had been a double-track main line in every sense between 1 July 1910 and 16 April 1968, regarded by many as the preferred route to travel between Britain's two largest cities. It was shorter than the Euston line, engineered for high speed and with its generous loading gauge it had permitted wider and more spacious coaching stock along with the largest and most powerful locomotives. It is arguable that the downgrading and subsequent singling in 1968 was dictated not so much by operational decline as need for a 'quid pro quo' to suit Treasury desire to offset the costs of electrifying the West Coast route out of Euston.

Adrian Shooter wrote to the Zonal Director of Railtrack Midlands in November 1996:

> Of the infrastructure options considered, only one offers a robust solution to meet our timetable aspirations, that is to double the track between Bicester North and Princes Risborough.
>
> The off-peak, half-hourly timetable could be delivered by doubling between Bicester and Ashendon (about eight miles) and for a few miles north of Princes Risborough. However, a more intensive peak service, which involves services from/to Banbury and Leamington, in addition to the Birmingham services, also involves trains crossing in the central section south of Ashendon, and in the vicinity of Haddenham.

The option of operating a more intensive peak-hour service from places north of Banbury and Leamington would also be required for the proposed new parkway station already being planned for Budbrooke, north of Warwick. With this prospect in mind, Shooter continued:

> We are committed to our mission statement, part of which states that 'all day, every day, we aim to offer a welcoming, reliable and value for money service'. We do not want to pursue an infrastructure option which compromises our commitment to reliability – a fundamental prerequisite of the Chiltern experience. An option which perpetuates two single line sections builds in unreliability in perpetuity, and is sub-optimal.

As well as being more reliable from the point of view of delivering a timetable, the preferred option eliminates several turnouts/crossovers and involves less signalling than the present infrastructure. Railtrack's financial exposure on performance will be reduced.

This infrastructure also maximises your flexibility to sell paths in the longer term, as it will not be built in such a way that only Chiltern's precise current requirements can be delivered on it.

The letter to Railtrack continued to emphasise the additional opportunities Railtrack would be creating for itself by undertaking the track doubling:

It seems to us that there is a very significant upside for Railtrack's profitability, including after the end of the first franchise:

- the reliability of the infrastructure will be enhanced permanently
- the doubling creates saleable capacity – Chiltern is not seeking exclusive use
- paths on the WCML are likely to be premium value after modernisation and the Chiltern route will be available for Railtrack to sell to 'secondary traffic', e.g. as part of the Cross-Country network, for freight, for open access

Shooter added a rider pointing out that it would be possible to take piggy-back freight traffic to London at a fraction of the capital investment required on the WCML. The letter concluded by suggesting ways in which Railtrack might receive a share of the benefits of the investment in return for taking a greater share of the cost and revenue risk of the service being introduced. Putting this in context, it is worth noting that investment in track and signalling on the Chiltern route totals £350 million over a fourteen-year period, compared to £9 billion invested in the West Coast upgrade.

When the new train operating companies needed infrastructure enhancements necessary to allow them grow their business, they immediately found themselves enmeshed in Byzantine procedures. Not owning any assets themselves, they had to persuade Railtrack (subsequently Network Rail) of the long-term profitability and strategic viability of the scheme in question. While on the one hand, railway investment is very expensive and needs a pay-back time of up to thirty years, most franchises are usually of short length, such as Chiltern's initial seven years. Also, the Rail Regulator requires a minimum of 7.5 per cent return on capital in all Railtrack's core business, more if the risks are deemed greater. If this was not complicated enough, the aspirations of the train operating companies had to be approved by the Office of Passenger Rail Franchising (OPRAF) for inclusion in their franchise plans, to which the train operators would then be held accountable. But this was not all; not only had Railtrack to be convinced but also the Office of the Rail Regulator (ORR). It was the ORR who decided what income Railtrack would have through setting the track access charges that operators would have to pay. ORR is responsible for ensuring the overall accountability of railway finances to the public interest.

Railtrack, for its part, would need convincing that the expenditure was in its long-term interests, and that the revenue stream, the only way a train operating company can finance the pay back, is sound and will continue long into the future. Also, in 1996 Railtrack had got rid of most of its in-house engineering staff at the time of its privatisation. Its top executives, mostly lawyers and accountants, had little knowledge or experience of railway operation and only two out of fourteen members of the Railtrack Board had railway experience, while many of Railtrack's senior capacity operational managers with a railway background had spent most of their professional careers in the rationalisation culture under which the nationalised British Rail had been required to operate.

On the other hand, given that Railtrack was now being asked to cough up an estimated £9.2 million by a company that had virtually no asset base, which might well not exist in six years' time and therefore could not guarantee any long-term ability to repay this substantial sum, a certain caution by Railtrack seemed not unreasonable!

In anticipation of this, Chiltern was keen to emphasise to Railtrack that the level of risk in this investment would not be any higher than that of its core business. They discussed their plans with the Rail Regulator who indicated that he was inclined to take a similar view. Other key points were:

- the cost risk on the project will almost certainly be taken by the contractor, not Railtrack;
- the deal will provide Railtrack with a fixed revenue stream as its access contracts do;
- the risk of the franchise becoming insolvent is one present in its core business;
- future uncertainty about its fixed income exists with regard to current access charges, because of regulatory review, just as it does for the supplementary charges for this investment at the end of the first franchise;
- even £9 million is small expenditure in comparison with Railtrack's business overall.

The Regulator's policy was that Railtrack, when considering the time for repayment of investment, must take account of the life of the asset created as well as make an assessment of the likelihood of operators wishing to pay for use of the asset in the longer term. Thus, if an investment was to be paid for during the life of a franchise, Railtrack's risk would be virtually zero, and a level of return less than 7.5 per cent would be justified. Chiltern's view therefore was that if Railtrack was asking for a return of this level, then by implication Railtrack should take some residual risk.

Further anticipating events, Chiltern noted that by 2004, the year following the end of its franchise in 2003, modernisation of the Euston line was expected to allow the introduction of four trains an hour in the peak on a one-hour twenty-minute timing between London and Birmingham. Thus Railtrack negotiators would put a question mark over the certainty of revenue from the Chiltern investment after 2003. For its part, Chiltern's consultants predicted a steady increase in passenger revenue extrapolated beyond the end of the franchise for a number of reasons, not least that Chiltern always saw the potential value of the markets south of Birmingham (Solihull and the proposed new parkway station at Warwick) and the fringes of London (High Wycombe), rather than London to Birmingham end to end. Somewhat perversely, Railtrack refused to accept that Chiltern would benefit by any disruption to services on the WCML because, it claimed, there would be no disruption to services during modernisation! They insisted that any benefits resulting from WCML modernisation be discounted from Chiltern's revenue projections.

All these points were included in the business case Beckett put to the M40 Board on 28 March 1997. This only looked at two options, partial doubling between Princes Risborough and Haddenham and Thame, or the doubling of the full eighteen miles between Princes Risborough and Bicester. The second option offered greater potential profit through being able, at last, to run a full two-trains-an-hour service between London and Birmingham, but at greater risk; a fall in revenue of 20 per cent would reduce profits to zero.

As an aside, it would be churlish not to acknowledge generously the tremendous engineering feat that has been achieved on the West Coast line, and also to express gratitude to all those thousands of men and women, some from the far corners of the world, who for years have been slogging away night and day in all weathers, seeing little of their families, often while the rest of us were either asleep or celebrating a national holiday, in order to complete the project. At the same time, on the Chiltern route once the Evergreen 3 project has restored overtaking loops at Princes Risborough and south of High Wycombe, then even before electrification Chiltern will be competitive with the West Coast timings and at a mere fraction of the astronomical cost of that modernisation.

Chiltern's full two-trains-an-hour service began on Monday 13 December 2004. The occasion was marked by a brief ceremony at Birmingham's Moor Street station performed by then Managing Director Cath Proctor.

In May 1997, a new Labour Government was elected. Instead of re-nationalisation, it put Deputy Prime Minister John Prescott in charge of a new 'super ministry' responsible for Environment, Transport and the Regions. A White Paper was soon published outlining plans for a new Strategic Rail Authority incorporating the franchising director's role as well as providing a strategic focus for the nation's railways. Unfortunately, there was no Parliamentary time available to pass the necessary legislation and the Strategic Rail Authority was not legally able to assume its powers until 1 February 2001. Three years and six transport ministers later, the Strategic Rail Authority was abolished by the sixth, Alastair Darling.

By mid-summer 1997, Chiltern's plans seemed to have been finally frustrated. Railtrack had increased the capital cost to about £12 million and their insistence at discounting any benefits resulting from West Coast modernisation reduced Chiltern's projected revenue by £2 million a year. At the same time, complete doubling of the eighteen miles would cost Chiltern nearly an extra £4 million each year, comprising £2 million for additional operating costs (including train leasing) plus over £1.5 million for increased track access charges. Chiltern's new revenue projections now calculated an increase from complete track doubling of £1.6 million rising in 2003/4 to £2.7 million. In presenting this information to the M40 Trains Board, Beckett stated unequivocally that: 'Therefore, the project as originally proposed cannot be justified.'

Instead, the lesser scheme to double the track seven miles from Princes Risborough northwards was revived which would give a reduction in operating and access charges from £2 million down to £320,000. Nevertheless, and this was significant for the eventual outcome, the cost to Railtrack of signalling was 50 per cent higher for the partial doubling than for the complete double tracking. However, between the paper Beckett presented to the M40 Board on 10 June 1997 explaining why Chiltern now had to opt for a partial track doubling and the beginning of the actual work on site on 27 October 1997, events restored the preferred scheme for complete re-doubling from Bicester to Princes Risborough at the revised price of £13.2 million (eventually rising to £30 million).

Firstly, there was a recognition by Railtrack of the strategic need for an alternative route between London and Birmingham while the West Coast project was underway. Secondly there was the heavy extra cost of signalling required by partial doubling, and thirdly, there may well have been a political perspective. At the time of the May 1997 election, which led to a change of Government, there was a wish to see a major capital rail project going ahead. Additionally, Railtrack was keen to have a major project demonstrating it working alongside a train operator. As ever Chiltern were proactive, and with encouragement from the new shadow Strategic Rail Authority and in consideration of its relatively small size and risk-free nature by comparison with the West Coast project, it was felt it was worth trying it out to see how it would work.

The quoted Railtrack estimate of £30 million was quite possibly an underestimate and the final costs could well have been nearer £40 million. This was largely because Railtrack had done very little or no development work prior to starting the project. The track bed had had very little beyond 'patch and mend' maintenance during the thirty years it had been singled. A serious problem concerned the embankments, riddled with rabbit and badger holes and now needing serious civil engineering work to once again support a twin-track main line. There was a particular problem at the former Ashendon Junction, situated between Princes Risborough and Bicester, where planning permission had to be obtained before the engineers could remove earthworks built for the original flyover.

But how on earth was Chiltern going to find the annual £3,375,000 in extra costs for track access charges, additional train leasing and additional operating costs? Chiltern here proposed something rather innovatory in the form of an escalating access charge, similar in concept to the profit share scheme being devised for the West Coast project. A dual solution was devised whereby Chiltern would pay an additional track access charge starting at £250,000 in the first year, rising to a maximum of £1.5 million in year five. At the same time it was agreed that, as soon as Chiltern started to make a profit from the track doubling, Railtrack would receive 25 per cent of that profit. Railtrack was much more inclined towards having a share of increased profitability rather than just a fixed price. In July 1997, the Railtrack Board formally accepted and signed the deal.

The schedule as planned would have seen the work completed by September 1997 and certainly by May 1998 to coincide with the expected arrival of the new Clubman trains.

Work between Princes Risborough and Bicester started many weeks later than planned with weekend possessions throughout the autumn and winter of 1997 and the spring of 1998. Initial work involved clearing back trees and foliage, strengthening embankments to permit the carrying of a double-track main line, levelling the surface for the new track formation, laying a membrane to prevent clay seepage into the track bed, laying tens of thousands of tons of fresh ballast and cable ducts for the new signalling.

Then between 17–25 January 1998 there was a total shut down with replacement bus services between Princes Risborough and Bicester, supervised with cheerful efficiency by area station manager Cathy Compton. The old single line was slewed back to form a new down line and make space once more for the new second track. To anyone braving the bitterly chill winds at the time to visit the site, the railway presented an impression of immense activity with orange-clad figures in white hard-hats as far as the eye could see, rails slewed at amazing angles, curious and fascinating machines moving up and down and frenetic activity at Haddenham and Thame to have a platform ready for the following Monday morning. Passengers were complimented on their patience. This was also the first major work for Chiltern involving Laing Engineering, at that time Chiltern's minority shareholder who were sub-contracted by Railtrack along with GrantRail.

Reference has already been made to the bureaucratic minefield faced by would-be train operators in Britain's newly privatised railway in those early days. Yet, amazingly, OPRAF now issued Schedule 7 penalty notices against Chiltern for all the cancellations resulting from the nine-day total line closure! This was in spite of the stated objectives of OPRAF to increase the number of passengers travelling by rail and to stimulate the development of the railway services by promoting a high level of cost effective investment in the network.

When the track doubling was nearly complete, frustration provoked Chiltern to write to OPRAF pointing out that Chiltern, along with partners Railtrack, Porterbrook and Adtranz, were investing nearly three times the level they were committed to do in their franchise and expressing strong feelings that this broader picture seemed rarely to be taken into account, with OPRAF press bulletins focussing on what was going badly rather than the investment going into the industry. It led Chiltern to observe that they appeared to be delivering a major network improvement, the first of its kind to be proposed by a franchisee despite, rather than with, the help of OPRAF. OPRAF's lack of positive support for the proposed Warwick Parkway scheme or the plans for the re-opening of part of the Watlington branch from Princes Risborough to a parkway station near the M40 were also noted.

A further frustration was the denial of much in the way of delegated authority to the OPRAF manager for Chiltern, who had day-to-day responsibility for liaison and oversight of the franchise yet was unable to make decisions without referring back to OPRAF's high level committee who, on many occasions, had prevented sensible changes to the Public Service Requirements (PSR) for the benefit of passengers and so on. The letter's next section, **The Spirit of the Agreement, Not the Letter**, continued: 'The Franchise Agreement is a very inflexible instrument. Of course, we knew that when we signed it. However, an inflexible instrument can be changed or interpreted where it is clearly sensible for both parties to do so…'

Then followed examples, beginning with the 'Handover Package', a sensible precaution dealing with procedures to keep trains moving in the event of a franchise failure. Chiltern pointed out that instead of the complicated package that had taken up masses of preparation, all that was really required was for the OPRAF franchise manager to keep a list of the railway managers' telephone numbers.

Many other instances were quoted. Commenting on the penultimate section, **Commercial Initiatives Versus Franchise Commitments,** the letter continued:

This is a distinction that has been used by your people many times to justify giving us no credit for major investment when negotiating a change to the Franchise Plan. The argument has gone: 'No, we will not agree to amend the Franchise Plan on item x, in exchange for investment that you are making in item y, because investment in y is a commercial initiative you are taking, and you would have done it anyway.' This is a distinction which puzzles us greatly. The vast majority of commitments we made in the Franchise Plan are in there because they are about developing the business – they are *all* commercial initiatives, which just happen to be written into the agreement. Their existence helped us to write down the subsidy requirements we bid for. **You are not paying us extra subsidy for us to deliver the Franchise Plan – you are paying us *less* subsidy because of the Franchise Plan.**

The letter concluded with a plea for OPRAF to work more in the spirit than the letter to assist Chiltern achieve the aims of both organisations.

In the case of railway privatisation, it is a truth now universally acknowledged by all parties that the plans were cobbled together with far too much haste, whatever their intrinsic worth or otherwise. The last thing needed is a conflict between those driven by commercial requirements yet committed to improving services for the public and the guardians of the public interest. Commercial flair and enterprise are axiomatic for reducing the burden on the public purse. The reorganisations of 2004 and 2005 gave an opportunity to address further the shortcomings of the original legislation. Whether the decision to micro manage the railways from the Department for Transport will resolve or further frustrate these key issues still remains to be seen.

Franchise directors, however, have to work within the existing legislation, whatever their personal feelings. Chiltern received a prompt and positive reply recognising the significance of the track doubling and Warwick Parkway projects, but reminding them that while OPRAF can be pro-active as a facilitator of such projects, it cannot take on the role of lobbyist on behalf of operators. This would not be consistent with its duty to safeguard the Government's position over any contingent liabilities arising and potential transfer of risk to the public sector. It also recognised that this is a difficult area where the official position can sometimes be wrongly interpreted as a holding back of support.

In fairness to the Government, some other franchisees had presented problems at the opposite end of the scale from the Chiltern situation which did require detailed accountability to ensure improvements for passengers. For example, readers may remember the ruthless cost-cutting in the early days of privatisation by some of the franchisees – with so many essential workers made redundant it was virtually impossible to deliver their published time-tables, while at the same time those perpetrating these cuts soon went back to the Government to say their subsidy was insufficient and they needed more help from the taxpayer. Two of the biggest players did this. Happily, the worst of these examples is history and senior Chiltern managers confirmed that the subsequent incorporation of OPRAF into the Strategic Rail Authority improved working relationships.

In March 1998, Chiltern gained the first ever National Railways Innovation Award, for their achievements in commissioning new rolling stock, in introducing new ways of purchasing tickets, installing automatic barriers at Marylebone and restoring eighteen miles of dual track. This was one of the few events of 1998 to lift the team's spirit.

Railtrack's promise to complete the track doubling by 24 May 1998, in time for the start of the new summer timetable, did not happen. Laing and GrantRail completed the civil engineering on time but there were problems with the computer software for the new signalling. Chiltern had spent an estimated £162,000 on marketing, timetabling and train planning, then on 29 April, just twenty-five days before the start of the new timetable, Railtrack informed them it would not be ready in time. Very hastily, Chiltern had to advise passengers, withdraw the new timetables and run on the existing winter timetable throughout most of the summer. As regular commuters will remember, Chiltern would have been advised to continue with their old timetable for even longer!

'Events, events, dear boy!' was the reply former Prime Minister Harold MacMillan once gave in reply to an interviewer's question as to what were the worst things he had to deal with while in office. Before 1998 was over, there were many times when Shooter's team must have felt the same.

Railtrack pulled out all the stops and the new double track was handed over on 19 July. The first of the new Clubman trains had entered revenue-earning service on 26 May. Like the track doubling, this was later than scheduled. Unfortunately, train building at Derby, a traditional industry in that city going back to the middle years of the nineteenth century and the origins of the

Midland Railway, had paused some three years earlier and the workforce redeployed. Now new owners Adtranz had had to recruit and train a new workforce in the sophisticated techniques required for automated train building almost from scratch. When the first trains came off the production line, there were many teething problems, particularly with the electronic control systems. Sir Richard Morris, in his contribution (see Part 2, Chapter 16 'My Railway Journey') describes the trains displaying increasing heights of eccentricity with doors either not closing or not opening, toilet doors jamming, people being trapped in the corridor connections between coaches, public address systems causing hilarity by telling passengers arriving at Birmingham Snow Hill that they had just arrived at Marylebone, air-conditioning failing and so on. As Sir Richard said, 'We paid the price of being first.'

It was fortunate that Shooter was a professional engineer who, by coincidence, had previously been in charge of the maintenance and repair of the first generation Class 115 DMUs on the Chiltern lines. While immediate pressure was put on Adtranz at the highest level to sort the problems out, steps were also initiated to bring routine maintenance at Aylesbury depot back 'in house'. This shrewd move led not only to improvements in fleet availability but also a reduction in costs with both Angel Trains and Porterbrook Leasing, the companies which legally own both the older Class 165s as well as the new Clubman trains, now paying Chiltern to maintain them thus offsetting the leasing costs. Even today, however, although passengers appreciate their comfort and civilised interior design, the mechanical reliability of the earlier batches of the Clubman fleet, despite intensive attention, have never matched that of the older Class 165s they were designed to complement.

Chiltern was naturally keen to demonstrate the potential of its Clubman trains on their new double-track main line. But unresolved problems remained, with speed restrictions continuing for many months to come compounded by other issues. Reflecting on this inglorious period, a senior Chiltern manager admitted they had been guilty of naivety in trying to progress on too many fronts at the same time. The very complex and overly ambitious timetable amounted to a 33 per cent increase in services. With other operators also increasing services, line congestion north of Aynho Junction also caused timekeeping problems. This made the remaining single line stretch from Aynho south to Bicester a greater constraint than expected and the net result was Chiltern's reliability and punctuality plummeting further. Also, lack of attention to manpower planning meant a shortage of drivers and deficiencies in fleet maintenance. At this time, Chiltern did not have the management processes to effectively deal with the complex changes demanded of the operating system. At this low point, Beckett and his senior colleagues remember occasional feelings of despair.

One example of the operational eccentricities concerned the new double track between Bicester and Princes Risborough. At this time only the original single line, now the down (northbound) line was truly bi-directionally signalled. The new up (southbound) line was not yet. This had the effect, when one train was running late, especially during the morning peak, of sometimes having two trains apparently racing each other on adjoining tracks. Many was the time when the regular commuters from Haddenham and Thame would be standing on the overbridge trying to guess at which platform a train would arrive first!

By the time August 1998 arrived, Chiltern's poor performance had meant them being summoned to account by the franchise director on no less than four separate occasions. In a press release announcing a £2.5 million package of compensation benefits for Chiltern passengers on 19 August OPRAF stated:

> Chiltern has been called in by the Franchising Director on four separate occasions in the past year for cancelling (due to driver shortage) more than 1 per cent of trains in each of four four-week operating periods. They will also exceed this level in the current period, which ends on 22 August [3 August was a particularly black day for Chiltern, with fifty-four cancellations]. Mr O'Brien has deemed this to be a breach of their franchise agreement. In addition to requiring Chiltern to implement an action plan to remedy the situation quickly, he has negotiated a substantial package of passenger benefits.

It continued:

> Chiltern Railways is in the process of implementing a large investment programme, and this
> has led to disruption in the short term. Its contract is also one of the toughest in the industry in
> terms of the number of trains they are allowed to cancel before being called in, reflecting previ-
> ous good performance on that line. But passengers want a service they can rely on now, not a
> promise of a return to good service at some unspecified time in the future.

On being called in on this fourth occasion, Beckett remembers it rather like being summoned
to the headmaster's study. Shooter and Beckett were handed a fine notice for £500,000. They
were given a short space of time to return with reasons why they need not be fined so worked
exceedingly fast to come up with the £2.5 million package of compensations and improvements
for passengers. What particularly upset Chiltern's staff was that, having come up with a package of
benefits to the public worth five times that of their potential fine, OPRAF promptly issued a press
release stating that Chiltern had been fined £2.5 million!

The actual compensation package was broadly in two sections, the first detailed the compensation to passengers. Anxious to salvage something from Chiltern's now lost reputation, these
generously offered all annual and quarterly season ticket holders one week's free travel at the expiry
of their existing tickets. In addition (and also including season ticket holders as well), all passengers
would be given a 100 per cent refund, in cash if preferred rather than the usual vouchers, if their
train was late by more than one hour, and 50 per cent if it was delayed by more than thirty minutes.

Other benefits included the provision of security guards at major stations until 11 p.m. each
night (which in 2009 was extended to last train arrival), new public address systems at all stations except Marylebone which had just had a new system, the refurbishment of the toilets at
Marylebone and many other principal stations within the next twelve months, and at Bicester
new all-weather passenger shelters for the London-bound (up) platform, together with the instal-
lation of lifts at either end of the passenger footbridge for the benefit of disabled people and
parents wheeling buggies.

The second part outlined the action plan to bring Chiltern's reliability and punctuality back
to its previous high standard. It noted that 92 per cent of all cancellations over the previous ten
months were due to only three causes. Train failure alone was responsible for 48 per cent, driver
shortage accounted for another 21 per cent and failure of Railtrack infrastructure 23 per cent.
To tackle the train failures, there would be an accelerated programme to install new engines and
replace other worn parts in the Class 165s and the provision for emergency use of spare trains
at Marylebone and Aylesbury. All this was pledged to be done by the end of 1998. Driver shortage was a perennial problem (see also Part 2, Chapter 13 'The Operations Director's Story').
The establishment needed by Chiltern was 141. In August 1998 there were 128. By the end
of September, Chiltern pledged to recruit an extra 10 per cent on top of establishment and to
maintain this margin.

Infrastructure problems were to be resolved in conjunction with Railtrack, particularly covering various measures to safeguard power supplies. At all major stations retail and platform staff
were to be trained in the manual operation of points in the event of a total power failure, and
contingency plans were agreed with Railtrack for emergency block working in the event of total
signal failure. A performance manager was also appointed to resolve issues with Railtrack and
London Underground. The congestion problems at Birmingham Snow Hill were to be addressed
urgently and Railtrack was urged to implement plans to update the antiquated signalling between
Banbury and Leamington Spa, which was now a major contributory factor in line congestion.

What happened on that black day, 3 August 1998, when Chiltern had to make fifty-four
cancellations? It was caused by a rat entering a Railtrack location box, an essential part of the
sophisticated signalling and Automatic Train Protection (ATP) system that operates on Chiltern
Railways, where it munched steadily away on the electronics and surrounding insulation until it
electrocuted itself, incidentally setting all signals to 'danger'. Its mummified corpse is now preserved in the company chairman's office.

Timetable issues were tackled vigorously. Acknowledging that the 1998 summer timetable had been too ambitious, they made a careful analysis and from the start of September knocked out some peak-time services. Once remedies had been arrived at, letters of explanation were sent to all user groups, acknowledging frankly that performance was still below standard and explaining the measures being taken to rectify the situation, including details of the planned cancellations.

The response from user groups tended to the 'more in sorrow than in anger' kind, a typical example from Cherwell Rail Users in Banbury on 27 August stated:

> The general feeling of our members is that if your proposals restore the reliability of Chiltern Railways services to the high level we associate with your company, then they are acceptable, because frankly of late things have become quite unacceptably bad. Naturally, our members who commute on a daily basis will be monitoring things as they experience them.
>
> We have an additional concern that many of the recent shortcomings have not only been due to line capacity but also specifically to failure of the new trains: for example, the air conditioning has failed (despite our being assured that it was the best in the world from Australia) as have the engines and the door mechanisms. We trust that Adtranz are taking drastic steps to improve their product reliability which on present form reminds one of the worst days of British Leyland circa 1970!

Meanwhile, things were not going well on other fronts. The Warwick Parkway scheme had generated much vocal opposition and a public enquiry was now scheduled for the autumn. In July 1998, consultants W.S. Atkins had issued a critical report which leading opponent Warwick District Council would use at the enquiry (see also Part 2, Chapter 23 'The Planning Officer's Story').

The reaction of Chiltern senior management, still reeling from the heavy compensation package, was to grit their teeth and knuckle down to delivering it, as well as presenting their strong case to the Warwick Parkway enquiry. Railtrack was also approached with a view to recovering some, at least, of the costs resulting from late delivery of the double tracking. Efforts to reduce delays were still frustrated by the dreary succession of temporary speed limits. Chiltern was also dismayed, and surprised, at Railtrack's failure up to then to give positive support for the new Warwick Parkway station.

The gist of Chiltern's case with Railtrack was that, although they had accepted there would be disruption and consequent loss of revenue during the track doubling, for which they had planned and budgeted, Chiltern had been twice hit financially by Railtrack, firstly through Railtrack's failure to give adequate notice of its inability to complete on time which left Chiltern with a hefty bill for wasted marketing costs, and secondly the additional costs of the seemingly endless delays, still onoing when Adrian Shooter wrote to Railtrack on 21 July 1998.

Throughout August and September 1998 the correspondence passed back and forth between Chiltern, Railtrack and, of course, law firms. By September there had been sixty-nine additional Railtrack possessions over and above what had been planned and budgeted for, nineteen of these had occurred since 19 July, when the line was supposed to have been handed over as complete. What angered Chiltern management was that, on a number of these occasions, no work had been possible because Railtrack had been unable to find drivers for the engineering trains bringing ballast, sleepers and rails. To Chiltern the cost, in terms of extra lost revenue and additional bus/taxi hire for passengers and Chiltern staff, plus the wasted marketing costs, were in the region of £1.5 million, and revenue was still haemorrhaging which was very serious for a small company. Railtrack was obdurate in the matter and maintained that late completion was always a possibility and that Chiltern had in any case saved the £200,000 early completion bonus that had been included in its costings. It was now mid-October.

At this point, heavy guns were brought to bear, exploiting the good personal relationship between Chiltern's Chairman Sir Richard Morris and Railtrack's Chairman Sir Robert Horton. After the exchange of a few, always courteous, broadsides, the matter was soon resolved amicably to the satisfaction of both parties.

During the autumn and winter of 1998/99, Chiltern was increasingly frustrated in its efforts to regain its reputation. As well as the signalling, there were frequent line blockages caused by failed

EWS freight trains which persisted until the more reliable General Electric Class 66s entered service. In January, the *Birmingham Post* did an article on rail services in the Midlands quoting figures given by the Rail Users Consultative Committee for the Midlands, the forerunner of the sadly now defunct Rail Passenger Committee. This showed that complaints had soared 600 per cent in the previous three months. Of the 1,620 complaints recorded, 899 were against Central Trains, 287 against Virgin Cross-Country and 264 against Virgin West Coast. Midland Main Line recorded eighty complaints but Chiltern just six.

Additional cuts were subsequently made to the timetable in January 1999. In Whitehall, the Department for the Environment Inspector was still considering evidence from the Warwick Parkway public enquiry. The shadow Strategic Rail Authority (sSRA), under its energetic first chairman, Sir Alastair Morton, began to assume the duties of OPRAF as well as attempting a ten-year strategic plan for the nation's railways.

There was a welcome moment of glory for Chiltern in January 1999 when, despite still being in the doldrums over performance, Chiltern was awarded the Charter Mark by the Prime Minister. In the bulletin sent immediately to all staff, Shooter stated:

> This morning we were awarded the Charter Mark by the Prime Minister – the award for provid-ing excellent customer service.
>
> Many of you will remember that we won it in 1995, and held it for three years. That was at a time when our train performance was better than it has been over the last year. So it really says something about what the judges thought about us that they decided to give us the award again.
>
> The judging was tough. As well as a written application, an assessor visited us for a day in October last year and spent a long time talking to staff and passengers. He also travelled incognito on several trains, including Clubmans.
>
> In his report to the judges he said he was particularly impressed with the helpfulness, friendli-ness and commitment of staff. *This was the reason we won the award.* He emphasised that, even when things were not going well, we deserve the award because of the staff. Congratulations everybody.

Soon after, the Government announced a ten-year plan for transport, backed up with £180 billion investment, but changed transport ministers again, replacing John Reid with Helen Liddell. Shooter began planning in anticipation of making an application to the sSRA for a franchise extension later that year.

Then it was back to the bad times for Chiltern. If real rats had caused the mayhem that led to Chiltern's fifth call-in by OPRAF, the issue now was cats – metaphorical fat ones! For some time discussions had been underway for John Laing plc, Chiltern's minority shareholder, to buy out the director's shares and become the effective owners of Chiltern Railways, via a holding company to be known as Laing Rail. Mark Beckett confirmed that Adrian Shooter was initially not keen on the idea. After all, his personal commitment was much more than any financial investment, but he was eventually persuaded that it would be in Chiltern's long-term strategic interest. However, just then, in February 1999 when the railways were getting a thrashing in the media on an almost daily basis, much of it caused by the swinging fare increases imposed in January, Chiltern again hit the headlines.

On Thursday 11 February, 1½in-banner headlines across the front of the *London Evening Standard* proclaimed 'Rail Fat Cats Share Millions'. The paper continued:

> A new row over railway 'fat cats' erupted today as it emerged that five directors of a poorly performing commuter train company stand to make about £3.5 million by selling the franchise. [Describing Chiltern as a *commuter* train company was really twisting the knife!]

Passenger groups and trade unions expressed outrage. The following day similar articles appeared in the *Birmingham Evening Mail*, the *Birmingham Post* ('Row over Chiltern's very fat controllers'), the *Daily Express* ('£3.5 million windfall for fat cats who can't run a railway'), *Daily Mail* ('Misery line rail bosses sell for millions') and *The Independent* ('Slow train bosses set for millions'). Even

Beckett, who had not been involved with the original management buy-out and in no way stood to benefit financially from the negotiations with John Laing, was also door-stepped by the *Daily Mail*. By a pure coincidence, with an increase in their family at that time Beckett and his wife were planning to sell their small house in Aylesbury and move to one with slightly more room. Picking up on the 'For Sale' sign outside, a reporter waited for him to arrive home and took photographs of it, clearly intended to use if possible to show that Beckett was going to be a beneficiary of the takeover.

With the benefit of hindsight, at that time such reactions must seem fairly predictable. For those individuals who were the target of the attacks, it was hard to take. The financial strength of Laing, who had long cherished ambitions of greater involvement in the rail industry, would secure the continued growth and development of Chiltern Railways. Although taken over the previous twelve months, Chiltern's punctuality had plummeted, now with the more robust timetable and an ending to the speed restrictions on the new double track, at last things had begun to improve.

Yes, the directors now found themselves wealthy beyond their dreams, but what if, when they had re-mortgaged their homes to raise the initial investment capital required, their plans had failed or been hit by an economic downturn and some of them had been out on the street with their families? Would the press have even noticed? Yet, without exception, none of the original Chiltern directors was particularly wealthy. They were ordinary people but with extraordinary commitment who in the event achieved something quite remarkable.

The takeover by Laing was approved in July 1999 and two of the directors, Owen Edgington and Alex Turner, retired. Turner now works as a consultant to the rail industry while Edgington, forever a railwayman, can sometimes be seen driving steam trains at weekends near Peterborough on the Nene Valley Railway. The rest carried on: Cath Proctor who, like Beckett, was never involved with the original buy-out, moved up to take over from Turner as marketing and sales director, Allen who stayed as finance director and is now the longest-serving and one of the most highly respected finance directors in any railway company. Shooter stayed on as managing director. When, in reply to an *Evening Standard* reporter's question as to how he felt about Chiltern's poor performance, he stated he was ashamed, he meant it.

Representatives of Rail User Groups at Derby viewing the prototype Clubman. Chiltern marketing director Alex Turner is seated far left. (Raymonds Photographers, Derby)

Above: Unveiling the first of the Clubmans, Class 168001, at Derby. Left to right: Sir Richard Morris, Adrian Shooter and Adtranz CEO Stig Svärd.

Right: Driver Mick Clare testing the Class 168001 at Leicester. (Chiltern Railways)

Chiltern Managing Director Adrian Shooter showing off prototype Clubman Class 168001 to Labour Transport Minister Glenda Jackson. (Raymonds Photographers, Derby)

CHAPTER 7

FORWARD!

When things have been difficult it is sometimes a good idea to have a party, and in the spring of 1999 Chiltern Railways cheered themselves and everyone else up with a splendid lunch at Marylebone in commemoration of the centenary of the arrival of the Great Central Railway in London.

All the great and the good of the railway industry were invited, along with representatives of the various passenger groups with whom Chiltern liaised. A beautifully produced and illustrated booklet was published containing a wealth of archive photography. In his Foreword, Shooter referred to the original grand vision of Sir Edward Watkin, who planned his Great Central Railway, never aiming merely to compete with other main lines from the north into the capital (an incorrect assumption unfortunately perpetuated by some railway historians) but with a grand vision to continue on all the way from Manchester, across London and on to Paris via a Channel Tunnel which he started to build but, sadly, never completed. A singular lack of political will combined with opposition from the military authorities who feared it might allow foreign invasion effectively stopped its completion for another century (it was a similar lack of foresight that in the 1960s allowed most of the Great Central, the only main line in Great Britain built to accommodate continental-loading gauge rolling stock, to be closed and abandoned). Shooter went on to give his opinion that, if alive today, Sir Edward, along with the redoubtable Sir Sam Fay, would both draw comfort to see at least the southern part of their railway arise, phoenix-like, from near total closure to become a heartening success story; the old Great Central motto of 'Forward' still appropriate.

Meanwhile, after only three months in post, the Government replaced Helen Liddell as Transport Minister with Lord (Gus) MacDonald.

At last some cheering news for Chiltern. On 6 April 1999 Beckett was able to report to the M40 Board that planning permission for the new Warwick Parkway station had at last been granted by the Department for Environment, Transport and the Regions (DETR). At the same time, Railtrack had agreed that the station could be constructed and owned by a third party. It was noted that a key factor in persuading the DETR had been support from employers' organisations in Warwick, Leamington Spa and along the M40/M42 corridor (see also Part 2, Chapter 23 'The Transport Planners Story' and Chapter 24 'The Warwick Parkway Project Manager's Story').

At this same Board meeting, it was noted that, along with improvements to performance, passenger numbers and revenue were increasing again and so the decision was taken to order ten more Class 168 Clubman vehicles in time for spring 2000.

A year previously, in April 1998, the M40 Board had approved a five-year business plan. Based upon improving passenger revenues, financial projections were now revised upwards and also used as the basis for a business plan for an extended franchise. By the end of February 1999 station sales were up 25 per cent over the previous year and significantly over budget. Along with the transfer of OPRAF to the sSRA came a new franchise manager for Chiltern, Graham Cross (Cross subsequently joined Chiltern Railways in January 2004 as strategic development manager, became head of business planning in 2006 and replaced Mark Beckett as director of business development when Beckett left Chiltern in 2007).

The first formal indication of Chiltern's intentions to seek a franchise extension came in a paper from Adrian Shooter to the M40 Board on 29 June 1999. In setting out the context, Shooter explained:

> The Government has indicated a willingness to enter into discussions with Train Operators about extensions to current franchises. Dr John Reid, the Transport Minister, has set out six criteria that must be addressed in bids. These included:
>
> - the track record of the Train Operator on train performance and investments above those committed in franchise agreements
> - accelerated or additional investment and new train services
> - tougher standards for punctuality and the maintenance of stations
> - the active promotion of integrated transport that encourages the use of public transport
> - steps to give passengers greater say in the services provided
> - proving to the Government that the tax payer will get a better deal by
> - extending the franchise rather than inviting fresh bids in 2003

Shooter explained to the Board that a team was already working up the bid and would begin discussions with sSRA later that summer armed with the core proposals. The document continued with a vision for Chiltern Railways in the twenty-first century as 'a railway which operates at a profit, without subsidy, carrying double the current number of passengers. The railway would provide fast, frequent and reliable train services using modern trains in the M40 Corridor, serving high-quality stations which are easy to access and staffed by a highly motivated team of customer-focussed people'.

The 'Rules of the Game' had been first hinted at by the Government in Dr John Reid's speech at the National Rail Summit in February 1999. Subsequently, OPRAF had started putting together a renegotiation team. More recently, on 21 June, Sir Alastair Morton said that he would be ready to start talking in the autumn and that 'nothing was ruled out' but continually emphasised the need to invest in capacity. Shooter had spoken personally with Sir Alastair just a few days before, on 24 June advising him of Chiltern's intentions to apply for a franchise extension. Shooter had been advised 'not to leave it too late!' and August of that year had been agreed as good timing. By now there was a clear consensus emerging within the rail industry and the sSRA that the fundamental to be addressed was investment in capacity. The problem for Chiltern was that key parts of its network were already close to, or actually at, capacity. The growth potential of the network would not be realised given current constraints.

Chiltern had therefore to confront three key issues including how to achieve a major increase in capacity, how to ensure that Chiltern was seen in the eyes of the sSRA to be part of the solution, and thirdly to gain the positive support of Railtrack without which the bid would not succeed, as had been already made clear. Richard Middleton, the commercial director of Railtrack had been given an objective to deliver five franchise extensions that calendar year and it was therefore crucial to convince him that Chiltern had to be one of the five. In the event, this was handsomely achieved and given the tension of some months previously over the first stage of track re-doubling, that it was achieved at all is a compliment to the personalities concerned.

Shooter was also concerned to ensure the sSRA, which like OPRAF until then had been generally supportive of Chiltern, did not see them as superseded once Virgin's West Coast route was upgraded. Measures were taken to ensure the Chiltern route was seen as a vital long-term arm of the network. These included the re-development of the old Moor Street station in Birmingham as a 'mini-Marylebone,' two trains every hour from Birmingham to London with faster journey times, the building of Warwick Parkway and a range of infrastructure investments to deliver more capacity and better performance particularly at the London end of the route. This consisted of proposals for re-laying quadruple tracks at those places where they had been

taken up in the 1970s along with signalling upgrades. The original Class 165 Turbos were getting tired, each vehicle having run up a colossal mileage and plans to either replace or refurbish
them were included.

Curiously, at this time Shooter was not pressing for the re-doubling of the last remaining
single-line section from Aynho to Bicester, believing it was possible to maintain the two trains an
hour without it. He had a concern that doubling it would open up the way to competition from
other operators. Nevertheless, he went ahead having the project surveyed and costed by Laing
Rail and other parties involved with the first track doubling. By August 1999, Shooter had now
become convinced that it was not only sensible but in fact essential for Chiltern's future strategy.
At the same time, the prospect of reopening the Oxford to Princes Risborough via Thame line
as an alternative commuter line from Oxford to London was investigated. A recent comparison
showed 50 per cent more passengers travelled from Cambridge to London by rail than from
Oxford and the existing Great Western route via Didcot was close to capacity. So, as summer
moved into autumn, Shooter and the Chiltern team concentrated on their bid for franchise
extension.

However, before the end of the year, tragic events put the Paddington line once more at the
forefront of everyone's mind. On Tuesday 5 October 1999, the 08:06 Thames Train departure for
Bedwyn in Wiltshire, as the subsequent Cullen Enquiry determined, drove through a badly positioned red signal, SN109, which was also partly obscured by low sunlight, and collided head on
with an incoming HST from Cheltenham. At impact, the combined speeds of the trains was in the
order of 130mph and in the ensuing collision and fire thirty-one people died. This was the second
serious accident on the approach lines into Paddington within two years, something that had not
happened throughout the 150-year combined history of both the Great Western Railway and the
Western Region of British Railways.

The fiercest criticism in the Cullen Report into the Ladbroke Grove accident was reserved for
Railtrack, which was condemned for its 'lamentable failure' in not responding to the enquiries into a
number of earlier serious SPADs (signal passed at danger), as well as its 'institutional paralysis'. SN109
had been passed at danger on no less than eight times since 1993. By an unhappy coincidence only
days before the Ladbroke Grove accident, HM Railway Inspectorate – then part of the HSE – concerned at the rising number of SPADs nationwide, had published 'Report on the Inspection carried
out by HM Railway Inspectorate during 1998/99 of the Management Systems in the Railway
Industry Covering Signals Passed at Danger'. One paragraph from the preface summed it all up:

> SPAD incidents probably give rise to the highest safety risk facing the rail industry and there-
> fore demands an appropriate level of resources and commitment to reduce the likelihood of an
> incident. Railtrack and all train operating companies will need to ensure that they have sufficient
> resources to identify and assess risks and take corrective action. It is also absolutely essential that
> this matter has the commitment necessary from senior directors and that they take a detailed
> personal interest. It is of concern to HMRI and indeed to the whole industry that incidents
> of signals passed at danger have increased during 1998/99 as compared with the immediately
> preceding years.

When incidents like Ladbroke Grove happen, all professional railway people at every level feel a
personal burden of responsibility, even though most would not be directly involved. Shooter sent
a letter from Chiltern to all its passengers on 8 October which began:

> The tragic events of this week have quite understandably brought the issue of rail safety to
> the forefront. I appreciate that many of you will have questions about safety on your railway. I
> would like to answer those questions and reassure you that in continuing to travel with Chiltern
> Railways you can do so with confidence.

The letter continued to explain, in layman's language, how the ATP system fitted on all Chiltern
trains, provided an additional level of safety. The letter concluded:

No words today can change the events of Tuesday or the damage it has caused to so many lives, but I promise you that if there are lessons to learn we will learn them and everyone of my team will continue to play their part in ensuring your safety every day.

At the next Board meeting, on 26 October, Shooter presented a paper he and Beckett had drafted entitled 'Safety Management and Signals Passed at Danger'. The paper examined the implications for the company of the recent train crash at Ladbroke Grove and proposed a strategy for enhancing the management of safety more generally. The six pages of the document were written in technical language but essentially proposed implementation of a number of the recommendations Lord Cullen was to make two years later.

Specifically, the paper covered the procedures that are implemented on Chiltern if a driver passes a signal set at danger; the technical equipment to reduce the risk of SPADs and their consequences; the use on Chiltern of ATP; the potential to extend it to Birmingham (never accomplished) and the programme to fit Cab Secure radio to all Chiltern trains. This latter does not prevent SPADs, but does enable the signalman to tell the driver to stop in emergency. Also included were the fitting of Driver Reminder Appliances and TPWS (Train Protection and Warning Systems) by 2003. In addition, Chiltern implemented, with immediate effect, five enhancements to the existing driver training programme.

A major part of the paper reviewed existing safety responsibilities and concluded that now Chiltern was larger and more complex, it was intended to appoint a safety management professional of high standing to overhaul this area of activity. Two years later, while presenting the results of his enquiry, Lord Cullen observed:

It was highly probable that the crash would not have happened if the turbo-train had been fitted with ATP.

On 30 March 2000, Sir Alastair Morton presented his Vision for Rail Growth speech to the Railway Forum, sending a copy to Shooter with a note attached drawing attention to what the sSRA would be expecting from TOCs, saying he thought it might be a useful checklist. Sir Alastair looked forward to the time when improved London commuter services may well cost less per passenger kilometre in subsidies than the Inland Revenue forgoes in corporation tax when a company car drives into London. Sir Alastair's message to the TOCs was clear:

Perhaps I need to elaborate a little about TOC investment at this time of franchise replacement. First, let me make clear it can be on or off the balance sheet of the franchisee owning the TOC. It can be direct capital, or supporting the burden of new investment costs for the early years of use until income rises to provide return of capital. We perceive that TOCs will sign long-term leases for new and more rolling stock; that they will lease or purchase a multiplicity of equipment from information to ticketing to security systems. But further than that, we expect TOCs to promote and participate in station-related infrastructure; from car parks through bus stops to the actual platform facilities and structures, and on beyond that to new platform, track and signalling developments in the approaches to any station which will enhance the system's capacity in their franchise area and improve their services. And then we look to them to promote and participate in new track links in the system; and, above all, we expect TOCs to invest and invest again in training to improve skills, safety, cleaning, customer service and, indeed sales development. We even want to hear from TOCs seeking new franchises just what they are doing to seek out and seduce new users around each station. Only growth will bring profit to the new franchisees and we want to have confidence in their ability to achieve growth. Subsidies will not be so spacious as to guarantee profit regardless.

Sir Alastair's remarks must have been very encouraging for Shooter's team. They noted the importance of obtaining positive support from Railtrack and by a happy coincidence, a good friend to Chiltern and personal friend of Shooter, Richard Fearn, had re-appeared on the scene as the zonal director for Railtrack Midlands by late 1999. This was Dick Fearn who in a previous incarnation as BR divisional manager, Thames and Chiltern, had been responsible for implementing Chris Green's Total Route Modernisation scheme in the late 1980s. Happily situated as Railtrack's zonal director, north-west, where his family roots lay, and with teenage children at critical stages of their education, he was reluctant to move but Shooter's enthusiastic encouragement as well as the prospect of adding more pieces to his 'jigsaw' eventually persuaded him. Fearn and his Railtrack team were to play a very key role in the next stage of Chiltern's development.

With his old friend and colleague settling into his new post, Shooter lost no time in beating a path to the Railtrack HQ to discuss Chiltern's development plans. These included track doubling between Aynho Junction and Bicester North, re-signalling all the way up the Cherwell Valley, platform expansion at Marylebone, refurbishment of the original station at Moor Street in Birmingham – made redundant when in 1987 the route through Snow Hill was reopened, and now an ideal expansion of capacity – and a new maintenance depot at Wembley. Initially, Shooter dealt with the Railtrack account executive for the Chiltern route, Dyan Crowther. It was Dyan who, in discussion with Fearn, first conceived the idea of giving the Chiltern development plan greater recognition by giving it a title. Although the whole scheme was mainly put together by Beckett, it was Crowther who came up with the name 'Evergreen', familiar to many regular Chiltern travellers. An appropriate title, since the Great Western Railway planted evergreen trees at its new station developments in the early twentieth century, and these can still be seen growing today alongside the platforms at Bicester North.

The reason Crowther and Fearn were trying to raise the profile of Chiltern's plans within Railtrack at that particular time, between the rail disasters of Ladbroke Grove and Hatfield, was growing concern both within Railtrack itself as well as the Government at the state of Railtrack's finances (for a fuller version of how Chiltern's plans got approval from the Railtrack Board as well as the SRA, who were going to have to fund most of it, see Part 2, Chapter 10 'The Irish Connection.'). Suffice to say that the game was won by a combination of sheer determination and shared vision by Fearn and Shooter, plus astute 'gamesmanship,' a dash of office politics and some smart opportunism. The story of the second phase of track doubling spread over two years, overlapping with Hatfield, Railtrack running out of money, Gerald Corbett leaving and being replaced firstly by Steve Marshall and then, as it went into receivership and became Network Rail, by John Armitt, a former professional railwayman.

By May 2001 Stephen Byers had become the fifth transport minister since 1997 and he replaced Sir Alastair Morton at the SRA with Richard Bowker who was previously with Virgin Trains.

Meanwhile in April 2000, the Chiltern/M40 Board had received a list of core franchise requirements from the sSRA. (The SRA did not yet have legal status until February 2001). By the end of April, The Chiltern/M40 team had agreed Heads of Terms for their franchise renewal bid with their solicitors Hollingworth Bissell, prior to having their Best and Final Offer approved at an Extraordinary Board meeting meeting in June.

Chiltern was not without competition. In the summer of 2000 the Go Ahead Group, who at that time had the franchise for Thames Trains, announced its intention of bidding for Chiltern. Their plans differed little from those already announced by Chiltern, but without the broader strategic vision of Chiltern. In the event, Go Ahead was not selected for final consideration . This decision may have been influenced in part by the evidence on their stewardship of Thames Trains beginning to emerge from the Cullen Enquiry into the Ladbroke Grove disaster. On 10 August 2000, Chiltern had been given notice that they were the preferred bidder for the new franchise.

On Saturday 9 September another celebration took place, this time at Banbury station, to mark its refurbishment together with the 150th anniversary of its original building. Festivities began at 10 a.m. with the arrival of a train carrying the directors and their guests to a welcome by the Mayor of Banbury. Most were dressed in mid-Victorian costume, which caused some merriment – the ladies looked most elegant in their crinolines but found sitting down was not an option! – and the train being a normal scheduled service. Family activities included face-painting, helium balloons, goody-bags, bookstalls and plenty of refreshments. Basket-carrying young ladies in Victorian costume (Railtrack office staff) strolled the station handing out balloons and traditional Banbury cakes. The sun shone, the Hook Norton Silver Band performed lustily, with a variety of delightful music, some of which had been played at the original 1850 opening. All in all it was a very happy day. A legacy of that happy event is the large mural on the wall of the new entrance hall, one of Banbury's largest pieces of public art, by local artist Nigel Fletcher, sponsored by Railtrack and depicting the original 1850 wooden station building. It was based on a Victorian print in the possession of former *Banbury Guardian* editor, Ted Clark.

On 8 October 2000, the new Warwick Parkway station was officially opened by the Secretary of State for Transport, on time and on budget. Then, just over a week later, at 12.23 p.m. on 17 October 2000, the 12.10 p.m. King's Cross to Leeds train derailed on a gentle curve near Hatfield, travelling at the permitted line speed of 115mph. Four people were killed. It was almost exactly twelve months since Ladbroke Grove. The subsequent investigation showed that the rails had disintegrated under the train, an example of the phenomenon of gauge corner cracking.

Although the fatalities were blessedly fewer than at Ladbroke Grove, no other railway crash in British history seems to have caused such profound political, social and psychological mayhem. For a more thorough exploration of this tragedy, Ian Jack's *The Crash that Stopped Britain*, Granta Books, London 2001, is highly commended. It covers the root causes and consequences with an excellent description for the non-technical person of the metal fatigue involved as well as a penetrating and chilling analysis of how the privatisation process had fragmented responsibility and co-ordination for much routine rail maintenance. In addition, Jack does not spare the politicians, whom he believes were ultimately to blame. In his opening pages Jack observes:

> Historical comparison made it almost a minor incident (e.g. the three-train Quintinshill collision 1915; 227 dead). But no other railway accident in British railway history – or, I would guess, in any other country's history – has led to the degree of public anger, managerial panic, political confusion, blame and counter blame that came in the wake of the Hatfield crash. In fact, outside wars and nuclear accidents, it is hard to think of any technological failure which has had such lasting and widespread effects. A week or so later, when overfilled rivers began to flood low-lying England and the first people were emptied from their sandbagged homes into boats, the unsettling impression grew of Britain as an unsound country, weakly equipped, under-skilled, easily made chaotic and only superficially modern; an incompetent society. 'We must be the laughing stock of Europe,' people said (and might have been correct). The reason was elementary: movement. People could not move, in an economy – the world's fourth or fifth largest – which depended on millions of everyday, necessary journeys. Few trains ran; those that did ran unreliably, even to the revised schedules that sometimes doubled or trebled the normal journey times. Travellers tried other methods; motorways became impassable, domestic flights overbooked. At railway stations, even aboard a train itself, would-be passengers were advised to travel 'only if your journey is really necessary;' the train may depart but it may not arrive – nothing could be guaranteed. In any case, what **was** necessity, how were we to rank it? Arriving at the office? Reaching a funeral? Getting home? The question hadn't been asked in Britain since the belt – tightening poster campaigns of the Second World War. People old enough to remember the Second World War, its long trains packed with troops crawling through black-outs and air raids, compared that period favourably with the present. There was an enemy then; Britain was a more capable nation.
> (Quoted by kind permission of Ian Jack, *The Crash the Stopped Britain*, Granta Books, London 2001)

The Chiltern network suffered less than most from temporary speed restrictions post-Hatfield. Chiltern ran its full published timetable; it was not easy, but it was done. Also, unique among train operators, Chiltern's rate of staff sickness and absenteeism actually fell during this difficult time.

Later in the year Chiltern issued a franchise replacement fact-sheet which was made available to all interested parties, including user groups and local authorities. It promised, in the event of Chiltern Railways winning the franchise extension, £370 million of investment by Chiltern, along with a total investment of £1 billion in new railway lines, new stations and new journey opportunities. Specifically, the first section dealt with safety matters, the extension of ATP, the new radio equipment for driver's cabs and a new driver simulator at a purpose-built training centre. A major upgrade of all Chiltern's routes was detailed, to be delivered in four phases:

Project Evergreen – Originally scheduled for completion by October 2002, this had three phases:
- track doubling north of Bicester
- two additional platforms at Marylebone, additional signals at Neasden, slewing the track at Beaconsfield, additional signals between High Wycombe and Bicester as well as on the Aylesbury branch
- (eventually jettisoned) four tracks between West and South Ruislip and through Beaconsfield station

West Midlands Capacity – By the same date, the original Birmingham Moor Street terminus will be re-opened, along with more capacity on the approaches to Birmingham and more signals between Banbury and Leamington Spa.

Aylesbury–London Upgrade – Whilst the work described above is taking place, further improvements will be under detailed development to upgrade the Aylesbury–Amersham–London route to main-line status.

The upgrade of the Aylesbury-London route is still on the drawing board in 2010. Chiltern trains share tracks with London Underground between Amersham and Harrow, and therefore any enhancement schemes are linked to LU's own plans – which are due to come to fruition between 2010 and 2016, including a completely new train fleet and resignalling. This will finally enable the Aylesbury route to enjoy some of the journey time benefits experienced on the High Wycombe route.

The other sections outlined measures to provide more and faster services; measures to improve punctuality which were based upon the concept of the Integrated Control Centre at Banbury; measures to improve the quality of the rolling stock, to reduce overcrowding and improve capacity, programmes to enhance the quality of the total experience and Primary Aspirations, which deals with the enhancing of the Aylesbury–Amersham route mentioned above.

Under Major Expansion Plans, five 'secondary aspirations' are listed, including a major interchange at West Hampstead which would offer across-platform exchange for passengers between the six different companies whose lines converge at that point; the East–West Rail Link; the New Route to Oxford; playing a major part in Crossrail; rebuilding the Great Central Railway from north of Aylesbury to a major new parkway station near the M1/M6 interchange and ultimately to Leicester itself. This section is accompanied by a map which is reproduced opposite.

Within the Franchise Agreement, a process to further develop, reach agreement on and then deliver these 'secondary aspirations' was set out. This enabled development work on Evergreen 2 to be completed by 2005, with the project delivered by the end of 2006, and subsequently Evergreen 3 to secure approval early in 2010.

Back in 2001, the jettisoning of the then third phase of Evergreen was down to cost. Railtrack had a limit of £146 million on Evergreen. At this stage, all three phases, plus the new Wembley depot, were estimated at £250–300 million, therefore phase three was scrapped. The total cost of Evergreen 1, plus the new depot and Evergreen 2 (new signalling from Banbury to Leamington Spa) now totalled £146 million.

However, even Chiltern Railways management team still had room for improvement. Earlier in 2000, during the course of one of their periodic audits, the SRA did identify one or two issues relating to process management. Perhaps the dismal period from 1998 was also still remembered. Fortunately for Chiltern, they had previously recruited as a non-executive director John Nelson, the last managing director of BR's Network SouthEast and something of an acknowledged expert on process management.

The M40 Board reacted promptly to the SRA concerns and at their June 2000 meeting Nelson was asked to assist Steve Murphy to investigate the problem and formulate proposals for a remedy. At the same time, Murphy was appointed managing director of Chiltern as part of a general Laing/Chiltern restructuring that saw Shooter become chairman of both Chiltern and Laing Rail.

CHILTERN RAILWAYS FRANCHISE
MAJOR PROJECTS TO BE DEVELOPED

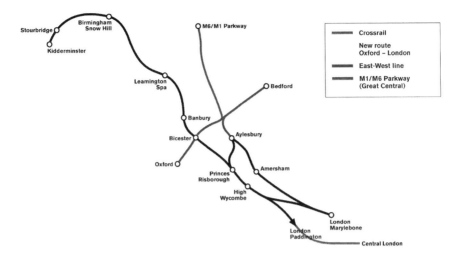

▬▬▬	Crossrail
	New route Oxford – London
▬▬▬	East-West line
▬▬▬	M1/M6 Parkway (Great Central)

Track-doubling on the Evergreen 1 project between Banbury and Bicester, 2002. (Chiltern Railways)

If process management is about identifying which processes add value to a company and removing those which are simply a cost, then the key to success is rooted in the culture of the business. It is essentially about raising performance and perceptions. Primarily, through people, their abilities, skills and above all, their motivation. On that score, Chiltern would seem to have already been doing rather better than many other companies.

However, Shooter was correct in seeking to earth this potential problem quickly. Chiltern was under the spotlight on two major counts: not only was the management team sweating on the task of achieving an extension to their existing franchise, but Chiltern, along with its new owner Laing, was also seeking to grow the business dramatically by bidding in conjunction with a new partner, Swiss Federal Railways, for the proposed new Wessex franchise in 2001. If successful, this would have increased the size of Laing Rail from £50 million to £250 million a year. For any bid to succeed, the effectiveness of Chiltern's management practices would need to be beyond question.

Consequently, at the October 2000 Board Meeting, the decision was made to appoint a process manager for Chiltern whose task would be to deliver in full the quality process capabilities identified by the SRA consultants. The current means by which Chiltern delivered its company strategy and business objectives would also be reviewed, along with any consequent necessary changes to existing company training. Further tasks would include ensuring a fully integrated management system with an effective review process together with any necessary changes to company culture. Finally, in order to protect Chiltern from any future criticisms by the SRA, and to ensure full compliance with franchise obligations, options were to be identified for appropriate accreditation.

During the run up to the winning of the franchise extension in February 2002, the negotiating process was extremely fraught. As already shown, it was a period characterised by combinations of tragic railway accidents, financial mayhem and administrative paralysis at Railtrack leading to its eventual collapse, along with other events including the financial fallout from 9/11, all of which made for Transport Minister Stephen Byers what must have been a very difficult stewardship.

The Chiltern franchise bid was basically led by Beckett and two others. Ian Wells, the then financial director for Laing Rail, dealt with the negotiations and documentation with the banks while Beckett did the negotiations with Network Rail and the SRA. The other person who was directly involved was Helen Bissell. Bissell had previously been a BR corporate lawyer. She worked closely with Chiltern all the way through and became considered virtually as part of their team. Chiltern also still used Cameron McKenna for the legal support for the funding documents for the bank.

Work on franchise replacement had started in earnest in 1999, with Shooter's paper on the strategic overview. Between the announcement of Chiltern as the preferred bidder in August 2000 and the signing of the twenty-year franchise extension on 18 February 2002 were eighteen very tense and difficult months. Long days were spent at Eversheds underground meeting rooms in the City by Mark Beckett, Ian Wells and Helen Bissell, meeting with Graham Cross and Cedric Pierce from OPRAF. So frequent were the meetings between these five that over the following two years they incidentally became good friends which aided a generally constructive approach all around. The same could not be said for the meetings with Railtrack, by that time in administration, over the final phase of track doubling. Things were very fraught and rather stiff with cross words and rooms full of people including two administrators who would not let Railtrack do anything. That was, of course, their job: to see that absolutely no risks were taken.

If these negotiations were very difficult, those with the SRA were generally much more reasonable. The SRA was still working out its procedures for franchise renewal. The Chiltern proposals were clearly liked, but the stumbling block was the financing of Project Evergreen, in particular phase 1, the remaining section of track re-doubling from Aynho to Bicester. With Railtrack clearly in deep financial trouble, it would fall to the SRA to pay the capital cost of the scheme, rising inexorably with each consulting engineers report on, for instance, the poor state of the embankments and the work required to restore them for main-line use for freight as well as passenger trains after thirty years of neglect. Being Government money, the Treasury was central to the discussions and, while Chiltern urgently needed to sign the new franchise to obtain rescheduling of its subsidy to accommodate its new and increased capital investment in trains and some infrastructure costs, the Government was not unreasonably reluctant to sign before final clarification of the costs of Project Evergreen. Over all of this was the shadow of 'post-Hatfield'.

On 26 February 2001, Shooter put a report to the M40 Board, in which he stated bluntly:

The Board should be aware that the financial position of the company will be in jeopardy if the current negotiations with the SRA do not produce a rapid and satisfactory outcome.

The financial results of M40 Trains have been affected by the lack of bid-for subsidy and the impact of Gauge Corner Cracking. However, it is also important to note that the underlying trading position of Chiltern is buoyant. Sales were not affected by Gauge Corner Cracking to the same extent as most other operators... If it had not been for these two external factors, the Chiltern budget for 2000 would have been achieved, and the main risk to the 2001 budget remains the subsidy issue, rather than any longer term impact on revenues.

The SRA's franchising programme is in some disarray, both because of defects in the process and because of concerns over affordability (e.g. the Regulatory settlement will be expensive for the SRA).

On the specific matter of the franchise replacement, the report continued:

> The signature of the Chiltern Franchise Agreement is being delayed by two factors:
>
> It is taking longer than anyone originally thought to get to a definitive cost for Project Evergreen. This is compounded by the SRA's refusal to sign a Franchise Agreement in advance of final costings, and their requirement to audit the costs to protect themselves from a national audit office investigation.
>
> Railtrack is currently refusing to commit to any new enhancement investment pending resolution of their post-Hatfield financial and credit rating problems.
>
> In addition, the General Election is likely to create a three-month hiatus when ministerial approvals will not be forthcoming.'

The essence of the difficulty was obtaining a Deed of Amendment to guarantee the £7.6 million subsidy which had been included within the Heads of Terms for the new franchise. The amount covered the period between October 2000 and 31 March 2002.

By the time Beckett placed his paper 'Project Evergreen, Proposals for a Way Forward' in front of the M40 Board towards the end of June 2001, there had been some profound changes. The SRA under Sir Alastair Morton was legally established. The Government had won the General Election, Stephen Byers had been put in charge of Transport and was initially seeking to merge the Rail Regulator with the SRA but was also not getting on too well with Sir Alastair, who was expecting the Government to back his ten-year Strategic Plan for Rail Development. Before the year was out, Stephen Byers had replaced Sir Alastair with Richard Bowker from Virgin Rail and had closed down Railtrack altogether, replacing it with the not-for-profit Network Rail under a professional railwayman, John Armitt.

Ministers were also dusting off the plans once more for London's Crossrail scheme, which if implemented as far as High Wycombe would have very profound implications for the plans of Chiltern's Project Evergreen, particularly their plans for track quadrupling south of High Wycombe, since the Chiltern plans for the track work already agreed with Railtrack/Network Rail did not allow for services stopping at South and West Ruislip to proceed from there into Paddington. Neither did they allow for the overhead catenary required for Crossrail.

At the same time, the schedule of planned total line closures on the WCML were dramatically changed to include long total closures at weekends and holiday periods between August 2002 and January 2003. This cut across the already agreed schedule between Chiltern and Railtrack/Network Rail which would have dovetailed it with the closures on the Chiltern route thus allowing work to begin on the Aynho–Bicester track re-doubling while ensuring that at least one route between London and the West Midlands was running all the time. Now this was not going to be possible.

The build up of work on the West Coast line also created a scarcity of appropriately skilled people available for Project Evergreen. This, along with Railtrack/Network Rail's risk-averse paralysis post-Hatfield, caused further difficulties. Simultaneously, the doubling of the frequency of Virgin Cross-Country services was causing serious congestion on the shared section between Aynho Junction and Leamington Spa, and putting at risk Chiltern's own plans to augment services.

Nevertheless, the paper shows Chiltern remained focussed on ensuring the delivery of the majority of benefits to passengers as planned. The strategy for delivery running through the paper was a robust combination of greater market testing of contract prices for significant parts of the project, a rigorous overhaul of the basic costings and a more pragmatic re-scheduling of the various elements of Evergreen which altogether would reduce the committed cost to the SRA and hence to the taxpayer. The paper was aiming to encourage a signing of the new franchise agreement in September 2001.

That did not happen, and Chiltern plans endured a further blow when Transport Minister Stephen Byers scrapped plans for the proposed Wessex franchise in July 2001, with the disturbing comment that there would be no more long-term franchises. The sheer cost in time, money and effort already put into this project by both Chiltern and Swiss Federal Railways had been very considerable indeed. SBB pulled out immediately, as a short franchise made nonsense of their plans for substantial investment. They had ambitious plans for integrated public transport, particularly in the Bristol and Plymouth regions and for which a reasonably long pay-back time was axiomatic.

Peter Grossenbacher was the senior manager from SBB who headed up their team working with Chiltern. On reflection, Grossenbacher contrasted what he termed the 'outstanding' professionalism of the Chiltern people with his analysis of Britain's railways in general stating, 'The UK is muddling through and runs its railways on a hand-to-mouth basis. Britain's privatised railways generally seem focussed only on making money and the customer comes last.' In its home country, SBB enjoys working with the Federal Government to implement twenty-year rail development plans.

Chiltern persisted with developments which it felt were needed whether or not it was eventually awarded the franchise extension. In July 2001 the Integrated Control Centre was opened at Banbury on land previously occupied by the old Higham's coal yard. The overall aim was to enhance Chiltern's performance in line with its franchise requirements. The paper to the M40 Board on 22 May 2001 drew upon experience of overseas railways who had brought together in close working collaboration the train operators (e.g. Chiltern), the owner of the infrastructure (Network Rail) and the party responsible for maintaining the infrastructure (Amey Rail), achieving substantial improvements in performance. In particular, the initial capital cost of £0.98 million and annual running costs of £178,000 would be offset against improvements in the performance of the infrastructure (in terms of reduced failure rates and improved response to residual failures) and hence would be a key instrument to help Chiltern achieve its 93.75 per cent PPM performance figure from December 2003. This commitment, to fifteen out of sixteen trains on time, all day, every day, was a key commitment in the twenty-year franchise. Looking back, it seems straightforward. In 2010, many franchised operators achieve similar levels of performance and Chiltern's own has now climbed to in excess of 95 per cent. Back in 2003, however, things were very different; post-Hatfield the railway nationally was climbing back from a very poor level and so 93.75 per cent was a challenging target. For Chiltern, good performance is another tool to attract passengers. By giving them security that they can rely on their train service to get them to their destination on time takes away one potential negative feature of rail travel.

Key features would include joint planning of the train service, infrastructure and fleet maintenance, rapid failure recovery and remote condition monitoring of infrastructure and on-train assets. The ICC allows for the assimilation of operational, signalling, condition monitoring (infrastructure and trainborne) and retail data (e.g. passenger loadings). This data would be analysed to allow signallers, drivers, retail staff and depot staff to make strategic operational decisions in the context of real time information.

The 'experience of overseas railways operations' referred to Shooter's initiative in arranging annual management exchanges with Japan Railways. Shooter was impressed with the Japanese concept of 'Kaizen,' which in the specific railway concept meant constant striving for higher excellence through gradual step-by-step improvements. Shooter hopes one day to see Japanese standards of punctuality and reliability achieved on Chiltern Railways. For the record, the Tokaido Shinkansen, Japan's high-speed 'Bullet Trains', operate eleven sixteen-vehicle trains each hour, 285 trains carrying 357,000 passengers per day. With regard to punctuality, a report by Carl Baker of Porterbrook Leasing, quoting from an official JR Central Annual Report, concluded:

> With respect to punctuality the average deviation from schedule per train, including delays caused by uncontrollable factors such as earthquakes, typhoons, heavy snow etc. is 0.6 minutes per train. The safety record of the Tokaido Shinkansen is flawless; during 37 years of operation there have been no passenger fatalities or injuries due to train accidents.
> (reproduced by kind permission of Porterbrook Leasing)

Well, that puts leaves on the line into perspective! Incidentally, Japan Railways is vertically integrated. Their executives do not see how a railway can work otherwise.

At long last, on 18 February 2002, and coinciding with the start of the re-laying of the double track from Aynho to Bicester, to great relief all around Chiltern and the SRA signed a twenty-year extension to its franchise.

From the signing of the new franchise, events both planned and unplanned came thick and fast to Chiltern. The unique twenty-year franchise was based upon both Chiltern's previous record of investing £154 million as well as their pledge of significant future funding to improve capacity and other customer benefits. To ensure the interests of all parties were safeguarded, the franchise rules specify periodic reviews, termed Passenger Service Output Updates (PSOU). The general idea is that Chiltern has to demonstrate both results achieved in line with its franchise objectives, and equally demonstrate planned future investments of sufficient worth to merit the franchise continuing. The first of these was scheduled for 2005 but because of the Gerrards Cross tunnel collapse, was re-scheduled for 2007. The second was due in December 2009.

In 2002 Chiltern, jointly with Railtrack, received the 'Best Rail Route 2002' award. Chiltern also received the same award in 2003 and 2004.

In 2004, by which time Chiltern's income had reached £69 million, the much-needed two extra maintenance bays were completed at Aylesbury depot.

In 2005, Chiltern started building a new maintenance depot at Wembley as part of their Evergreen 2 project (see also Chapter 5).

On Thursday 30 June 2005 all Chiltern services were disrupted for seven weeks by the collapse of the tunnel at Gerrards Cross and also subsequently by the London bombings and the Wembley fire (see also Chapter 1).

Once Chiltern had recovered from these disasters, work continued on two major new projects. The first of these, Aylesbury Vale Parkway, lay some two and a half miles north-west of the newly expanded Aylesbury depot where the original Great Central/Metropolitan main line, now a singled freight line, crosses the A41 trunk road. The scheme was to build a new parkway station to serve a projected massive housing development planned in conjunction with the District Council, Buckinghamshire County Council, John Laing and also this time with the support of a central Government looking for means to address the urgent need for thousands of new homes.

In concept, Aylesbury Vale Parkway was a part continuation of 'Metroland', the generic name ascribed to the Metropolitan Railway Company's various schemes in the first half of the twentieth century for affordable housing in the rural edges of London with the aim of enticing city dwellers to move to pleasant countryside far removed from city grime and, of course, then use the railway to commute back into the city. *Metroland* is also the name of the delightful documentary film conceived and hosted by John Betjeman and produced by the BBC in 1972.

Using valuable previous experience with Warwick Parkway, but with even more complicated land ownership to be dealt with, Laing led a representative consortium of all the interested parties. Graham Cross represented Chiltern after Beckett moved on. Buckinghamshire County Council worked very closely and put money into the associated road schemes. The railway infrastructure and station building were relatively straightforward and completed on time. However, the roundabout and short approach road to the station were a Section 106 planning obligation on the developers, who were required to build them before starting on the houses. Unfortunately, in 2007/8 the bottom fell out of the housing market. The developer's plans were frozen, as were plans for roads. Cross had nightmares about the station opening without road access but, fortunately, energetic action by Buckinghamshire County Council eventually put a package together with the developers that resolved the issue and the new station was officially opened on 3 July 2009 by Transport Minister Lord Adonis.

A further significant event in 2005 was an approach from Renaissance Trains, led by non-executive director John Nelson. This was to restore direct train services, after a thirty-year absence, between Wrexham, north-east Wales, Shropshire and London. Acting as promoter, the Renaissance Trains team repeated the successful approach of the late 1990s which saw the development and implementation of Hull Trains, which started running services very successfully over the East Coast main line from Hull to London, King's Cross in 2000. Both services are possible through the liberalisation of competition following privatisation. 'Open Access' permits any new operators to gain access to the network, and provided they can demonstrate a robust business plan without 'cherry picking' of existing business, a licence will be granted. Chiltern's franchise holder, M40 Trains, agreed to a 50 per cent stake in the venture and after two further years detailed work, a seven-year licence was granted by the ORR to the Wrexham, Shropshire and Marylebone Railway (WSMR) in 2007, with operations to start in spring 2008.

The senior management of WSMR came, not surprisingly, from Chiltern Railways. The MD of WSMR is engineering graduate Andy Hamilton who joined Chiltern in 1993 after seven years with British Rail. He became fleet manager in 1995 and was responsible for developing Chiltern's standalone fleet capabilities as part of Chiltern's privatisation. In 1999, Hamilton was made engineering director and from 2005 led the WSMR project.

It was unfortunate that WSMR services began simultaneously with the economic collapse so initial progress towards its clear economic potential will take time. From the beginning, WSMR paid Chiltern for support services such as IT, train cleaning and light maintenance at Wembley depot. Over time, the working relationship has become closer, and there are now proposals for the two companies to be merged – although the 'Wrexham & Shropshire' brand will be retained.

In 2006, Chiltern's Evergreen 2 Project was completed, including additional platforms at Marylebone and the restoration of Birmingham's Moor Street station, for which Chiltern was given the Renaissance Award.

The second major project re-focussed on the need for additional rail capacity between Oxford and London. At the time of the joint bid with SBB for the Wessex franchise, Mark Beckett and his team had looked carefully at rebuilding the largely abandoned Great Western branch line from Princes Risborough to Oxford via Thame. This was eventually rejected due to the cost of restoring a route that had not been preserved – houses had been built on the route and structures such as bridges removed.

However, the concept now resurfaced through Chiltern's involvement in the East–West Rail Scheme; the plans to eventually reopen in stages the direct rail line between Oxford and Cambridge as part of a strategic east–west rail corridor designed to provide capacity for freight traffic and for long-distance passenger services to be diverted from routes used currently which are either approaching full capacity or, in the case of freight, cannot accommodate the proposed size of train within gauge. One of the early ideas was for a new Bicester Junction station at the spot where the old Oxford to Cambridge line passes under the Chiltern route. From this now evolved the alternative idea of constructing a new rail link between the two lines at their point of intersection just south of the present Bicester North station and upgrading the existing line from there to new platforms at Oxford station, including some double tracking and 100mph line speeds.

The really clever aspect of the scheme though is the building of a new station, Water Eaton Parkway, in north Oxford. This would be strategically well placed for 'Park and Ride' with good road access to north Oxford and Kidlington, and a wide catchment area including Chipping Norton and reaching across towards Cheltenham. Market research showed that this relatively prosperous area was currently poorly served by rail and the average journey time of an hour or less from Water Eaton to Marylebone would be very competitive.

In combination with enhancements on the 'main-line' Chiltern route from London to Birmingham, the new Evergreen 3 project was born. An ambitious £250 million project, transforming the Chiltern route into a 100mph railway, the deal was concluded in January 2010. The project will deliver the capability to handle a larger number of fast trains, and is being delivered in two phases. The first phase sees new overtaking loops at Northolt-Ruislip and Princes Risborough, which allied to greater sections of 100mph running will enable a London–Birmingham journey time of one hour forty minutes from 2011. The capacity that this phase delivers will also enable accommodation of the half-hourly London–Oxford service from 2013. The new railway between Bicester and Oxford requires planning approval through a 'Transport and Works Act', the public inquiry for which is expected in autumn 2010.

One of the key attractions of the scheme was the minimum of new works required. The financial arrangements are similar to those for the second stage of track doubling from Bicester to Aynho Junction; Network Rail finances the build and Chiltern will pay back from farebox receipts, plus 6 per cent.

In 2006–7, Shooter and Rob Brighouse were working away at another franchise opportunity with a new overseas partner, MTR Corporation of Hong Kong. This time their efforts were successful and a 50/50 joint venture with MTR won the contract from Transport for London for the running of the London Overground system from November 2007. This comprises the Third rail DC electrified lines from Euston to Watford Junction, the lines from Willesden Junction to Clapham Junction, the North London Lines from Richmond in the West to Stratford and Barking in the east. Further stages will add a link from Highbury and Islington to West Croydon – part of which will open in 2010 – with an eventual link connecting back to Clapham Junction, thus completing a rail orbital route around London.

The attraction of London Overground is that it offered the opportunity to diversify the financial portfolio. Unlike the Chiltern franchise which has 100 per cent financial risk of downturn, London Overground is completely the opposite with only 10 per cent of risk. Nevertheless, the task for the management team is not straightforward, with a need to support a wide range of project investments by Transport for London totalling £1.4 billion on track and signalling upgrades before the 2012 Olympics.

London Overground's managing director is Steve Murphy, who, as readers of Chapter 2 will recall, was one of the first of Shooter's appointments to Chiltern in 1994 (see also Part 2). Subsequently Murphy was promoted to general manager of Chiltern in 1999 becoming managing director in 2002 and in 2004 was seconded to Irish Rail as general manager, Southern and Western. Murphy returned and was appointed managing director of London Overground in September 2007.

Along with the successes were a number of ventures which have not come off. In 2005/6, a joint venture with GNER parent company Sea Containers targeted a bid for the Great Western franchise. Despite a huge amount of local support, the team failed to prequalify for the bid proper. And over the years, there have been several attempts to bring the Snow Hill lines local services, which co-exist with Chiltern in the Birmingham area, into the fold. Formal bids were submitted as part of the twenty-year franchise in 2002, and more recently at the time of the appointment of London Midland in 2007. In both cases, this move – sensible for both passenger and operator – has not succeeded with the franchising auuthority.

Then, in 2006, came a potential bombshell that could have impacted very detrimentally on Chiltern. John Laing was sold to private equity company Henderson. Henderson concluded that their strategic vision for the future of Laing did not include railway companies and so once the required formalities had been completed, Laing Rail which included M40 Trains the owner of the Chiltern franchise, 50 per cent of Wrexham, Shropshire and Marylebone Railway and 50 per cent of LOROL, was put up for sale by auction.

Some fifteen companies expressed an interest in buying Chiltern, among them the state-owned German Deutsche Bahn (DB). Dirk Thater, Business Development Director for DB Regio, together with his colleague Karsten Nagel, DB's Head of Mergers, had spotted the opportunity to acquire Laing Rail. Other major companies bidding also included the Go Ahead Group, Arriva, Stagecoach, National Express and a French company, Keolis. DB had already previously indicated its interest in the UK rail market by acquiring the rail freight company EWS.

Not only was Chiltern's growth potential attractive for Deutsche Bahn both in the commuter and London–Birmingham markets, but DB were in expansionist mode generally. By 2009 railways in Germany were not yet privatised but were in the process of being 'liberalised'. This meant that DB was state owned but was being attacked on a number of fronts by proper private sector operators through a kind of regional franchising system where a region's services are put up for franchise and DB would bid but not necessarily get the franchise. Hence DB found itself losing market share at home but trying to compensate by acquisitions abroad. This also gave it a greater understanding of how franchising is done elsewhere. For example, the UK rail industry by 2009 had been privatised for fifteen years so that was the kind of experience they were buying into.

Having acquired both Chiltern and EWS, DB now had a springboard in the UK for future expansion. The 2008–09 recession hit the freight business very hard both on mainland Europe as well as in the UK so their balance sheet strength was clearly affected. Hence DB expansion plans in 2009 were more about competing in franchise bids than acquisitions through share purchase; for example their bid for Tyne and Wear Metro. It was a small expansion but it is DB's first attempt to do it. At the time of writing their offer was down to the last two.

The process was severely testing for those closely involved. Adrian Shooter and Tony Allen had been there before, in 1996 at the time of the management buy-out (Chapter 3) but the others, Steve Murphy and Graham Cross, found it a weird experience. The 'Estate Agents' for the auction were KPMG. Cross found it extremely interesting being sold; he had to learn masses about his company and now think about it in quite a different way from when he simply operated in it.

The team was required to spend four days at the KPMG offices talking to the four short-listed bidders including DB. They did management presentations and underwent close interrogation about the finances and their vision for the future. The team's priority was to convince the potential buyers that they were not acquiring a static business but a broad canvas on which to expand. One of the most testing aspects of the exercise was not merely having questions fired at them, but all the time knowing that those same potential buyers were simultaneously wondering whether or not they would want to retain this particular management team! Not merely a series of scary presentations but also a series of testing job interviews.

Chiltern's regular customers were also very concerned at the danger they might be acquired by one of those second-rate bus companies that since 1996 had done so much to discredit any potential benefits of rail privatisation in the UK. Then, on 21 January 2008, Adrian Shooter sent a letter to all interested parties entitled 'Chiltern Railways – New Shareholders Announced'. The second paragraph began:

> I am delighted to tell you that Laing Rail, including Chiltern Railways, has been bought by Deutsche Bahn AG, the German railway company. Chiltern will become part of DB Regio, the division of Deutsche Bahn responsible for operating regional and local services. The sale is subject to approval from the DfT, TfL and the Office of Rail Regulation.
>
> This is excellent news for passengers and stake holders. Our new owners are fully behind the continuing development of Chiltern Railways. We look forward to continuing to provide the safe, reliable, welcoming and value for money service you have come to expect.
>
> I am also pleased to say our new owners have asked me to continue in my role as Chairman of Chiltern Railways, and to manage Laing Rail's other interests in Wrexham & Shropshire and London Overground. I look forward to the continued development of our group of companies at this exciting, positive time.

Four days earlier, Dr Martin Lamm, Legal Counsel for Deutsche Bahn AG, had written to Mr Haydon Walker at the Department for Transport in Marsham Street confirming DB's wish to proceed with the acquisition of Laing Rail, requesting an official Change of Control and adding:

> It is our intention to keep Chiltern's existing management in place, namely Adrian Shooter, Anthony Allen and Graham Cross, as well as the key managers in all operational functions. Instead of the current non-executive Directors, high-level DB representatives will be appointed replacing those current members representing the Seller. The interaction between Chiltern and DB will be mainly focussed on DB's Business Unit DB Regio with a direct reporting line of the Chairman of Laing Rail Limited to the top management of DB Regio AG.
>
> As a general business principle, DB has high regard for local management responsibilities we consider this to be crucial to deliver excellent customer satisfaction.
>
> On an operational level, DB will share best practices between Chiltern, LOROL, WSMR and its other international, German and UK (EWS) operations to further support the business.

This was greeted with great relief all around, as well as gentle smiles at the irony of the UK's best private railway company now being 100 per cent owned by a 100 per cent state enterprise.

From 2008 Chiltern has no longer received a Government subsidy, and operated an intensive daily service of over 300 trains, roughly a five-fold increase on 1984.

In conclusion, it is difficult to overestimate the strategic significance of Evergeen 3 for the future potential of this main line between London and the West Midlands as well as the proposed new link to Oxford, this latter being the first new rail link to be opened between to major centres of population in one hundred years. Chiltern's investment of £250 million is the largest domestic passenger infrastructure project to be funded without recourse to the taxpayer since before the Second World War, and, all in all, Chiltern can be forgiven its apparent lack of modesty in proclaiming these plans. As this former Great Western main line goes into its second century in July 2010, it is clear Chiltern would agree with the poet that 'the best is yet to be'.

CHAPTER 8

A DAY IN THE LIFE OF CHILTERN RAILWAYS

The day starts at Banbury with Driver Rangitsingh Chawda. We may just be starting our day, but Driver Chawda actually booked on at 10.52 p.m. in London the night before. Before we depart, Driver Chawda prepares his unit for its day ahead and once all preparations and checks have been completed, we are joined by train host Barry Stiles for the first movement of the new day. The train departs Banbury at 4.48 a.m., empty and bound for Hatton where it reverses and then runs, still empty, to Warwick Parkway to form the first commuter train of the day from the north of the route. This train has been added in recent years after feedback from the growing number of passengers using Warwick Parkway since it opened in 2000.

The time now is 5.40 a.m. and as the first commuters board the train at Warwick Parkway, the same scene is being repeated at other locations along the length of the route as they are served by their first trains of the day. A wide variety of staff along the route from car-park attendants to ticket office clerks are booking on for their shifts, giving life to stations from Birmingham Moor Street in the North, across to Aylesbury Vale Parkway and down to our terminus at London Marylebone in the south, encompassing a variety of local communities and conurbations along the way.

Back on board we are leaving Leamington Spa and new passengers are greeted with an announcement from Train Host Stiles. We are informed about the train's stopping pattern, our expected arrival time in to London Marylebone and to have our tickets and passes ready for inspection. Sure enough, shortly after leaving Leamington Spa, our train host appears and our tickets are checked quickly and efficiently. South of Banbury, the Chiltern route operates under driver only operation and so Train Host Stiles departs the service ready to work another northbound service once we arrive at Banbury.

From here until London, Driver Chawda is our point of call for information and we have announcements before each of the remaining stops as we travel through the rolling hills of the Chilterns. We are soon on the final leg of our journey and the countryside gives way to the North London suburbs before we arrive in to platform three at London Marylebone, two minutes early. We follow the groups of commuters as they make a bee line for the ticket barriers, well versed in station procedure.

At the ticket barriers, there is a steady stream of commuters passing through from the variety of trains now filling the platforms. For those whose tickets get rejected by the barrier the revenue protection team are ready to let them through manually. For those who do not have tickets then the excess window is open for them to purchase a ticket and/or be issued with a penalty fare. In the peaks, very few people travel without a ticket, but as with all things in life it seems there is always somebody trying to get something for nothing!

We note several passengers from Princes Risborough who arrive without tickets and are sold the relevant one. They have a good excuse though: with it being a particularly busy morning at Princes Risborough, Michael Garrucho the ticket office clerk allowed the passengers to travel so that they did not miss their train, and then got Phil Simms on the retail control desk to send out a pager message to let the revenue team know what the situation was, resulting in the problem being solved quickly and efficiently. We will see more from control later in our journey.

The first stage of track doubling. The scene at Haddenham and Thame station, showing membrane in place prior to laying of ballast and the new up line. (Chiltern Railways)

First track doubling, Haddenham and Thame, showing the new platform in place and the ballast laid. (Chiltern Railways)

Whilst on the station we observe a variety of staff going about their roles, ensuring that the concourse is clean, that passengers have the assistance they need at the ticket vending machines and with the departure boards. To the side of the concourse is a booth dedicated to providing information on train services, attractions and local amenities and bus services.

We venture over and observe an item of lost property being handed in by one of the on-train cleaners. Some weird and wonderful items have been handed in on Chiltern Railways over the years, but this time it is simply a mobile phone. This item will remain with the information booth clerk for a short period, in case the owner quickly returns, before being taken down to lost property to be catalogued and stored whilst attempts are made to reunite the phone with its owner.

It is now time for us to leave London Marylebone and head northbound once more, this time taking in a Chiltern service to Aylesbury Vale Parkway that travels along the shared infrastructure of London Underground's Metropolitan line. Shortly before the 9.27 a.m. departure time, Robert Fotofili (one of Marylebone's duty operations managers) escorts an elderly couple to the train and assists the gentleman in a wheelchair to board. This is one of four disabled assists that are due at Marylebone today which are all detailed on a daily report that is sent to the relevant location. With this information, Chiltern aims to provide a journey that is as easy and stress free as possible for those that require assistance.

We arrive at Aylesbury and have a chance to have a quick look around before our next train. In the distance we can see the activity of Aylesbury depot which is Chiltern's primary maintenance depot and in the sidings next to the station; we see an array of heritage units. Speaking of heritage units, our next train has arrived on platform 1 and is formed of Chiltern's 'Bubble Car', a unit that dates from the 1960s, but which has recently been refurbished with modern passenger systems.

We travel along the single line on the 10.38 a.m. Aylesbury to Princes Risborough, with the large windows of the Bubble Car giving great views across the countryside, even if the ride is a little bumpy! We arrive at Princes Risborough in time to make the 11.01 a.m. towards Banbury and are back on board the comfortable Clubman stock after our previous interesting journey.

With us now well into the morning service, ticket restrictions along the length of the route are relaxed and the mix of passengers on board begins to change. There is still a steady mix of commuters from most areas, but there is a noticeable increase in the number of families, retired couples and tourists who begin to use the trains. Along the line there are many destinations and attractions that are key tourism draws, not least Bicester Village designer outlet centre, Warwick Castle, Shakespeare's Stratford-upon-Avon and the various attractions in Birmingham.

As we arrive at Bicester North, large numbers of passengers disembark for the taxibus to Bicester Village to indulge their fashion shopping desires, but we continue our journey northbound. Shortly before we leave the train at Banbury we spot another item of lost property minus its owner, this time an umbrella. We hand the item to Mark Clewlow at the information point on the bridge at Banbury station, where it would then normally be sent down to the lost property office at London Marylebone to be stored. On this occasion the owner has already informed the ticket office at Bicester of the missing item and so Mark will send the item back with the driver of the next train southbound. A speedy reunification is on the cards here, so we head out and across to the Chiltern Integrated Control Centre.

Throughout the day, the railway is monitored by the Chiltern control in Banbury. This state of the art facility opened in recent years and allows controllers to monitor the railway in real time and see how well the railway is running compared to the plan for the day and to manage and react to situations that may occur from time to time.

We join the action shortly before midday in the control centre at Banbury. Following on from the smooth morning peak with only one train having registered as being late due to a minor issue, control are called into action when at 11.50 a.m. a call is received from Network Rail Control in Birmingham to report that whilst piling holes for the construction of a new building there was an explosion thought to be from a previously unexploded war time bomb. Being near to the railway line at Small Heath, there was the prospect that any safety zone put in place by the emergency services in the area could close the railway.

At 12.07 a.m., control receive the news that the railway is inside the 200m exclusion zone being set up and so no trains will be allowed to use the railway in the Small Heath area until further notice. Now the control centre swings in to action and decisions are made as to how to respond to the incident.

The guiding principle is to get as many passengers to their destinations as possible, and so ideally the trains will be terminated and then restarted in the opposite direction at the closest station to the incident (in this case Solihull). Unfortunately the track layout at Solihull does not allow this to happen and so the trains would have to turn back in nearby Tyseley depot to achieve this. The question now is, does Tyseley depot fall in the exclusion zone?

A call to Network Rail determines that it does not and so the next question is how this affects staffing. As a large number of drivers never need to go to Tyseley depot then they do not all sign the route and so this results in one train having to be turned at Dorridge where the track does allow this to happen.

Whilst the Duty Control Manager Alan Newman is making the high-level decisions, the other desks in the room are dealing with the ramifications for their areas. The fleet desk, manned by Greg Scott, is determining how this affects units being in the right place for their next services, for their refuelling and maintenance and how units need to be swapped around to return the train service to normal later in the day. To add to this there is a unit trapped at Birmingham Snow Hill and this will need factoring in when the route reopens.

We move over to the other side of the room where we have the retail desk (manned today by Phil Simms and Tracy Costello) who help ensure that passengers are kept up to date, manning the information point phones that are situated across the route, updating the information screens, sending out pager messages to staff across the company to keep people updated, organising taxis for displaced members of staff who need to get to their trains or back to their depots and generally being the first point of contact for customer facing staff across the route.

To add to the complexity of the day, there is an event at Wembley Stadium. This affects Chiltern particularly because our station at Wembley Stadium is the closest to the stadium and is well used in both the London and northbound directions. We will be visiting Wembley Stadium later in the day to see how this affects the railway, but for now there are a number of issues for Control to deal with.

The first of these is that the train plan for the day has been written specifically to cater for the capacity and timings needed for the event (and because of the complexity, today's plan was written by the Head of Train Planning Bevis Thomas), so when the duty control manager and the fleet controller are planning on how to return the service to normal, there is less flexibility than would normally be the case and also far greater numbers of passengers that will need to be accommodated in any changes made. These will need decisions later, but for now there is an additional issue to deal with.

On Wembley days when a major event is on, Chiltern run a special charter train for Club Wembley passengers. This train usually runs from Birmingham Moor Street and so is affected by the line closure at Small Heath. Some quick thinking and investigation by control finds that there is a driver available at Tyseley depot that has the route knowledge to divert the train to Birmingham New Street. This is obviously of great benefit to those passengers who now do not have to get a bus part of the way. In an ideal world more services could be diverted at New Street this way, but with only a small number of drivers signing the route and very little spare capacity around other operator's services, the charter train has to be squeezed through as it is!

With the railway still closed at its northern end for the foreseeable future, we leave control as they continue to manage the situation and travel southbound to Bicester North where we see how the railway plans for the Wembley event taking place this evening. We have already seen the preparations made for the charter train from control, but now to see how this works on the ground.

Platform staff are kept informed by the Wembley Events Manager Guy Horstmann of the charter train's progress and that of the still disrupted trains around it. With this information both the passengers of scheduled services and the charter train are kept up to date. The charter train will arrive thirteen minutes late, but considering the events of the day, passengers are good humoured and appreciative that delays have been kept to a minimum.

Right: A typical day at Marylebone. (Chiltern Railways)

Above: Banbury Booking Office Clerk Jane Haynes. (Chiltern Railways)

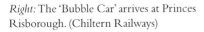

Right: The 'Bubble Car' arrives at Princes Risborough. (Chiltern Railways)

With the charter train departed we remain at Bicester North to assist with the additional volumes of passengers that use the station on Wembley event days. Stations such as Bicester North, Haddenham and Thame Parkway, Warwick Parkway and Beaconsfield with their large car parks are well used by both locals and as railheads from fans across the country. With direct services and a comprehensive service to return passengers after the event, travelling by rail is a very convenient option for many.

As the start of the event approaches we journey south once more, joined by fans heading to the games. On arrival at Wembley Stadium station there is a large presence of Chiltern staff, security guards and the police to ensure that the additional volumes of passengers have a safe and efficient journey to the stadium itself. As the event starts, it is break time for some of the staff involved, but outside a transformation begins as hundreds of barriers are placed across the Whitehorse Bridge above the station to form vast queuing areas for the various destinations to accommodate the large numbers of fans who will leave the stadium at the same time. The biggest reason for the barriers is to ensure the safety of all those involved. To put in to perspective how important the logistics are for this whole event, the evening peak out of London Marylebone on an average weekday will take approximately 8,500 back home. Tonight, close to an additional 4,000 people have travelled out of Marylebone with an additional 5,500 coming from the north.

As the event finishes and the fans pour out of the stadium, we observe the well-practised process of getting the crowds home as safely and efficiently as possible. With all call signs having been checked on the radio beforehand, everyone is in place and the trains begin to arrive. Passengers are directed in to the relevant queues for their destinations where they will be held until the platform is clear for them to await their train.

Everybody involved has a plan that tells them how long a train is, what type of units will form them and even where on the platform they will stop. This allows the controlling staff to ensure that the correct numbers of passengers are sent down to the correct platform in the correct place and at the correct time. When trains are being loaded with upwards of 800 people, it is important that everybody knows their role if the trains are to leave on time and get the crowds home.

With the train plan and everything on the ground running smoothly, 4,500 passengers are returned northbound and 4,000 passengers southbound in the seventy minutes after the event finishes: a success in anybody's book!

We leave Wembley Stadium on the return charter train as it makes its way back to Birmingham. With the route now clear again through Small Heath we can travel as scheduled back to Birmingham Moor Street and with an England win the mood on board is good. Abigail and Janet, two of Chiltern's catering stewards then come along the train and offer us a selection of refreshments for the journey home. The catering usually operates only in the morning, but like most things on Chiltern Railways, changed demand can be catered for.

As we pass through the stations at the north of the route we can see evidence of the depth of planning that goes in to Wembley days on Chiltern Railways. The station lights are on at Solihull and Dorridge after the end of regular service, not because they always are, but because it has been planned to change the timer for these specific days. It is only a small detail, but one that ensures passengers can safely disembark the later trains.

We cross the viaduct heading in to Birmingham towards the bright lights of the modern Bullring shopping centre and disembark the service at Birmingham Moor Street along with the rest of the passengers, the train host and the catering stewards. The driver will now take the unit back to Tyseley depot where it will stable overnight for cleaning and fuelling purposes before starting the whole process again the next day.

We make our way out of the recently restored station concourse looking back over the days events. It has been a busy one for Chiltern Railways, but thanks to the work of all concerned the disruption was minimised and over 95 per cent of trains on the day arrived on time and thousands of additional passengers made their way home safely.

(Author note: For this description of a typical day in the life of Chiltern Railways in 2009, I am indebted to new arrival on the staff, Tony Hickman.)

The Italian Café at Haddenham and Thame. (Chiltern Railways)

Above: Bicester taxibus. (Chiltern Railways)

Below: Winter scene at Haddenham and Thame. (Geoff Plumb)

(1) *Above:* Birmingham-bound Chiltern Clubman passing King's Sutton. Here the line lies for a few miles in Northants, a county celebrated for its spires and squires – this is one of the finest of the former. The location of the line in Northants justified the GWR in so naming one of its County class locomotives. (Chiltern Railways)

(2) *Left:* The Victorian Navvy with admirers; three of the author's grandchildren.

(3) Above: It is late and Aylesbury depot is filling up with Class 165 and 168 trains.

(4) Below: Wembley.

(5 & 6) This page:
The train-wash at
Wembley.

(7) Above: More vintage steam power. Ex–GWR (and ex-Barry scrapyard) No.6024 *King Edward I* at Haddenham and Thame, 9 June 2007, an enthusiasts' special train.

(8) Below: Ex–GWR 'Hall' class No.4965 *Rood Ashton Hall*, passing Haddenham and Thame with Charter Train, 5 May 2007.

(9) Above: Warwick Parkway. Note the wooden cladding. (Chiltern Railways)

(10) Left: The ground exterior of Marylebone station. The porte-cochère now shelters trains rather than the horse-drawn carriages of a century earlier.

(11) Above: Passengers on a typically busy day.

(12) Below: Wembley fans!

(13) Above: Deutsch Bahn.

(14) Below: When relaxing from running a railway, Adrian Shooter enjoys… running a railway!
Adrian Shooter driving his Darjeeling Himalayan steam locomotive on his Beeches Light Railway in
Oxfordshire. (Chiltern Railways)

Above: Integrating Public Transport at Haddenham and Thame. (The Oxford–Aylesbury bus calls every half hour.) (Chiltern Railways)

Right: Well-deserved award to Hadenham and Thame staff for customer service. (Geoff Plumb)

One of the first Wrexham & Shropshire services approaching Hadenham and Thame. (Geoff Plumb)

Above: VSOE charter train at Hadenham and Thame. (Geoff Plumb)

Below: Vintage diesel power approaching Haddenham and Thame. (Geoff Plumb)

Warwick Parkway station, 1999;
Adrian Shooter cutting the first sod.
Second from right is Richard Fearn,
then Zonal Director Railtrack
Midlands, later Chief Operating
Officer, Iarnrod Eireann. (Chiltern
Railways)

Warwick Parkway has been referred to as a club, not a railway station, because of the relaxed and friendly atmosphere. That is in no small part due to Judy Biggs, who has been station host since just after it opened in 2000. Judy says 'it's essential in this position to get to know our customers. They can often be under stress, or unsure what to do because they are new to Chiltern. I thoroughly enjoy my job and try to help people with things, like when they have forgotten something.' A friendly welcome is assured!

The Victorian cattle creep re-used as a passenger walkway. (See Part 2 Andy Harmer, 'The Project Manager's Story'.) (Chiltern Railways)

Warwick Parkway.
(Chiltern
Railways)

Above: Putting it back down again! (Alan Donaldson)

Below: Marylebone station, new platforms. (Chiltern Railways)

Above and below: Aylesbury Vale Parkway. (Chiltern Railways)

Above: Aylesbury Vale Parkway, starting construction. (Chiltern Railways)

Left: Aylesbury Vale Parkway; the new roundabout on the A41. (Chiltern Railways)

Above and below: Aylesbury Vale Parkway; station construction. (Chiltern Railways)

Above: Birmingham Moor Street and the Bullring. (Chiltern Railways)

Below: Announcement of purchase of Chiltern by Deutsche Bahn. (Chiltern Railways)

Above: Chiltern and Deutsche Bahn getting together. (Chiltern Railways)

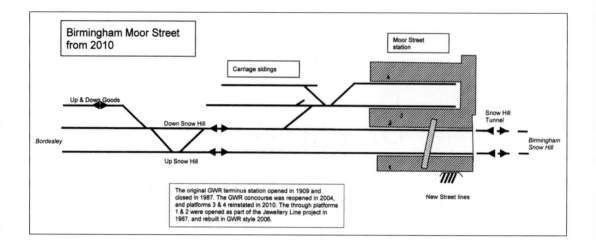

Birmingham Moor Street from 2010

Moor Street station

Carriage sidings

Up & Down Goods

Down Snow Hill

Bordesley

Up Snow Hill

Snow Hill Tunnel

Birmingham Snow Hill

New Street lines

The original GWR terminus station opened in 1909 and closed in 1987. The GWR concourse was reopened in 2004, and platforms 3 & 4 reinstated in 2010. The through platforms 1 & 2 were opened as part of the Jewellery Line project in 1987, and rebuilt in GWR style 2006.

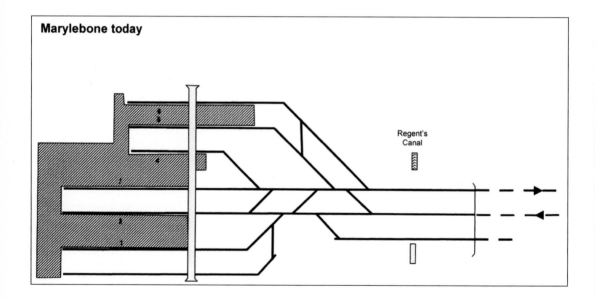

Marylebone today

Regent's Canal

PART 2

OTHER VOICES

CHAPTER 9

THE LINE THAT NEARLY DIED

Chris Green, Managing Director, Network SouthEast 1986–1992

My railway career began with British Rail as a graduate trainee in 1965. My first posting was to Banbury, little realising then that the station and the line, which is now known as the Chiltern line, would play such a significant part in my later career.

Banbury had just been transferred to the London Midland Region and there was a lot of tension surrounding the change from a Great Western to a London Midland culture. The first thing I noticed was how ancient and thin the Chiltern services were. We still had the link to Woodford Halse in those days but it was about to close, which felt sad. Nevertheless, my mentor at Banbury was the station master Don Holmes, from whom I learned much.

Although a Londoner by birth, I left Scotland to become managing director of London & SouthEast in January 1986 with some regret. We had used our relative independence in Scotland to create a totally new railway culture and I knew that London was going to be a very different challenge – on the other hand, I felt that we had done some things in Scotland that would successfully transfer to London.

ScotRail had succeeded in rolling back the Beeching cloud and had generated a public appetite for a rail renaissance. The ScotRail culture was aggressively positive in the face of strong deregulated coach competition. The London culture was still based on a slow decline and belief that offices would be relocating outside of London. Furthermore, what investment there had been had largely occurred south of the Thames; the commuter routes north of the Thames were not valued.

ScotRail faced up to the coach threat with investment, marketing and training. We were allowed to create our new brand – 'ScotRail' – and to invest in modernising our railway. In less than five years we had upgraded all 900 stations, replaced many of our trains, reopened sixteen stations and had even reopened an entire new line to Bathgate. Our railway was an expanding universe – we didn't close lines, we reopened them!

It was, therefore, a huge shock to arrive in London to find that one of my first jobs was to close Marylebone station, together with the railway as far as Northolt Junction. This felt like a very short-sighted decision, in fact I remember confiding to Adrian Shooter, the then-area manager for St Pancras, that the proposal felt 'barking mad'.

The closure proposal was, however, already public and had come about for two reasons. Firstly, the Whitehall wisdom was still locked into the view that rail was in a long, slow decline and this meant that the network should be shrinking. Secondly, the Prime Minister Margaret Thatcher had a Number 10 Transport Adviser called Alfred Sherman who was leading a personal crusade to convert rail travel into coach travel; he saw Marylebone as a big win.

In January 1986, all fingers pointed to Marylebone being the sacrificial lamb. Whitehall would avoid investing in a long-overdue Chiltern line upgrade and the coach industry would be given the invaluable asset of an exclusive new transport corridor into central London. The idea was to tarmac over the rails in the tunnels from Marylebone to Neasden and allow express coaches to drive through the narrow tunnels to a new coach terminal at Marylebone.

The reason that I had felt the whole scheme to be 'barking mad' had less to do with coaches passing at 50mph in tunnels with inches to spare, and more the fact that rail demand was on the rise in London again. It just seemed wrong to be giving up a high-capacity route into London, which could be bringing 500 commuters into central London every three minutes.

My first task was to find out how both the existing and future Chiltern demand was to be met when it lost its terminus. The rather vague answer was that London Underground would somehow absorb the Aylesbury line traffic into Baker Street by running extra electric trains; BR Western Region would somehow absorb the High Wycombe line into Paddington. Passengers would be expected to change into a diesel shuttle service between Amersham and Aylesbury.

Further enquiries quickly established that were there were no detailed plans that would stand muster at a public closure enquiry – but neither LUL nor BR Western believed that they could absorb the existing traffic reliably, let alone the growth that everyone now agreed was coming. It was also clear that the existing commuters intended to fight to the last to retain their direct service into London. The (RUCC), who would be running the closure procedure, were also very well aware that rail demand was growing and the proposed alternative capacity was becoming a figment of the imagination. Members of Parliament all along the route, of all political affiliations, stood four-square against the closure proposals and helped us enormously by ensuring we had a very rational debate. I owe many unspoken thanks to both them and the various rail-user groups.

I had great pleasure in recommending to the Board that there was no way that the Marylebone services could be absorbed onto other routes and that I could see no way of delivering the closure of Marylebone as a commuter rail corridor. The British Railway Board told Whitehall that it was ending the closure proceedings amidst much public jubilation – from all except the coach operators.

But this was just the beginning. It was one thing to reprieve Marylebone; it was quite another to catch up on the years of suspended investment in this unfortunate route. I had never seen such a rundown rail service in all my years with British Rail. The stations were unpainted and uncared for, the track still had the oldest 'bull-headed' rails with a ruling 60mph speed restriction, the ageing class 115 diesel units constantly broke down and Marylebone diesel depot looked as though it had just emerged from the Blitz. The signalling was out-dated, and whilst not the cause had been a factor in a recent fatal accident at Seer Green in 1981. There was black soot, broken window glass and bricks all over the floor. Indeed, the line's only claim to fame was that it regularly earned income as a film set for nineteenth-century films: it was easy money – nothing had to be changed!

But there was one main positive – both staff and customers remained doggedly loyal to their Chiltern railway. I remember standing in the horror of Marylebone depot – more 1956 than 1986 – and feeling the deepest shame for what we had done to this forgotten group of staff while the endless closure procedures had raged on. It was time that we put some pride back into the line.

In June 1986, Network SouthEast was launched and it was based unashamedly on ScotRail values. It was supported by 'Operation Pride', which was inspired by Marylebone depot, and was intended to start the clean-up of the entire London commuter network. It was further supported by the creation of nine route directors who took personal responsibility for each of the radiating routes out of London.

The Chiltern line was now in the vanguard instead of the rearguard. Network SouthEast had identified two 'Cinderella' routes which needed the most support in catching up with the new standards – and these were the Chiltern line and the London Tilbury & Southend. Success would be getting the two routes from the bottom of the league tables to the top – where they both now proudly sit.

How was it done? Mainly in equal quantities of leadership and investment: the Chiltern line was a small, self-contained railway that was lost within the giant London Midland Region, which had far bigger issues of its own. The first decision was to transfer the route to the Western Region, which was smaller, closer and had more time to manage staff and investment. Secondly, the Chiltern line was given its very own route director – Chris Tibbits was appointed route director of Thames & Chiltern and immediately started working with his new Western colleagues to bring the route into the twentieth century.

But how was it to be modernised? Fortunately, Network SouthEast had established very public standards on what it was trying to deliver: brightly painted stations; freshly upholstered trains; modern, 100mph welded track; committed professional staff. Most routes required different doses of the medicine, but the Chiltern line needed the lot – immediately!

The only solution was to make the case for a Total Route Modernisation of the Chiltern line now that the shadow of closure had been removed. Most of the cards were in Network SouthEast's hands, as the Board was allowing its new managing directors to set their own priorities. Network SouthEast decided to make the Chiltern line their showpiece transformation and make a virtue out of Total Route Modernisation. The idea was that both staff and public would really notice the difference if we achieved a dramatic transformation within the next five years. This was intended to be the beginning of a rolling programme of Total Route Modernisation that worked its way around the network.

The Chiltern line was blessed with two first class route directors in Chris Tibbits and Dick Fearn, who took on the awesome task of bringing the route up to the new Network SouthEast standards, while also maintaining an increasingly decaying railway. Chris Tibbits broadly got the investment authorities sorted and Dick Fearn arrived in 1989 to implement the delivery of the Network SouthEast goals.

The second task was to make a very public statement that the Total Route Modernisation of the Chiltern line had unstoppable momentum. The Secretary of State, Cecil Parkinson MP, came to Marylebone in 1989 to make the announcement at an exhibition on the concourse with a blaze of media cameras and user group representatives. The modernisation plan was launched and a huge illuminated jigsaw map kept customers updated on progress as each piece was completed.

The first visible change came in the stations, where a team of painters and builders quickly restored the entire complement of (fifty) stations – from London to Banbury to Aylesbury – to a bright, modern image complete with red lamp posts, the new network map and all the new marketing offers – such as CapitalCard, NetworkCard and the free off-peak parking – that had been so lacking on the route while it was under threat. Dick Fearn turned station upgrading into an art form with platforms paved in a beautiful red dutch tiling and Victorian buildings and canopies restored to their former glory.

The second visible change was in the trains. The Networker Electric train was announced for Kent in 1990, but it was actually preceded by the Class 165 Networker Turbo train, which was specifically designed for both the Thames and Chiltern services and delivered in 1991. Suddenly, Chiltern had the most modern and attractive commuter trains in the country! But the new trains needed a new depot if they were to work with Japanese-style reliability. Our best decision was the closure of the medieval Marylebone diesel depot and replacing it with a brand new facility at Aylesbury. The Board was able to sell the valuable Marylebone site for housing and Chiltern passengers got one of the best diesel depots in the country. The Chiltern Turbos were used to accelerate the timetable and to provide a regular interval service to London with trains that ran at 75mph.

The third visible change was in the track and signalling. Network SouthEast had started the task of renewing the entire (100) miles of ancient bull-head track to provide smoother, faster services. The process was to be completed by Adrian Shooter in the privatised Chiltern Railways. Network SouthEast could not, however, authorise the re-signalling of the early twentieth-century signal boxes without Board investment approval. This proved to be a frustrating challenge. The vision was to sweep away every existing signal box from London to Banbury (Ayhno Jct) and provide just one modern signalling centre, based at Marylebone, capable of working the entire railway automatically, under the watchful eye of one signaller. This would bring a revolution in train performance and customer information, as would the proposal to install ATP on the route so that no train could pass a signal at red or exceed the line speed.

This all proved to be one step too far for the Board Investment Panel, which knocked the scheme back on cost grounds and asked Network SouthEast to look at down-sizing to cheaper and more traditional solutions. We were so convinced that we had got the right answer that we simply waited two months and then re-submitted the original scheme again! Our determination paid off and the Chiltern line now has one of the most modern, safe and reliable signalling systems in the country.

The cream on the cake was a revitalised staff. If you stand with your staff in the bad times while also giving them the tools that they have been crying out for, you can transform unmotivated people into crusaders. If you then sit with them on customer-service training courses you can improve their behaviour and motivation out of all recognition. That is what was being achieved on the Chiltern line as I left in 1992 to become managing director of InterCity. The most impressive point for me was that 90 per cent of the staff was the same people who I had met in the blackened days of 1986 – they had now transformed themselves into some of the most committed and customer-friendly staff in the whole of the network. And they have kept it that way.

Privatisation of the railways was soon to follow in 1996 and the Chiltern line was lucky in its leadership once again. Adrian Shooter volunteered to lead the route into the private sector where it has prospered like no other route. Adrian took a route that had got the basics right and took it up to the next logistical level – he turned a robust commuting railway into an alternative main line to the West Midlands. Network SouthEast had not really looked beyond High Wycombe: Adrian restored continuous double track to Banbury, raised line speeds to 100mph and opened Warwick Parkway as a symbol of the new intercity dimension. He also won the UK's only twenty-year franchise for the Chiltern line.

The Chiltern Story is by no means finished and it is quite possible that it may one day find itself paralleling the proposed High Speed 2 line from London to the North. Whatever the future, I remain certain that we all made the right decisions when we retained Marylebone station and invested in a Total Route Modernisation back in 1986. Running a railway is like a baton race, and the Chiltern line has been fortunate to have had so many Olympic atheletes carrying the torch in the twenty years since its reprieve. Long may it continue!

Chris Green, Berkhamsted, April 2009

CHAPTER 10

THE IRISH CONNECTION

Richard Fearn, Chief Operating Officer, Iarnrod Eireann;
(formerly Zonal Director, Railtrack Midlands)

The modern Chiltern story dates back to the rescuing of the line by Chris Green and BR Network SouthEast in the 1980s. A question pondered by many since then is how on earth did anyone manage to persuade Mrs Thatcher's Government to put £85 million into rebuilding a line many in the Treasury wanted closed? The answer is basically the story of Chris Green and his perception of the growth that was occurring in London commuting territory as it increasingly became the centre of the new financial economy. To be thinking of taking out capacity was just crass stupidity to Green.

Green started a whole series of schemes geared to the overall objective of significantly increasing the capacity and quality of London commuting. As the managing director of Network SouthEast, he was in the right position to do that. In fact, he created the title Network SouthEast in 1986. Regarding Chiltern, through very skilful manoeuvring with the British Railways Board and with the Department of Transport, he managed to convince people that, instead of thinking about closing down Chiltern altogether and turning Marylebone into a coach station and all that nonsense, what was needed was a Total Route Modernisation. That was the actual title used and was conceived and enveloped in the late 1980s. These Total Route Modernisation schemes were developed between 1987 and 1989.

I didn't come onto the scene myself until I arrived at Reading as the new Network Divisional Manager for Thames and Chiltern in the last months of 1989. I took over from Chris Tibbitts – Tibbitts had in fact been very good at developing the investment cases and had been a great support to Green. However, he hadn't had the pleasure of implementing any of it. By the time I arrived in December 1989 the investment had been authorised, I had none of the bureaucracy to do but I had all the fun in terms of actually making it happen.

Over the years 1990–92, we implemented the Chiltern element of Total Route Modernisation. This included the purchase of a complete fleet of new rolling stock, getting rid of all the old first generation DMUs and bringing in the new Class 165 Turbo trains. It also included a lot of station improvement work, complete re-signalling of the route, getting rid of all the old manual signal boxes and creating the Marylebone Integrated Electronic Signalling Control Centre (IECC). It included the construction of the Aylesbury depot and at the digging of the first sod, I remember meeting the managing director of the contractors, who was a grandson of Sir Nigel Gresley, the great steam locomotive designer.

Over those years we created the first pieces of the jigsaw. You may recall that at that time we had a huge map of the Chiltern line erected on Marylebone concourse to illustrate how each section of the Total Route Modernisation fitted together 'like a jigsaw'. When each piece was completed – the improvements to Marylebone station, the building of the new depot at Aylesbury, the new signalling and so on – then that bit of the jigsaw lit up. Malcolm Rifkind was the Minister of Transport at the time and Bob Reid was the British Rail chairman, and periodically we would get them along, together with the great and the good from the route, and we would have a little ceremony to switch on that piece of the jigsaw. Sometimes we would have events out in the field – for example when we renovated Bicester, Wendover, and Great Missenden stations. It was always very nice on those occasions to be able to involve local schoolchildren. Back in 1992, we found a lady who was well over 100 years of age and had remembered the opening of the line through Bicester in 1910 because her father had worked on the scheme. We felt very honoured to be able to bring her back to see the opening, second time around.

All this was a very important phase for me. Ultimately, my job changed to become Divisional Director of Thames and Chiltern and I was there long enough to see the whole of the Chiltern bit through before I later moved on to South Eastern in Kent. We had a very important ceremony as well with the unveiling of the statue at Gerrards Cross, in commemoration of the navvies who had built the original line of 1910; one of my most cherished possessions is the original one-third-size sculptor's model for the figure, which was presented to me at the time. That idea came from a meeting with colleagues within Network SouthEast and we wanted to do something to say, 'We have re-built the Chiltern line, we've relaid the track, we've redone the signalling and so on'. The military people after a campaign would probably have a Tomb for the Unknown Soldier. Consequently, we thought on the railway it would be very fitting to have a statue to the unknown navvy, because the unsung heroes both in 1910 and the 1990s were the men who physically did it. So, we commissioned this statue, part-funded by the rock group Genesis with Phil Collins. Of course, they are all ageing rockers now in their fifties and sixties, but Phil Collins and Genesis in about 1992 produced an album called *We Can't Dance* and the third track on the record is called 'Driving the Last Spike', which was written as a tribute to the plight of the Victorian railway navvies. It dealt with how many of them died in camps from cholera, or from injury because of the almost total absence of safety precautions. It was a very, very harsh time. Anyway, I wrote to the band's agent telling him about our proposal for a statue asking if there would be any chance of them being able to play at the unveiling. In reply they wrote back saying they were not available on the day but instead they offered to contribute to the funding of the statue. It's appropriate that this model is with me now because many of the original navvies would undoubtedly have come from Ireland. So, I regard that period in my life under Green's leadership as the time when we set the stall out for the modern Chiltern Railways. I know things have come a long way since then, and great credit to all those in Chiltern Railways, but I take great pride that we laid out the template for future development.

Many of the stations were in good condition structurally. We didn't need or want to knock them down; they were part of the heritage of the route, but they were fairly lacklustre. There we were, wanting to create a modern railway with modern trains. At the time, Green was one of the few people recognising that the stations were our front door and that we must do something different. For example, we started to use Dutch paviers instead of tarmac for the platforms, which can now be seen at Aylesbury, for example, and other stations on the Amersham route. They have stood the test of time and when a new cable has to be laid, for instance, the tiles can be taken up, the cable relaid, and the tiles put back without that awful 'patchwork quilt' effect one has with tarmac.

We did also initiate something on Chiltern then that we were not doing on the rest of British Railways. It meant not just doing the heavy engineering and signalling of the track but also finishing off works and nice bits of restoration, which have been supported subsequently by the railway heritage trust. The 1970s and '80s, however, were very bleak times and those things were often not done; I always felt we were able to set a good precedent with some really good station restorations in the early 1990s. It is sometimes difficult if people feel one is focussing on the wrong things, but it seems to me that it is possible in any railway renewal to do the heavy things the people don't see, as well as also doing things that people certainly do see and appreciate. In mathematics there is a concept of things being necessary but not sufficient, and I always say whenever we are doing something, whether track renewal or resignalling, those things are necessary but they are not sufficient; we have to do more for the public to actually see the railway as a new place. You can have the most reliable signalling, the best track in the world, but if the trains are lacklustre, not well maintained, not well presented and unclean, if the stations are scruffy and vandalised and not well signed, and so on, you thereby give the impression of a very unsatisfactory railway. Although it might well have had massive infrastructure investment behind the scenes, it is still not sufficient.

Occasionally some of our work did not stand the test of time – for example, we created a new barrier line at Marylebone, which over time was completely inappropriate. Shooter was right to have it swept right away because the idea of automatic ticket barriers is far better. What that demonstrated is when something like Chiltern's Total Route Modernisation is really successful, it is very easy to then quickly move on to the next stage – we now saw the extra platforms, the new signalling all the way up the route, we saw the fantastic growth at Haddenham – all well beyond anything envisaged when it was opened just before my arrival.

I left Thames and Chiltern in 1993 to become the divisional director of the South Eastern Division in Kent. It was testing but I enjoyed it. I never thought I would have much of a chance to have anything to do with Chiltern again. As a little aside, I remember, at about the same time before I left, attending a leaving do on HMS *Belfast* for Green, who at approximately the same time was moving on, somewhat reluctantly, from Network SouthEast to take over InterCity. He stood up and said:

> Colleagues, I have just been looking at my investment budget in InterCity and comparing it with Network SouthEast. I am fearful. I've been asked to take the managing director's job and I'm taking it with a good grace, but I am fearful because I have a £50 million budget for the whole of the next financial year and I would just like to advise you colleagues that Dick Fearn spent that much last weekend!

Of course, the above is completely untrue, a complete fabrication! But I had this great rapport with Green and if the money was there I always spent it – just as colleagues are now trying to help me do here in Ireland, as I also did at Railtrack Midland Zone, because why waste an opportunity if it is there? I don't care whose money it is: European Union, Irish Government or British Government, if we can use it to make the railway a better place we should do it.

During the five years I was at South Eastern Connex took over. I left in 1998 to become Railtrack Director for the North West for the following two years. Then in the second half of 1999 I was offered the chance to become the zonal director for Railtrack Midlands. It was not immediately attractive, although a bigger job with better conditions of service, I was very happy in the North West until I met Shooter, who greeted me enthusiastically with, 'I hear you are coming back!' And I thought I should go because I've now a chance to put another bit of my jigsaw puzzle together! Shooter's Chiltern Railways was going from strength to strength and needed more capacity and here was a chance to play a part in that.

So in mid-1999 I found myself with Shooter, his team and the whole Chiltern network entirely within my zonal boundary, apart from the very occasional train to Paddington. That's actually an interesting little point because a lot of the train operating companies found themselves running across zonal boundaries. I am convinced that was just one of the things that helped pave the way to a productive relationship in terms of getting infrastructure schemes done. In the early days of privatisation, one of the major problems shared by many managers arose in having to talk to different infrastructure suppliers across several zones.

By the time I arrived in 1999 the first phase of doubling of the track from Risborough to Bicester was largely complete. That had not been without its pain and anguish but of course I can't comment because I was not there at that time, although I have heard the anecdotes!

That period during the second half of 1999 and the first half of 2000 was a period when OPRAF (later renamed the SRA) hadn't declared their hand in terms of the next franchises. Everybody was treading water, very soon after that it became clear that things were definitely going to change. Sir Alastair Morton was put in charge of the SRA and understood the need for long franchises if private investment was going to happen. At the same time, the setting up of the Welsh Assembly and Scottish Parliament precipitated a re-designing of rail franchise boundaries to make them more nationally identifiable.

During my first year I very clearly recall Shooter approaching us through the then-Account Executive for Chiltern, Dyan Crowther, who incidentally is now back with Network Rail as the Zone Director for London North Eastern. Crowther was approached by the Chiltern team, who said they now had a scheme that they wanted to develop and saw further infrastructure expansion as part of their bid for a twenty-year franchise. This was very clearly the game plan. We mulled it over within the Railtrack team and I clearly remember thinking very early on that there's a lot to this – it was not straightforward, even though Chiltern is a relatively straightforward TOC, with a relatively straightforward route. There's a whole load of stuff in this. At that time, the scheme included the remainder of the track doubling from Bicester to Aynho Junction, as well as re-signalling to obtain better headways, the Marylebone platform expansion and the new depot at Wembley. In all it was a very significant scheme.

No sooner had the scheme appeared on the table than the beginning of the end for Railtrack started. We went through a terrible phase with great tragedies, the accidents at Ladbroke Grove and Hatfield and then ultimately the Government deciding to scrap it. But at that time I was very excited about the scheme Chiltern had on the table, although my own personal investment budget for the Midlands was starting to be pulled back. All of a sudden what I would have called Phase 2 of Total Route Modernisation was starting to look very shaky indeed. Crowther decided we needed a project title and she came up with 'Evergreen'. She believed the scheme would fly if it had recognition and therefore we needed a name. I remember it very clearly – she said to me Project Evergreen and I said, 'Where did you get that from?' She said it was her idea – she deserves the credit.

Thus we gave the project a name, but very quickly Railtrack changed the game. Gerald Corbett was still in post, but was under huge pressure, going around telling us all that the finances didn't make sense and something had to change. This was after Ladbroke Grove but prior to Hatfield – the situation was not looking good. All the massive investment that had been going on during my time both in the North West and my first year in the Midland Zone was closing down. Then came Hatfield followed by nationwide panic about gauge corner cracking. I have to say we were very lucky on Chiltern as there was not much of a problem, unlike the West Coast Main Line, which was a disaster. At that time we could not run a train between London and Birmingham via the West Coast route in less than about three hours. We were in a terrible position and in the end it cost Gerald his job and we had a new managing director Steve Marshall, an accountant, a very nice guy and keen supporter of Brentford FC. Poor Steve found himself in the mire all of a sudden. He was a very decent guy but was not going to be able to rescue that whole situation. In the middle of this when he was genuinely trying to do his best, I sat down with Adrian in his office and said:

> I think you should re-think this. You should kick off the first phase of this, the track doubling from Bicester to Aynho which I do believe we can do and that gives us tangible infrastructure benefit, we can see the benefit of it. We all know in railway terms that signalling headway gives us tangible benefit but people don't see it so clearly, and the great and the good in the Department of Transport and SRA will not see that as clearly as they will see double track. So for heaven's sake let us finish the double track, put the line back to its main line status and let's call it Evergreen Phase 1. Let's just do that and, at the risk of temporarily losing momentum on the rest of the scheme, let us focus all our efforts on that.

I don't recall Shooter giving me a straight answer at that meeting but I do recall very soon afterwards him coming to me and saying he would go for this, but what could we do to help get through the then situation at Railtrack which by then was not able to approve anything?

Consequently, I rang Steve Marshall personally, whom I liked but who was in a very difficult situation under great pressure and about to go on holiday to Africa for a thoroughly well-earned break to follow another of his interests which he is now following professionally, wildlife conservation. My head of projects at that time was Ian Scholey, who was soon convinced of the real worth of the scheme, not simply another 'Adrian Shooter' scheme but something with national strategic importance. We sold the idea to the SRA, principally on the strength of providing a vital diversionary route. But the real problem was to convince Marshall that we should spend anything at all on the railway that he knew little about, and being influenced by loads of people in Railtrack simply saying this was just Dick again and his love of Chiltern! Marshall said that he would think about it when he came back.

Now at this point I had learned a trick from Chris Green, which is 'get on site' when people are hedging and worrying, because if you've only got authority to put up a Portakabin, you are still actually on site. And the minute you are on site it is a much bigger decision for someone to say 'get off site' than simply to stop you starting something in the first place. So I pleaded with Marshall before he went on holiday to allow me a little bit of authority to get the lads on site just to do some very simple stuff. So Marshall went on holiday leaving me with a small (in Railtrack terms) budget of £2 million and allowed me to let the contract to Carrillion do the first surveys. And I remember saying to Shooter, 'It's good stuff now, we're on site.' He then asked if we had authority for the whole scheme and I remember saying that of course we hadn't, as we still had the SRA to convince. But at least we were doing the preparatory works. From that point everything went swimmingly because nobody from Railtrack HQ or the SRA wanted to be the person to say 'We'll stop Evergreen'.

Everybody was sceptical at that time, and said we would not get the £60 million we needed. At that time on the railways very few positive stories were happening. The West Coast modernisation was going ahead but was bad news anyway, and virtually nothing else. .

Marshall returned from his holiday, by which time we had spent the £2 million, and we were really motoring, the Chiltern twenty-year franchise had been awarded and the project was almost unstoppable. But there was one thing that could stop it, the SRA, because having just awarded the twenty-year franchise, they were going to have to approve the funding for this project. Railtrack was nearly bust. Alastair Morton had left the SRA and Richard Bowker had been in charge for about three weeks. I was called in with a few of my people and no doubt Shooter was also called in separately. At this time there was a very senior chap in the SRA who sat close to Bowker called Stuart Baker. Bowker saw himself as a great financier but it was Stuart Baker who understood the trains properly, he writes railway map books, and he came along and said to Bowker 'diversionary route for the West Coast Main Line!' At this point Adrian was very astute and kept silent; actually, there is no way in reality he would want diversions over his railway, but you don't kick the guy who is trying to help you! So the game was won.

We were all anxious about the money because we knew within Railtrack/Network Rail that we were strapped and were playing with other people's money so the worst thing to do was over spend. By contrast, an under spend was going to be well appreciated! So we estimated in a way that created the likelihood of an under spend. Then something very positive happened. Once everyone was behind the project – including Network Rail, who simply said 'get on with it Dick but don't bother us at HQ', they knew it was SRA money and that everyone was committed – then the contractors realised it was very much in their interest that this scheme should go well. The result was that in all my experience with Railtrack and Network Rail, I have never experienced better management of a contract anywhere. The physical works were done by Amey and Carillion, while Laing was responsible for the project management.

So we had everybody backing it. I can't claim credit for the setting up of the big yard at Ardley but again it was so different from the way other Network Rail projects were handled because everyone was there, the Laing people, the Chiltern team, my own team, Carillion and Amey. I think credit for this team building must go to Laing. Everybody was in line. It was the best organised project I have ever had the pleasure to work with; everybody was focussed and of course, the quality of work then starts to come through.

One example that showed the organisation was the embankment work. Many of them were in a really bad way, having been subjected to what is politely described as a 'maintenance holiday'. When the line had been singled in the 1970s the track had been laid down the middle and subsequently wiggled around to accommodate weak spots. The problem with embankments is that over time drainage becomes an issue – many of them in the early days were made simply of ash and other waste material and were undermined by badgers and rabbits. It can be as simple as that, and over decades the embankment will weaken resulting in minor slippage, weakening of the lower levels, ballast running away and so on. Then one has poor alignment and twisting of the track. On a minor or downgraded line such as Chiltern was for thirty years, people say they can't spend much money so end up slewing the track away from the problem. Where a previously double track has been singled, one has scope to do that. Once you are going to go back to double track, you have to do it properly. Good soil surveys were done and extensive use made of what is known as gabion baskets, basically wire mesh baskets of small rocks. They are very successful because the water just runs through them. They act like a filter and, of course, they deter badgers and rabbits. The same technique was used at Haddenham to build the new platform.

In so many other Railtrack projects nationally, the contractors have gone their own way in order to save a crust here or a bean there and then Railtrack sometimes ends up with a problem. That never happened on Evergreen. The whole thing worked as if we were all working with the same cap badge.

Richard Fearn, Dublin, November 2004

THE NETWORK DIRECTOR'S STORY

John Nelson, formerly BR's Managing Director, Network SouthEast, and Non-Executive Director, Laing Rail, until 2008

I joined the railways in 1968 after graduating in Economics from the University of Manchester. I was looking for a career in management but at that time had no particular interest in railways and so applied for a number of management training schemes which included British Rail. I was accepted by them and joined the railways in September 1968, going straight on to a two-year management training scheme, the like of which doesn't exist these days, which immersed me in just about every aspect of the railways. I was attached to the Western Region of British Rail. Because my home was at the London end of the Western Region at Gerrards Cross, the rule was you were sent to the opposite end of the Region from your home – in my case, Exeter!

My two years training was followed by a series of general management posts mainly in the commercial side of the industry. So, for example, I ran the ticket and enquiry office at Liverpool Street; I was responsible for the stations on what is now known as the Great Eastern Railway; I went to Leeds as a passenger manager responsible for marketing the railways in West Yorkshire, involving working closely with the West Yorkshire PTE. This close liaison between British Rail and the passenger transport authority was new then, of course, but I then did the same job in Sheffield and South Yorkshire until I became personal assistant to the then Chief Executive of British Rail, Bob (Sir Robert) Reid. I worked with him for a year during which sector management was being developed, when the railways moved from a production orientated, regionally based industry to a sector-based commercial organisation with the production side serving the needs of the businesses. That gave me a further insight into how railways can work on a commercial, as opposed to a purely operational, basis. After a year with him, I then went to work in a very commercial part of the railway, the parcels sector. For a few years I was the person responsible for the Red Star parcels business throughout the railways; co-incidentally, Adrian Shooter followed me into that job.

In 1987 I was appointed the general manager of the Eastern Region of British Rail, which then represented about a third of British Railways covering all the services out of King's Cross to the north of England and Scotland, as well as East Anglia. Marylebone was by then in the Midland

Region. Marylebone in British Rail times was very much the forgotten bit of the railway – it switched periodically between regions. One year it was in the Midland region and another it would be in the Western; it was a kind of 'also ran' really and got very little management attention. I knew this because I commuted for a few years between Gerrards Cross and Marylebone and it had all the hallmarks of a forgotten railway. Considering it was a commuter service it was far and away the inferior of any other service into London.

Then, in 1991 I was appointed managing director of Network SouthEast, which I ran as a vertically integrated operation. Chris Green had been my predecessor although in his days the regions still ran the trains and the sectors specified the services, so there was a difference when I took it over. Chris Green then went to InterCity and ran that as a vertically integrated operation. The five-year period that I was there, from 1992–97, was one of the most fascinating periods of my life because this was the period when the privatisation of the railways was first proposed and then implemented and I was central to that. From 1994–97 my principal role, in addition to being responsible for the running of the railway Network SouthEast, was to prepare it for privatisation. That included the preparation of the Chiltern line.

Now interestingly when Network SouthEast was established as a vertically integrated organisa-tion, Chiltern was not at that time a separate train operating company. It was part of Thames and Chiltern, which ran as an integrated operation and Dick Fearn, who is now running Irish Railways, was the divisional director. When the railways were being prepared for privatisation there was quite a big discussion, as you might imagine, that took place between the railway authorities, led principally by me as far as Network SouthEast was concerned, and the Department for Transport and the Treasury, as to what precisely should be the individual units that were established as train operating companies franchises and they drew quite heavily on our advice as to what those units could look like. The policy then was to have small rather than large units, as initially it was thought that would be needed to attract private investors into the industry because (and people forget this), there was a fear right at the beginning that there would be no interest in railway franchises. It was expected that a lot of the interest would come from bus companies, who would be afraid of taking on big railway operations that they didn't understand or were deemed too complicated, so there was a drive for simplicity. Chiltern could obviously be a viable entity on its own – it was separate geographically and it served the political purpose of the time to have smaller, as well as larger, units available for franchising.

One of the key aspects to setting it up was to populate it with a management team. I was concerned at the time that there was inadequate commercial experience within our manage-ment teams in terms of running a company. Finance was also weak and these were the areas in the private sector that needed to be strengthened. Now the public policy at the time was to allow and indeed to support individual management teams in bidding for franchises. Obviously, for those teams to be viable we had to look at who was occupying those key positions and specifically Chiltern, because there was a weakness on the financial and commercial sides I took the decision that we would recruit people from outside the industry – Tony Allen and Alex Turner were both duly appointed. They were interviewed initially by Adrian Shooter and then I had to see them to decide if they were suitable. Obviously, they were as far as I was concerned.

This new management team was set up and Adrian was appointed as the managing director with my support and indeed on my recommendation. Chiltern was established, it was populated managerially and one of the first things we had to do was to determine the track access arrange-ments that would exist between the train operating companies and Railtrack. There was one particular matter, quite obvious to both myself and Adrian, which caused us to take a decision as a (shadow) Board that this company should no longer be primarily regarded as a London commut-ing operation, but had a more strategic role to serve other markets, in particular Birmingham and to the south of Birmingham. The key decision was taken to enable Chiltern, post-privatisation, to do what it has actually done – to develop its longer distance markets very successfully.

This was also the period when the Total Route Modernisation of the Chiltern line was being completed. It had been initiated by my predecessor Chris Green, as the strategy he pursued in connection with investment in the railways. Sometime during the 1980s, Marylebone and the line as far as Northolt Junction had been put up for closure with the intention of diverting the bulk of the services into Paddington, which was operationally feasible at the time. Of course, in those days British Rail was operating on a rationalisation remit, so it was perhaps logical that it should come up with that type of proposal.

It met with stiff political resistance and I am convinced that the reason that it did not happen was that the constituency, particularly in the commuting belt of the Chilterns, was very politically influential and the proposal was withdrawn. Once the proposal was withdrawn it was essential that something was done about the very bad state of the railway. There had been a fatal accident at Seer Green one day in about 1981, which initially led to the proposal to close the line but when that proposal was withdrawn, because of public pressure, something had to be done. Therefore, it was decided to replace everything at the same time, the infrastructure as well as the trains, and that was the proposal that recommended itself to Chris Green; Chiltern was one of the first to receive that treatment. Everybody who lives in the Chilterns will be eternally grateful to Chris Green!

All previous modernisations had produced a huge initial benefit and if you are turning something around that was nearly in the grave to something that is completely modern, you can expect a 'higher bounce' than in other circumstances. And that certainly proved to be the case, but I don't think many people expected Chiltern to maintain double-digit growth per annum year after year after year. One might have expected that for three or four years but it has lasted. That of course is a testimony to the strategies followed by Adrian Shooter and his team.

I parted company with the railways in 1997 to set up my own consulting business and do one or two other things, including Hull Trains. In 1998 one of the first things I did post-British Rail was to publish a large report, which was an assessment of all of the franchise bids that had been successful in the context of what I knew about the operating and financial structure of each of those businesses. I knew most of them because either currently or previously I had worked in them. So I produced a report which was an assessment of those companies and was invited to go on the BBC breakfast business programme to talk about it. I was interviewed by Geoff Randall who became the BBC's business correspondent and also a writer for the *Sunday Telegraph*.

A couple of weeks later the telephone rang and it was Adrian Shooter to say he had seen this interview and so had some other members of his team, and would I be be interested in becoming a non-executive director of M40 Trains? The chairman said that they needed somebody on this Board who was going to be critical and challenging in terms of some of the things that they were doing, and they thought that I might fit that bill. A meeting followed with Adrian and Sir Richard Morris at his club, the Atheneum, and a couple of weeks later I got a letter from Sir Richard to say they would be delighted if I would consider joining the Board. From my joining in 1998 until my replacement after the DB purchase in 2008, I have witnessed the transition from British Rail to the Chiltern Railway Co. under the ownership of a management buy-out and it was only one of two management buy-outs that were successful. And then the ownership changed to Laing and then DB. They have grown from an annual turnover of about £12 million in 1991 to their present approximate £100 million, with no Government subsidy, and it will obviously increase further.

They have done an amazing job and they have done some very innovative things. What they have done to Marylebone station is mould-breaking stuff. Not only have they created a fantastic modern station with good retailing and catering and all the rest of it, but they have also restored its Victorian magnificence – an amazing piece of railway architecture – and much the same at Moor Street. They have done much more besides, which is reflected in their customer approval ratings relative to other train-operating companies. That success rests entirely on meeting passenger needs and expectations, and exploiting their market. They have done it magnificently and are without doubt the most successful train-operating company within that context. Some of the others who have had slightly greater growth were those where it could almost have happened anyway, the obvious example being Thameslink. Chiltern is the prime example of post-privatisation railway companies where the progress has been achieved entirely because of the management strategy, and the team efforts of everyone on the staff. The only other company I would put into the same category is GNER under its original management and both realise, more than many companies, that keeping the staff onboard, highly motivated and committed is a critical part of achieving their business strategy and they have done that very successfully.

A small company, both geographically as well as in terms of the number of people involved, has been a strength of Chiltern. It would have been very much more difficult for a larger more dispersed operation to achieve quite that same level of staff commitment. There is a big challenge here to the franchising authorities who appear to be obsessed with the idea of much larger franchises which, I think without question, is the wrong policy. I think the experience of Chiltern, and the whole of the railways over the last twenty years, has been that if you focus on a market, if you focus on the customers, if you focus on the staff, then you deliver a much higher quality and generally more profitable and cost-effective railway. Generally speaking, you can only do that with particularly focussed types of operation, which means smaller rather than larger affairs. At the moment I am, in general, a little bit pessimistic about the way this might go nationally.

However, every organisation has its weaknesses and at one point Chiltern did have an issue with process management, which was picked up by the SRA during a periodic audit. It would be fair to say that within the rail industry I am known to be very committed to the idea of improved process management. This stems from my own experience within the industry and particularly the exposure to the concepts of total quality management about twenty years ago. Whether this was because I already believed in it or not, or didn't realise what quality management was, I don't know! But I have a strong belief in two aspects of management that is best summed up by getting things done through people. Getting things done through people is about process, and it's about putting in place the effective management systems and processes to get things done. It doesn't matter what it is, it might be making station announcements, it might be running the trains to time, and it might be cleaning the trains, etc. It's about having effective processes and control systems to plan for things in place to monitor their implementation and then to adjust and improve.

This requires a number of things, including understanding the dimensions of a process element, a task, and also presumes an ability to measure that task so you can see how effective you are in delivering that action. In relation to Chiltern, the SRA had a view – a correct view in my opinion – that for a company to be considered for running a franchise, they would need to demonstrate their understanding of quality management processes and systems. They decided no company could be awarded a franchise unless they could demonstrate this. Accordingly, they decided to make an assessment of a number of Train Operating Companies as a pilot exercise to inform their own policy. They would then know how they would take this forward and they undertook an audit of three or four train companies, including Chiltern. They involved a company called Cap Gemini and funnily enough in one of my consulting capacities I was also working with them. so I got both sides of this story, one from Cap Gemini and one from Chiltern. I also got involved with Steve Murphy, who was given the task of looking at this audit. The conclusion was that in many of the more important aspects of running a company, Chiltern got ten out of ten. They were people- and customer-focussed, and understood. Where they were perhaps not quite so effective as they needed to be was in process management. Chiltern were better than most in just about every aspect, so they came out of this as the best of the companies that were piloted despite their process issues.

I then got involved with Steve and we looked specifically at two aspects of running a company. One was safety and the other was train service performance we looked at both those things in process terms – new systems and methodologies were developed which brought improved processes to both those areas. I think the results that Chiltern has subsequently had with their train service performance have derived from the work that was done at that time.

My association with Chiltern has mainly been 'highs'. Every time they face a new challenge they seem to meet it. The passenger and revenue growth has been incredible. I think the boldness of their strategy is a complete credit to them and is in stark contrast to a number of other companies who have said, 'Oh! We can't invest in this until we get a renewed franchise or whatever.' Chiltern did none of that. Chiltern, right from the start, adopted a strategy where they didn't go running to the SRA or the franchising authority every five minutes making threatening noises saying if you don't give us another five years we won't invest in this or that. Chiltern just went ahead and did it, on the not unreasonable assumption that it was necessary to further the interests of the business. Subsequently, even if they were unsuccessful in being awarded an extension to their franchise, it didn't really matter because that was what any future franchise operator would do anyway! That was a good approach to the risk.

The Board of Laing Rail fulfilled a very useful role for Chiltern Railways in holding them to account and I think we were able to do that for a number of different reasons. I was able to contribute because of my own background and understanding of railways. Without a non-executive on the Board who has that ability, there is a great risk that the management themselves are the only repository of knowledge and they don't get challenged. Or if they do it is not a professionally assembled challenge. So I think that was a useful thing. But other people who have been non-executive directors have brought tremendous experience and added value to the scene. For example, Sir Richard Morris was an outstanding chairman and clearly his experience of project management and commercial life generally was a tremendous benefit to Chiltern. Other colleagues that I've served with as non-executive directors from Laing, people like Alan Cheney, Andy Friend and Derek Potts all brought a slightly different experience and background which was used to constructively challenge. That is the key, we were never negative about our role and I think that was tremendously beneficial because train operating companies exist on quite narrow margins – if you get it even slightly wrong you are in serious trouble. This explains why Alex Turner was initially very nervous about the whole enterprise, and he was right to be nervous, but all credit to Chiltern – they've succeeded where many others have failed. Chiltern have never had to go back to the Government for more money. This is a very tight ship and it needs to be run as such.

Are there any downsides? They got into serious trouble at one point in 1998 with train service cancellations and that was due to poor process, which they put right. Generally speaking, I would say they have managed the introduction of their new rolling stock well, though I am still of the view that the biggest risk to the company is the management of their fleet. They've not, I think, always been quite as effective in managing costs as they have in managing revenues. But I wouldn't say that was a low, nor would I say that marked them out as being inferior to any other train-operating company. In fact, by comparison with most train-operating companies they continue to run a fairly tight ship. I think some of the things we've done have proved to be perhaps not quite so good strategically in the light of experience. For example, running to Stourbridge and Kidderminster was probably not a brilliant idea but these are really quite small criticisms when you look at some of the major victories.

Warwick Parkway must be one of the most outstanding successes. I remember being absolutely astounded at a Board meeting when we discussed the need for Warwick Parkway. We were informed that Railtrack had been approached about building it and rejected it because they didn't really see that as a core activity! At that point we all realised there was something wrong with Railtrack! And, of course, their loss was Laing Rail's gain – if Railtrack had been managed with the same commercial insight and energy that Chiltern was being run, then one might have had a very different story to tell about the success of that particular company, but alas it wasn't to be.

So I think there are very few downsides. We are now looking at moves in other directions and those are obviously huge opportunities for Chiltern, but again they are accompanied with some degree of risk because they involve getting into larger operations. That is the way of the world, whether you agree with it or not, that's the way it's going to go. I think companies like Chiltern can contribute enormously to some of these other operations if they are given the opportunity to get involved, and I hope that they will, but they mustn't over extend themselves.

John Nelson, London, August 2004

CHAPTER 12

FROM THE RED STAR TO THE EMERALD ISLE AND BACK AGAIN

(Steve Murphy, the Second Managing Director's Story)

Firstly, let me say there is no truth in the legend that height is a primary requirement for managing directors of Chiltern Railways!

Although my family has many Irish connections, I was born and brought up in East Ham and Essex. Both my parents were from Ireland and came over in the 1950s when they were eighteen or nineteen. We moved out to Essex and my father became the chief union negotiator with Ford. This was in the 1970s and 1980s when the Ford settlement used to be the benchmark for the private sector. So I was brought up in a trade union environment, went to the Campion school in Hornchurch, a state voluntary aided school run by the Jesuits, followed by university in Wales at University College Lampeter, where I had an absolutely fantastic three years studying Geography, playing lots of football and generally enjoying myself. Then, when I was about to graduate in 1991 I started to look around for the best graduate-training schemes and the two that stood out were the British Railways scheme and Ford. The British Rail scheme had a very good reputation as something that gave you a very good general grounding – for example, one would spend time looking at operations management, marketing, human resources, finance and absolutely everything. With many other graduate schemes, after a couple of months your speciality would be decided for you. British Rail appealed. The other scheme that I applied to was Ford's, which I knew quite a lot about because of my father's involvement. I was fortunate to be offered both and I chose to go with British Rail. The interview and selection process was very rigorous. I spent two whole days at their training centre at Watford, called The Grove, where we were set all manner of management exercises, some quite difficult, including a variety of interview situations with senior managers. In the evenings the interviewers would mingle with the fifty or so of us at the bar; this was all part of the selection process.

I got through all that and joined British Rail where I was attached in the first instance to Red Star, the parcels and delivery group within British Rail that had had a very successful and profitable period in the 1980s and when I joined in 1991 it was just coming to terms with some very aggressive competition from the likes of TNT, DHL and also the advent of fax machines. I spent a year doing a combination of the British Rail graduate scheme which consisted of a series of residential courses at The Grove covering the theory of how you do everything; human resources, disciplinary procedures, financial management – it was very thorough. In short, by the end I was fully equipped at least in the theory of everything. I spent the remainder of my time going around parts of the Red Star business, as well as the main railway. On Leeds station I did cleaning gangs and bits of shunting, all sorts of things. Also at Preston, an interesting station where the station manager's office was an old carriage in a siding that he had converted. I enjoyed meeting a variety of very interesting characters during this period. At last I was given my first post of responsibility, Red Star depot manager at Euston. It was shift management with early, lates and nights at the busiest depot in the country with over a hundred staff. It was the main hub for deliveries into London and the South East, as well as despatching 'Brute' cages onto overnight trains for the North and Scotland. It was very labour intensive so immediately I was trying out all the theories I had been taught at the Grove about managing people, and learnt where they were helpful and where you needed to work it out for yourself – a real lesson in managing people which has proved very useful.

I did that for about a year and a half. Adrian was the boss during this time and it was he who had originally recruited me, hence the story about my cold lunch. I had got through the British Rail graduate entry procedures but Red Star took on their own graduate trainees. There were six or seven of us and they would only choose one or two permanently. We were all down in the old British Rail canteen at Euston and we had only just got our fish and chips and stuff when Adrian started saying, 'So, what's the next ten years going to hold for UK freight then?' just as we were about to tuck in, so we had to think up something that might sound vaguely intelligent and relevant! So that's how I got on the course with Red Star. All down to cold fish and chips!

After about eighteen months at Euston with Red Star I thought I would like to try something else, preferably connected to marketing. It was the commercial areas that interested me most during my training. So, I went to see the graduate development manager, a very understanding chap, Dr Brian Redfern. He said I could either apply for the job of the British Rail chairman's personal assistant, quite a prestigious job, or there's this chap Adrian Shooter who was going off to set up Chiltern Railways. That might be an interesting opportunity because it's quite unique; the company is being set up from scratch, offering the opportunity to be right at the start of something. I mulled that over for a bit and decided I would not be a very good bag carrier, so I rang Adrian up and asked if he had any jobs going. He asked me what I had been doing at Red Star since he had left and invited me over for an interview. That turned into two or three interviews and each time I would be asked to come back to do another presentation. A typical example would be something like, 'How would you quadruple the size of the Chiltern business in the next five years?' I would go away, ride around on the trains and think up ideas. Finally, I was interviewed by Adrian and Owen Edgington, the original operations director, and from that they decided to offer me the job of specifications manager. I was thrilled to bits.

At that stage the only other employees I can recall were Adrian Shooter, Owen Edgington, Julie Abbott, Alex Turner and also within a few days, Cath Proctor and Martin Talbot. There were no offices, just a few desks with a phone in Euston House and I commandeered one of those, every day I had to figure out what I was going to do. There were no set jobs, I just had to make myself useful.

Specifications manager was a typical British Rail title, almost designed to create a certain mystique, but in reality it was simply deciding what time the trains were going to run and what the service pattern would be. So I came across and met the train planners. The first advice I was given was not to change anything to do with the service pattern, and in particular not to change the service pattern at West Ruislip. I think they had had a difficult relationship with the West Ruislip user group.

I hadn't done timetable planning before so there was a risk there from Adrian's point of view and it was an example of the way he tended to do things. I think it unlikely that any other part of British Rail would have put me in as a specifications manager at that stage; normally one would have to have some background in it, but the advantage was that I looked at the timetable as a customer and I could see all these gaps, which helped me see how we could improve and enhance services. Fortunately, because the rolling stock and infrastructure were new there was plenty of opportunity. So we used the assets more productively and turned trains around more quickly, improving the frequency and going for quite high availability targets on the stock every day. One of the most noticeable places was Princes Risborough, which when I joined would have a train every couple of hours off-peak, so we got it to hourly, then every forty minutes, and then half hourly. We were able to do this without any major investment because the investment had already been made.

Alex Turner worked closely with me on all this and everything we did was designed to make the service more accessible and more understandable to customers. I was new to passenger railways, Alex had come in fresh to the industry so we asked a lot of the obvious questions, such as why was the single fare not half the return, what were all these cheap day singles all about and how come the return was only 10p more than a single – all questions the customers had been asking for a long time. Because British Rail had become very sophisticated about pricing, it had overcomplicated it. It was a sophisticated way of managing the yield but it had not explained it to passengers. We did some simple things to make it more understandable and I remember having simple posters with big bold prices and the three fares you could get. We took the same approach to the timetable and a lot of work went into making the timetable more readable and laying it out so that it was more understandable. The original British Rail timetable we inherited was quite difficult to follow, with all those funny arrows that directed you to different columns. We also developed the use of A–Z timetables for station use as part of that process.

The other thing we started to do at that stage was to go out and make contact with the user groups up and down the line, which was probably one of the most successful things we did because British Rail, being a big centralised company, hadn't done that. We found people were delighted to see us, they hadn't seen anyone for a long time and every single time we got loads and loads of ideas on how to improve the service. Discussions covered the service patterns, station environments, prices, all things of key importance to customers. We had lots from Cherwell, from Nick Walker at North Chilterns user group in Haddenham. Reg Whittome at Marylebone and many others were also very influential. Much of what the user groups were telling us was about how to sort the train service out to ensure we would get more customers; it was free consultancy – fantastic!

So we took advantage and did a lot of that stuff, we couldn't find reasons not to do it. In some senses, the people who were advising us, the user groups, were more informed than us and some of them were pretty good amateur train planners. Then you get into a virtuous circle where because you are consulting, the people are more likely to come forward with ideas and when they see the ideas being implemented they are even more motivated to come back with more. All that consultancy built up very successfully and had a lot to do with how the perception of the railway management for Chiltern started to change from British Rail days. There was a feeling that we were people they could work with.

Passenger numbers really took off and we were routinely getting 15 or 16 per cent revenue growth each year, which had been unheard of under British Rail. The British Rail forecast for Chiltern had been that growth would be flat after 1994 because the upsurge after investment would have happened. Then, as we got into 1995 I began to be aware of privatisation and the fact that we were now going to be bidding for the right to run the line as a private company. Up until that point, Adrian and the other directors were held accountable by British Rail's Network SouthEast, John Nelson and his deputy, Euan Cameron.

The time the directors were working on the MBO bid was a really interesting time. Adrian and the other directors had no experience of making such a bid, so everyone was learning it as they went along. I remember it as being incredibly intensive and it took them all away from the day job for a number of months. I remember there was a process called 'vesting' Sarah Hewitt, our company secretary, who went on to South West Trains as a revenue analyst, was quite central to this vesting process. Sarah Hewitt did a lot of that for a year or so before she moved on and Mark Beckett then arrived and gradually got more involved with the bidding process. But the interesting thing for the likes of Cath, Ian Walters and me was that at that stage the directors like Alex Turner said, 'You guys are going to have to run this because I'm going to have to go off and win the business.' So, at a young age, the three of us were all about aged twenty-six, we were pretty much running the company day to day. It was a fantastic opportunity, daunting as well, but we took a lot of decisions over that year and in hindsight it was a very useful learning experience for us.

The bidding process and the presentations must have been a very tense time for those directly involved. I remember Alex Turner briefed me with a golfing analogy, 'Just keep the ball on the course for the next few months, don't try and do anything dramatic, just keep things steady', which is what I pretty much tried to do along with Cath, Ian and various other people. With hindsight it was a unique opportunity and we managed to run the business pretty successfully between us. Of course, we won the seven-year franchise.

Immediately after that I can remember an enormous list of franchise commitments; all sorts of things we had to get in place over the next few months, changes to the service frequency and so on. That's when we also started to see a bit more of Laing through Alan Coakley, who came over to be the project manager for this huge raft of commitments. He used to turn up every week or so with a checklist you were responsible for and ask if you were going to hit your deadlines. That was my introduction to project management. It's worth reflecting back just a little here: during that period from 1994–96 the company was so small that we had the entire management team in Western House at Aylesbury. On a day-to-day basis, although I was the specifications manager, I'd get involved with train crew issues and safety issues, because you would hear all these conversations going on around you. Because there weren't many of us, about thirty in all, you'd be asked to help out. I remember the train planners weren't available for whatever reason for a couple of weeks so Martin Talbot and I had to put together train crew diagrams which we had never done! That sort of thing used to happen all the time. Another day you would have to help out the safety manager, it was great. In 1996 we also put a bid together for the Thames franchise, which I thought was pretty good but in the event it turned out to be too expensive.

From 1996 onwards we started to tick off that huge raft of commitments and we decided then to carry on doing more of the same. We started to think about Clubman trains in 1997. I was marketing manager, under Alex Turner, and responsible for the timetable and pricing and Cath Proctor would have been retail manager. Mike Bagshaw was our timetable planner. This was the time things started to go wrong through over-ambition. In all honesty, between the period 1994–98, we'd never had to think about performance. It was just a given. Every day it would be 98–99 per cent because there was all this unused capacity. One could continue ramping up the train service and planning the timetable was almost entirely a commercial job. Because we didn't have to worry about performance, the sort of decision was, 'If we put on three more trains at Risborough, how much money will we make?' We were over ambitious with some journey times on our London–Birmingham service in 1998. We had a few timetabled at under two hours. Unfortunately, this coincided with a number of other things. We had introduced the Clubmans and they had all sorts of teething problems, we were ramping up the timetable again in terms of frequency and journey times, while at the same time we had quite seriously underestimated the number of drivers we required to run these services and this driver situation was the most critical. We were down a significant number, so on a day-to-day basis we could not resource the service. We didn't plan that particularly well because we were so busy thinking about all these wonderful new services we could run, rather than plan the resources. Once you get behind on drivers, it takes a long while to recover because it takes seven, eight or nine months to train a driver.

The driver shortage situation was dire and I remember being summoned to a Council of War with Adrian and Owen Edgington to decide what we were going to do pretty quickly to turn the situation around. We looked at a whole range of things and we gave some of our key operational managers an enhanced remit to look after performance. Some of our train crew supervisors were specifically tasked with right time departures. This was also the time we got whistles down to the staff and all those sorts of things. We got on with the driver recruitment and managed to get some in quickly from some other TOCs and started to re-cast the timetable. We were in quite a bit of trouble because we were in breach of our franchise with the number of cancellations and were fined by OPRAF and had to provide a couple of million pounds worth of compensation by way of passenger improvements. It was an interesting period and I remember the run-in to Christmas was pretty dire because it's always the worst part of the year anyway, in terms of performance, and if you have a fragile plan and not enough drivers you really cop it; we certainly did!

However, in January and February 1999 we picked up quite a bit and started to come out the other side. It was the back end of 1998 and early 1999 that I first joined the Board as customer service director, responsible for all the retailing. Things then started to settle down, the timetable recovered, we got some more Clubmans and enhanced the service again with the additional capacity. Then in November 1999 I was asked to become general manager and that was because Mark Beckett went off to take charge of franchise bids and put a team together for the Wessex bid. This was under the Alastair Morton SRA regime, which was very expansive, aimed for twenty-year franchises, huge investment, and everything was awash with money – it was going to do all sorts of fantastic things.

The most significant thing that happened next was the Hatfield crash in October 2000. It had just happened when I went on an exchange visit to Japan with colleagues from Network Rail and Chiltern for a couple of weeks. When I came back the railway nationally was just collapsing and the network was covered in speed restrictions because of the perceived risk of gauge corner cracking. We had between twelve and twenty speed restrictions between Birmingham and London, which essentially meant we could not adhere to the timetable in any shape or form and virtually every operator in the UK at that time decided that the way to respond was to run a much reduced service. We took a very critical decision at that time to continue to run the entire timetable, knowing that our punctuality would be a lot worse but we felt it was what our passengers wanted us to do. It was a very important decision for Chiltern because it is very noticeable if you plot customer satisfaction over the period: on the graph the Chiltern line does not deviate. Surveys showed that customers were just as satisfied as they had been before, which is quite remarkable because punctuality was dire. What was happening was that people understood that we had this major problem to deal with and there was enormous support for us because we were running the full timetable and people knew that all the other companies were chopping a lot of trains. Gradually the speed restrictions came off as we moved into 2001 so that we were back to a normal timetable by about May.

The impact generally on the railway industry of Southall, Ladbroke Grove and Hatfield was profound. My personal feelings at the time were similar to anyone else, mostly ones of shock. The way we find out about these things is usually through our pagers, often when we are sitting in meetings and it's just shock, no different to anyone else really. In fact, I sometimes think the people in the industry are more shocked because we spend our working lives trying to ensure these things don't happen and because we know the effort that goes into those things. When it does happen you are even more personally affected. Also, we live with the knowledge that these things do happen and one can't make things completely risk free. It's mainly just shock, and then you start to talk to colleagues about how it could have happened. The other thing in railway companies is you always ask yourselves, could that happen here? Have we got similar risks? And you start checking those issues, so for us after Hatfield, the Railtrack Midlands zone started to look everywhere for gauge corner cracking. With hindsight, people generally think that was overdone. But after Ladbroke Grove, we did checks to see if we had any signals that drivers had reported having problems sighting, so there's always some immediate work after something like this because you check for similar things yourself.

The long-term effects of all this have been enormous and quite fundamental. As a manager in the industry, and also as a director sharing the collective responsibility implicit in that position, there's an obvious plus side in that everyone is focussed on safety and that's how it should be, the wrong behaviour is when everyone is so scared that they become totally risk averse and that can present itself as people not wanting to do anything because they are so scared of making a mistake. Even simple things such as deciding to commission some new signalling, who is prepared to put their name on a piece of paper to say this is the right signalling system given the use that it is going to be put to, given the funds you want to spend on it, the economic return you want from it and given the safety requirements you need to make? All of these decisions need to be seen in the round and people need to be quite brave now to make those decisions, given what the industry has experienced and how it has been interpreted outside.

All the people I know in the TOCs and in Network Rail, which is now re-focussing as an engineering company and concentrating on its core responsibilities of providing a safe and relia-ble railway, are very focussed on their safety commitments and if you think about the jobs people do in the industry, the last thing people want to see is a major incident because the personal burden is huge. I haven't met anyone in this industry who is not acutely aware of their responsi-bilities and who does not do their utmost to run a safe railway, although I think in all truth you could say that Railtrack in its early days was not focusssed enough on its job as an engineering company. But the people who make the day-to-day operational decisions have always under-stood that and are very committed.

I've now been with Chiltern for ten years and when I go to Ireland I shall take with me Chiltern's mission statement that is above my office door and retain those core values. Whatever service you are trying to run, that is what you should be trying to do as an operator; offer-ing a safe, reliable, welcoming and value-for-money service, and looking after your customers. Fundamentally, that is all any railway company is there to do, no matter what your particular profile of revenue and passenger subsidy may be. Nowadays, I don't think that I could work with anyone who did not share these core values. I shall certainly miss the drive and enthusiasm at Chiltern because one of the defining things about them is the sheer energy about the company, which can mean that sometimes in the past we may perhaps have gone off once or twice, and done things before we had planned them properly. That can be the down side! But the positive is that we get on and do things, it is perpetual motion. Being part of a dynamic company is very exciting. I can remember that in British Rail there were some pockets where there were people who made it their job in life to find reasons not to do things; that is hugely demoralising and drains you of all energy. Here, where there is this constant buzz and energy, I feed off it and I will miss that tremendously because I'm sure that is pretty unique. But I am going to do my best to bring some of it over to Ireland.

Steve Murphy, 2004

In 2004 Steve Murphy joined Irish Rail as general manager, Southern and Western. The role involved delivery of capital investment as well as leadership of 2,000 staff through a major change programme. During the following three years, Murphy increased inter-city punctuality by 10–15 per cent and secured capital investment approaching £1 billion. Ireland now has the fastest grow-ing railway in Europe. In September 2007, Murphy returned to take up the position of managing director of London Overground, Chiltern's sister company.

CHAPTER 13

THE OPERATIONS DIRECTOR'S STORY

Owen Edgington

I started on the railway in 1960, much to my father's horror because he thought I was going to go into his butcher's shop in Bordesley Green, Coventry Road, Birmingham. But I'd always been mad on railways and had been a trainspotter since I was about six years old. In fact, my mum used to kick us out of the house and tell us to go to Small Heath station to watch the trains; she'd be done for child abuse nowadays!

I left school in the June and started as a cleaner at Saltley Loco in the August. I was fifteen and I absolutely loved it. The work was filthy dirty and the conditions, by today's standards, were absolutely appalling but it was what I wanted to do. I worked with people I liked a lot, we had a lot of fun and after a year I went as a passed cleaner to be a junior fireman. We were always short of men at Saltley because the big attractions were the car factories where they could earn £20 a week and we were on £7 a week; a slight difference in income! But I got passed out as a driver in 1969, staying from 1969–74 as a passed fireman, which meant if they were short of drivers I was driving, but if they had plenty of drivers I was back at second man. Because of the closures that were happening all over the country there were lots of men who were senior to us and with British Rail everything was done on seniority, on 'years of service', so if someone came to the depot who was senior to you it just kept pushing you back and back. So in 1974 I moved to Waterloo as a driver coming back to Saltley in 1980, then went as an instructor driver at Birmingham Stanier House on modern traction training. In 1982 I went to St Pancras as a running inspector, followed by Cambridge as assistant train crew manager, then up to Liverpool Street. That was round about 1986/87, looking after safety standards and performance for drivers and the train services. That was quite problematic because of all the difficulties we had with infrastructure, track and overhead lines out of Liverpool Street, plus the fact we were always struggling for men in the London area. We were always short of drivers so that didn't make life easy but then I was approached to go and work with Trainload Freight.

What we didn't realise at the time was that Anglia Region was set up as a precursor for privatisation and I have to say there were lots of good things in the Anglia Region that we didn't carry on into privatisation, which shows you that civil servants don't learn! For example, my boss at Anglia was Graham Eccles. Without doubt Graham was one of the best operators I worked for, he had control of all the civil engineers and the over-head electrification engineers and the signal engineers, train crew depots and the maintenance, which a lot of these organisations hated because they had been free-standing and really a law unto themselves under British Rail. That stopped when Graham Eccles got hold of them and drummed into everybody that focussing on improving performance was the key to everything else.

Anyway, after Anglia, I went to work for Trainload Freight, which was the precursor to EWS. I ended up in charge of safety and train crew standards for fifty-two driver's depots and it was a John O'Groats to Lands End job, which I quite enjoyed. We achieved much in Trainload Freight, including many useful productivity gains. Previously I'd been with Adrian Shooter, introducing the first driver-only passenger railway from St Pancras to Bedford, and at Trainload Freight we extended driver-only operation of freight trains to 80 per cent of the network, which was a major step forward in productivity and to some extent it was a safety plus as well because having a driver in sole charge there was less room for confusion between two parties.

Then, in about 1995, Adrian asked me to come and talk to him. He'd been approached to run what became Chiltern Railways by the British Railways Board. Adrian and I shared exactly the same philosophy, the fact you were there to run trains for passengers, not to run trains for timetablers, signalmen or operators.

The other thing is we both passionately believe in safety which as a professional railwayman we don't discuss as such, we discuss incidents, but safety is a 'given' – it's part of running a railway, it's intrinsic to have a safe railway. You do look for trends and you monitor all the incidents within Chiltern. The first item at the top of every agenda at every Chiltern Board meeting, and I know it is still the same today, is 'safety'. That covers the safety of the passengers, the safety of the staff, safety of workshops – anything to do with safety is discussed in minute detail and people have to resolve the issues. I had a lot of time for Adrian as a manager because I'd worked with him at St Pancras. He's very dynamic, leads from the front and is not always comfortable to work for because he's totally demanding. Totally relentless! For example, he'd phone me every Sunday evening religiously at 9.30 p.m. and would want to know what had happened to 'his' railway from Friday night! He also did something that as far as I know no other managing directors do, or at least very rarely. Adrian would ride in the front of the train every day and talk to drivers, talk to station staff and he would phone you up if he had a problem and it would then be your problem! He constantly badgers Railtrack/Network Rail and it is performance, performance, performance, because that's what the customer wants. Given the amount of money people pay in fares, they have a right to expect the trains to run on time and to be clean.

When we started at Chiltern we had no option but to bring in an entirely new set of managers and also I got rid of quite a few supervisors as well because they weren't committed enough to the industry. I don't mean they were bad managers, I just couldn't see them being managers or supervisors within the Chiltern environment. One of the first things I did at Marylebone was to take off the 'private' sign from the station supervisor's door. It's not private – he's there for the passengers if they've got a problem because he is the interface between them and the railway. Part of the problem was that in British Rail days, Marylebone had been a very quiet place and perhaps had tended to attract too many people who just wanted a quiet life.

We had a vision of what Marylebone station was going to look like. It was going to be busy, there were going to be trains arriving and departing every few minutes. One of the things Adrian is very good at, and I believe in it too, is to get all the supervisors and managers together and tell them exactly what you want. Some people thought we were mad when we said there would be a train leaving Marylebone every few minutes in the peak hours. People just looked as if to say 'Yeah? In your dreams!' But we knew that within the limits of the signalling system that was achievable, and that was what we wanted. The other thing was we wanted the trains full up, because if they were not full up they are not making any money. So, we did have a vision of how it was going to be.

The other thing we did – I loved the fact that people thought we were mad the way we did things at Chiltern – was to double the number of carriage cleaners. The reason for that is that the first thing you see when you walk on a station, especially a terminus station like Marylebone, is your train standing there. That's your first image of the railway and I used to say to my carriage cleaners, 'You are very important people, it's not a menial job, it's important to the business because that is the image of the trains.' Way back, we did an experiment once, I only cleaned the front of the trains, religiously, just the fronts, didn't clean the sides, but the fronts were pristine. We didn't carry it on but the public perception of cleanliness went up. It's that impact as you walk on the station, coming and going from work. Obviously we didn't go on with that because we wanted the trains to be clean all over. Another thing we did was to get every manager to have a notebook and to write down on every train they travelled on whether they were clean, how much paper was on the floor, whether the windows were dirty, a whole raft of things and all that came to me and I had to chase the maintenance depot if the trains weren't up to standard, or if we had ongoing faults that hadn't been rectified.

Another thing about Chiltern is the very strong interface I had with the fleet managers, both Andy Hamilton and his predecessor, who was tragically killed accidentally when on holiday in Africa. They were up for it, and because they were all relatively young managers as well – I didn't count myself as one of the young managers – they were committed and they wanted the railway to succeed. Without being naive, they were proud of it and I'm always proud to say I worked for Chiltern. I think if you've got pride in something, you give it the extra shot. When I think back, if we had a problem, Martin Talbot, Richard McClennan, who went on to Virgin, Carl Stanley who moved on to Central, Andy Hamilton, they would come in at 3 a.m. and try and sort that out – they wouldn't expect to go home until 5 or 6 p.m. the following evening. In fact, sometimes I used to have to send them home! They would just work too long. They just had this huge commitment to the job. If, for example, we were short of supervisors, one of the managers would do the supervisor's job without being asked or instructed to. Now I worked just six months short of forty years in the industry, and I can't think of any railway that I've worked in where you didn't have to phone up and tell someone. On Chiltern, many is the time I'd phone up and be surprised because one of the managers was doing the duty controller's job. You'd say 'What are you there for?' and they would say, 'Oh so and so went sick and I couldn't fill the gap.'

Running a railway is very ground floor with the interface between the control centre, stations, maintenance depots, driver's depots and Railtrack Control. One of the things we achieved on Chiltern, which was always an ambition of Adrian's and mine, was to have the Integrated Control Centre where you have the Railtrack controllers and the Chiltern controllers all together. That took a hell of a lot to achieve. Ideally, they should also be with the signalmen. Signalling shouldn't work in isolation from other groups of staff. If you want to put bulletproof doors on the signal box as they have at Marylebone that's fine but they should work together so that the signalman can be aware of the problems that his actions can cause. For example, how many people are on the platform at Banbury, or how many people are left behind at Hatton if they decide to run a train through – in the control centre at Banbury they can see it.

One of the other benefits of the time was that Adrian sent me to Japan to experience at first hand the benefits of integration between the signalman, the train driver, the people who look after drivers, track and train maintenance people: they all slot together and sit in one big room together. They are not all compartmentalised in little boxes because they all run the railway. If any one of those things lets you down, the railway doesn't function. That was one of the problems under British Rail in traction policy. They didn't ask the people responsible for running trains what they actually wanted. Instead, the engineers decided what they thought was 'sexy'. What you need at the end of the day is this commonality of purpose throughout the grades to achieve the goal of having the trains run on time. I know it is Adrian's ambition to achieve Japanese levels of punctuality, but I think in a UK context that is currently impossible, simply because of the huge Japanese investment in their railways.

The other thing we did at Chiltern was to spend lots of money and time having seminars for drivers and station staff. You state the obvious to them, that what we are there to achieve is to run every train on time, never-ending, every day, because that is what you need to do. The other thing is that we are there to serve the passengers, even if they can sometimes be a pain in the backside! Chiltern policy is also to have managers on some of the ticket barriers at Marylebone at peak hours. Not every day, but so they can understand the problems both the staff and the passengers have.

It took us a long time to get to grips with the drivers at Marylebone because there was, and still is, difficulty in recruiting in London. Although, in an industrial wage context, drivers are very highly paid – there is a misconception drivers earn low money, that is total nonsense; average earnings on Chiltern in 2004 are in the high 'thirties,' so these people are well paid – but the big problem with the London depots now is accommodation because there is a huge mobility of drivers. Under British Rail, if you cancelled a train it was no big deal; you hadn't got a driver, end of story. It should have been an issue but it wasn't.

Anyway, I struggled to fill the driver vacancies at Marylebone and it took a long time because it takes almost a year to train a driver. It used to take years longer in steam days. Now the actual techniques are much easier to grasp and a complete novice could take the controls of a modern DMU and with someone like me standing behind them and telling them what to do, they could drive the train safely. They wouldn't particularly know what they were doing but they could do it. But when you are talking about loose-coupled or semi-fitted freight trains or vacuum-fitted passenger stock in steam days, the techniques of driving were very different.

In the old days there were also more accidents to railwaymen. When I was a fireman, I can think of at least two occasions when shunters were killed, shunting loose-coupled wagons in yards. On one occasion a guy lost his legs in Lawley Street sidings and another lost an arm at Washwood Heath sidings. During my fireman days, two guys that I knew were killed. One was crushed to death between the coaling stage and a locomotive at Burton-on-Trent depot and another got killed by an EMU outside Walsall. It wasn't that the railways were intrinsically unsafe, it was just that the operating methods, the way we shunted freight trains, was a bit of a dodgy procedure! It couldn't be tolerated today because of the health and safety legislation. But then it was a very different environment. Today we run mostly fixed-formation trains. People are not wandering about on the ground where wagons are being unloaded to the extent they were previously, so the railway is definitely safer in that respect.

Nevertheless, safety was something instilled into us from day one in the industry. That was part of your job, to work trains safely whether you were a driver, signalman, manager, whatever your job happened to be. That was what you were supposed to do and everyone knew that. The one thing we instigated on Chiltern and I think on some other companies as well, was for the safety manager to report directly to the managing director. The advantage with that is that it's far better to have someone outside the organisation that picks up on things because one of the problems in any organisation is that there is a tendency to accept small variations to the instructions because it becomes custom and practice. It's not anyone doing something deliberately unsafe or not wanting to stick to the instructions, it's that practical and daily usage become the norm. Cutting corners can become the norm. I must have sat on two or three hundred enquiries on health and safety, especially when I was at the Area level within BR and with Trainload Freight. Some of the things that stick in your mind are, for instance: 'We never thought that would happen.'; 'I thought Joe Bloggs had done it and Joe Bloggs thought I'd done it.'; 'But we've always done it that way and never had a problem.' But they didn't obey the operating instructions! That's why the incidents happen. I can honestly put my hand on my heart and say, certainly within Chiltern, that safety would never ever be deliberately compromised.

One of the things that really helped Chiltern's safety record was getting ATP. ATP now runs on virtually 100 per cent of Chiltern trains. By that I mean that every train that can work with it and every piece of track that can be equipped has been equipped. One of the biggest problems we had with it was with the suppliers. I don't want to get involved with all the history, but back in British Rail days they had been led to believe that all of the British Rail network would be equipped with ATP, then they had been shot in the back because British Rail changed its mind and only the Marylebone line would be equipped with it. The reason for not doing it was that it was prohibitively expensive. When it started, Chiltern had a choice, either to pull the plug on it or to run with full ATP. Adrian and I decided we wanted full ATP. We both knew, especially Adrian with his engineering knowledge, that it didn't need a lot to make it reliable and efficient. Some of the Railtrack civil engineers didn't like it at all, not because they didn't believe it wasn't safe but simply because they felt it would be a distraction from the many other priorities they had all over the system. If ATP wasn't going to be extended to the rest of the system, why should they spend hundreds of hours making it work? Adrian spent many hours badgering Railtrack to get the job done. The difference between TPWS (Train Protection and Warning System) and ATP is that ATP gives total train control. TPWS will stop a train within a safe distance from a signal at danger. To minimise the risk of serious accident if a signal set at danger is accidentally passed, there is an 'overlap' distance of a quarter of a mile, or the metric equivalent, built into the calculated stopping distance between signals within which the driver should be able to stop the train. Currently, following the Ladbroke Grove accident, there is much concern about signals passed at danger (SPADs). One of the differences between our procedures and, for example, that of SNCF, is that on French railways if a train passes a signal set at danger but nevertheless manages to stop within the overlap, then it is not recorded as a SPAD. In Britain it is. The TGV has a version of ATP. I have certain sympathy with the French attitude that SPADs should be judged by risk. But basically, ATP is a safer system than TPWS at speeds below 140mph. For the last thirty to forty years, airlines have had cost/benefit analysis on safety measures. If you do a cost/benefit analysis on ATP in some ways it just doesn't stand up. Nevertheless, the risk of being killed or injured on the railway, compared with the roads, is minuscule. High-speed trains need to have some form of ATP because at over 140mph drivers can't think that quickly.

Owen Edgington, 8 March 2004

CHAPTER 14

THE MARKETING DIRECTOR'S STORY

Alex Turner – Getting the Job

I first noticed an ad in the *Sunday Times* in September 1993 saying 'Commercial directors required for rail privatisation.' My wife told me it was time to get back to work after six months' redundancy from W.H. Smith.

I'd grown up in East Anglia, attending Colchester Royal Grammar School before reading Classics at Bristol University. My career to that time had included Rowntree, Ernst and Young, United Biscuits, Fine Art Developments and British Rail.

At first I was not keen because of my previous experience of the public sector as a consultant and I was more interested by an opportunity to go into television with HTV in Bristol. To my surprise, after a shambolic screening interview by a head-hunter, which felt like going through a sheep dip, I was shortlisted for no fewer than four jobs with different parts of British Rail.

The first interview with Adrian Shooter was the third of three consecutive interviews on that same morning without a break, so maybe I did look a bit dishevelled and stressed out! It was also true that my heart wasn't really in it at that point. But in preparation I had actually spent a day riding on Chiltern Turbos and visited a few stations including Banbury, which seemed a real heap, yet had a full car park – it looked expensive to sort out! It seemed to me that the trains were a bit 'Mickey Mouse' compared with HST's, but new and probably fine for the job. In such a well-off catchment area there had to be growth opportunities surely?

My first impression of Adrian Shooter, apart from his height, was that he seemed to know the industry really well and have a good grasp of the importance of trying to satisfy the needs of the customer. His common sense approach was refreshing after the style of one or two of the other managing directors I had been interviewed by recently. He obviously wanted to do an MBO and was keen to build a 'private sector-style team'. I was confident that Owen was the man to run the trains; Cath Proctor seemed a lively young manager with bags of enthusiasm.

At a later interview John Nelson (the British Rail Director for Network SouthEast) assured me that it wasn't all green teacups and green paint on the walls – he seemed surprised that I had thought it was. The phone call from Adrian Shooter came through when I was sat on the sofa with my kids watching *Bottom* and it all seemed a bit bizarre – what was I getting into here?

Early days at Euston House

Adrian's first act on day one was to take me to the staff canteen at lunch time and inform me that if I ever drank on duty I would be fired on the spot. I wondered how a marketing man could exist in such an environment! The canteen was full of grey men in grey suits. Where were all the women managers?

From January to April 1994, until Thames and Chiltern were separated, we were a management team without a business to run and that was frustrating. We were cocooned on the seventh floor. Owen Edgington said it felt like the retreat of the German army from Moscow, as huge battalions of staff moved out or were disbanded in the death throes of British Rail. I hated every single day of those three months.

To try to keep sane and prepare for the future I went out around the stations only to find that the irregular, infrequent off-peak timetable meant I kept getting stranded for an hour or more in what I had imagined to be quite big stations like Princes Risborough. Something wrong here, I thought!

Adrian got me to help him and others develop a mission statement for the new TOU:

> We want to become recognised as the best passenger railway in the UK. We aim to offer a reliable, civilised, value for money railway. Our business will prosper because people will use us regularly and recommend us to our friends.

This mission statement recognised the importance of word of mouth endorsement as a primary marketing tool. I was very happy with it and remain convinced of its powerful place in the story, particularly since Adrian pushed it constantly and even had it displayed on a large poster above his desk. Some booking offices still have it too! It was later developed further through the involvement of a wider group of managers who replaced the word 'civilised' with 'welcoming' and added the phrase 'all day every day' to stress the importance of moving away from being 'a nine to five Monday to Friday railway'. The word 'safe' was not included even though, or perhaps because, it was taken as read as the fundamental requirement. [Note: The word 'safe' was added later, at the time following Ladbroke Grove and Hatfield when customers may have taken the view that it wasn't a 'given'.]

Adrian also developed a few supporting goals such as 'to listen to our customers' and 'to provide an environment in which our staff can develop their skills'. It was all textbook stuff and it worked.

A new start at Aylesbury

The relatively modest new Chiltern HQ situated on the second floor of a solicitor's office in Aylesbury, rather than an imposing situation in London, was all part of Adrian's determination to have a flat management structure and keep overheads to the minimum. However, it was immediately clear that about forty office staff were planned for it and it was inadequate. Nevertheless, the office had a good feel about it, open for business and nothing like the anonymity associated with the public sector, though the marketing team didn't have the space to be noisy and do their job properly. We had the core of a potentially good marketing team but it had to be strengthened later by some newcomers from the commercial world.

Adrian soon recruited an experienced finance director in Tony Allen 'to look after the numbers'. Tony immediately showed that he intended to roam everywhere in the business to understand it properly and challenged everyone, including the marketing director! He often seemed keener to spend money on marketing than I was, a first as far as I was concerned from a finance director.

Adrian made it clear my focus was on external customers, not on Railtrack and contracts like most rail commercial directors. This was the right decision and another example of Adrian thinking deeply about what he needed to do to be successful. My clear aim from my first day was to grow the revenues in a largely fixed-cost environment. My main achievement was to persuade Adrian that we needed to grow the peak business, including season ticket holders. The British Rail approach was crazy in its emphasis on off peak. It consistently pushed up its season ticket prices well ahead of inflation as a deliberate act of policy to reduce the need for extra capacity. We needed to provide peak travellers with a seat on punctual trains. If we did this they would speak well of us to their family and friends and off peak would grow faster than before. And it worked a treat!

We could afford to lease more vehicles if we managed to sell about 90 per cent of the extra weekday peak seats provided, therefore off-peak seats would be a 'free good' to offer at attractive prices for the rest of the day and at weekends. I never doubted we would, nor did Tony Allen. He and I thought we would potentially need one extra coach each year for five years. Our fleet then was then running at seventy-five vehicles. How many vehicles have they got now for goodness sake!

Our first step was to lease an extra four vehicles from Thames which were being used on the Reading–Gatwick route, these had been originally built for Chiltern and had been 'nicked' by Roger McDonald at Thames. Even this very modest step prompted a very negative response from the economists at British Rail head office.

Stretching the business

How were we to grow the business in a situation of fares regulation and limited capacity? Analysis showed our maximum train length in 1994 was only four coaches and the average was two! These were short trains running short distances to places like High Wycombe and Aylesbury. What about stretching the business to Banbury and beyond? This would yield higher fares per seat and loads of potential for off-peak leisure travel in addition to longer distance commuting, so we researched places in Oxfordshire like Princes Risborough and Haddenham, and also Warwickshire – primarily Warwick and Leamington. All were growing in terms of new housing and were increasingly popular places from which to commute and are now much more popular, of course! These poor folk were driving to places like Coventry for a train to London because of Beeching. Could we get them back by reducing our journey times and increasing the frequency?

Chiltern was always intended as an inter-urban rather than an inter-city service. Very few people were crossing the imaginary border at Banbury; the traffic in 1994 was at either end into each respective city. We now set out to get them travelling by train along the route of the newly completed M40. The 'natives' were friendly and welcomed us like the long lost sons of the Great Western! A marvellously warm bond was soon established and this proved to be extraordinarily powerful in guiding us along the right path. If it worked last time, why not now? We have often said that nearly all our best ideas for improvement came from our customers, and it was true – rail user groups please take a bow!

To start with we had to be much cheaper than West Coast out of Euston, of course, and we were fortunate in inheriting a silly £20 day return fare, valid all day, between Snow Hill and Marylebone. This was a very little sold ticket before we got cracking but proved to be a useful marketing tool in building awareness and trial of our route. Some of our longer distance commuters still talk of those days when Chiltern was the 'cheapskates' railway'! A downside of this is that the fare regulation has crystallised the weekly season ticket at around £100 because that happened to be what was quoted by the fare book in 1994. No amount of patient persuasion has allowed a sensible relationship between this weekly season ticket and the daily open return, now around £50.

The stations which suffered as a result of this stretching strategy were the inner stations at either end of the route. Some pain was inevitable if we were to provide sensible long-distance journey times and we always faced a difficult juggling act, which I believe Mike Bagshaw and Steve Murphy performed with great skill. Of course it flew in the face of our 'listen to the customer' approach but we convinced ourselves they had decent alternatives at each end of the line such as London Underground (also Piccadilly etc.) and Centro services. In any case, as far as I was concerned we had no alternative. This was business. In fact I would like to have gone further, Hatton and Lapworth being good examples as Keith Gascoigne, then chairman of the local rail users association, well knows!

Our 'stations out' marketing policy

I brought with me from the retail world (W.H. Smith) a concept which was largely unknown in the railways and one that has worked a treat for Chiltern Railways. I called it 'stations out marketing'. The standard British Rail approach was to induce people into think about using a train via expensive TV ads etc. British Rail entered their living room and said 'come to us'. I did the opposite. I assumed that many people wouldn't be interested in using the train, but that some had a higher propensity to use a train than others, especially those living near a station or knowing someone who was already a regular rail user. So we went out to them, using the stations as our marketing agents.

How did that work? The concept is that you focus on making the station, or shop, as attractive and user friendly as possible so that people who use them tell their friends. You start with the ticket office and work outwards into the local community. So the sequence includes:

-windows open longer during the day when people needed them
- better-trained, friendly ticket office staff, including several recently retired blokes who had been in management positions in industry and enjoyed serving customers without much pressure
- better fares information near the ticket office windows, especially on key fares to London
- posters on platforms about railcards and key fares such as one-day travel cards
- leaflets and pocket timetables door dropped to local homes within two miles of the station
- research shows they are four times more likely to use the train than the national average
- timetables displayed in local libraries etc
- always moving in gradual steps outwards from the station in to the local community

Only when all this had been done did we spend money on advertising media such as local press, radio and posters. There was much higher wastage with these techniques and our budgets were always stretched.

I don't think that 'stations out' would have worked if we hadn't brought in station masters like Donald Wilson at Marylebone from a quite early stage to make sure that staff and station premises were being looked after properly. British Rail had tried to do all this via endless requisition forms to head office and it didn't work. Instead, we gave them responsibility for their own maintenance and staffing budgets and also sales targets to work to. They decide when a tap needed replacing in a toilet or whether to repaint the staff areas. All this worked a treat and we were surprised to find just how motivating the targets were to the ticket office staff. It meant someone was taking an interest in what they were achieving. But the targets had to be realistic and Cath Proctor did a great job in piloting the whole project before it went live and then making sure that the targets were stretching but not demoralising – a fine balance.

Keith White was my retail manager and he did a good job in keeping on top of the staffing levels and making sure that my wilder ideas were translated into concepts the ticket offices could cope with. I was especially impressed by how well his maintenance teams kept the stations well presented and maintained, usually removing graffiti within a few hours to discourage further attempts. And it usually worked!

Establishing a marketing team

After a year at Aylesbury, I persuaded Adrian to allow me to move my little marketing team to Marylebone station offices, which were largely unused up to that point. Quite a spooky atmosphere and some people thought the offices might be haunted. It took me quite a long time to get used to drivers not saying hello when we crossed on the stairs – their mess room was on the second floor. It took a couple of years before this all changed and we enjoyed a good relationship.

I remember finding a huge model train set in the middle of the area that was to become our marketing offices! It soon went, possibly in the skip, as we spruced the place up and turned it into commercial offices, much used later by other managers passing through from Aylesbury.

I recruited one or two people whom I had known in commerce to balance out the career rail people I had inherited and it worked quite well (Mike Barnes, previously managing director for an advertising agency, and Ian Kenworthy, a former estate agent). By this time I had also hired an excellent little London ad agency, Pocock and Co., who did marvellous work, including such classic lines as 'Brummie good value!' It helped that Stuart Pocock was from Wolverhampton and understood the Midlands well. PR was supplied by Liz Fraser and her team at Key Communications near Paddington station, who did a fine job in supporting the 'stations out' policy, especially in developing better links with local and national newspapers and radio stations.

We were frequently asked to give interviews and we rarely refused, especially if we had a bad news story to deal with – we thought this was essential if we wanted to them to give coverage to our achievements. Previously, Thames and Chiltern had not found local press terribly supportive. We worked really hard to turn this around.

A seven-day week

For a period between January 1995 and early 1996 my role at Chiltern Railways, as with the other directors, had three main elements that combined to make it practically a seven-day week of work: We helped British Rail prepare the documentation for 'sale' of the franchise; this involved many tedious days sitting with lawyers, OPRAF representatives, and investment bankers from Kleinwort Benson. This included quite a lot of weekend work towards the end and I well remember the bulky legal documents arriving by courier from London every Saturday morning, all to be corrected and sent back to London by the Monday morning. This was excruciatingly repetitive and tedious work and it consumed most of my weekends.

We prepared our own management bid for the franchise, as advised by Grant Thornton. A key task was to develop new revenue and cost projections for a seven-year period. All this work had to be done out of hours, usually after work and at the offices of our advisers.

Our day job was to run the railway and keep passengers and staff as happy as possible amidst of all the (mostly adverse) publicity about the impending rail privatisation programme.

Doing all three things at once I found to be immensely demanding, not to say tiring, and I can well understand when it is said that most people only have one MBO in them during a lifetime. Of course Adrian seemed as fresh as a daisy throughout! I can remember feeling no elation or even pleasure when we won the bid, only relief that the task had been completed and worry as to the scale of the challenge that lay ahead in achieving the demanding revenue projections upon which our winning bid was based.

This reaction concerned both my wife Anne and me at the time, for good reason as it turned out. Although my revenue projections were comfortably surpassed, it was the cost estimates that proved to be hopelessly off the mark! I have no doubt that this period exhausted my emotional reserves and I was never the same again during the rest of my time at Chiltern Railways. Indeed I was off work for several weeks from September 1996.

Adrian was extraordinarily supportive and understanding during this difficult time in my professional life, as was my staff that had to cover for me. Adrian even had my secretary watching me closely for a while. On more than one occasion she sent me home when I tried to come in to work for more than the initially agreed three days per week. Although at this time my illness meant an increased workload for my team, they remained incredibly loyal. After returning to work full time, I began to feel that perhaps it was time to move on, not least because of the burden of the long hours spent travelling to and from work. In the end, I left Chiltern in 1999.

All in all I am proud that I left behind a solid team, most of them are still there today. In particular I'd like to think that I helped groom Steve Murphy and Cath Proctor for their future key roles with Chiltern and elsewhere.

Would I go through it all again?

It was undoubtedly an exceptional experience and I count myself very lucky to have been chosen by Adrian to take part in his adventure. It has also made me comfortable for the rest of my life financially since I sold my shares at the very peak of the stock market boom. These are big upsides.

But did I enjoy it? Maybe I am too much of a worrier, but I found the terms of the franchise deal quite frightening and I was concerned that a decent economic downturn might wreck our plans and projections. I always thought that the deals should have included an element of risk sharing with the Treasury so that they could share in any 'super profits' and also give us some protection from circumstances beyond our control. It is absolutely no surprise to me that so many franchises have needed to be bailed out by the taxpayer – as our feisty chairman Sir Richard Morris predicted they would all along.

I also hated the four-hour commuting from the Cotswolds, especially on dark winter mornings when I knew I would not be back until 9 or 10 p.m., also in the dark, just in time to have supper and go to bed only to undergo the same travelling again next day.

Many was the time when Anne had to almost literally kick me out of bed at 6 a.m. to catch the 06:50 from Kemble, the train which was subsequently involved in the Ladbroke Grove crash.

I was always happiest out in the community selling the railway to local councils, rail user groups and businesses. We had a great story to tell and much to learn at the same time as to how we might improve further. I was genuinely touched at my final meeting of the M40 Rail Forum to receive from Hugh Jones a book, *The Final Link* by Edwards and Pigram, describing the original construction of what is now the Chiltern route from Birmingham to London. I guess not many rail marketing types have enjoyed similarly warm relationships with their long-suffering passengers. That makes me feel we did some good as well as made some money. That is a nice feeling to cling to.

Alex Turner, 24 July 2003

CHAPTER 15

THE FINANCE DIRECTOR'S STORY

Tony Allen

I'm a Londoner, born in North London about a mile and a half down the road from White Hart Lane in 1949, so naturally my football support goes to Tottenham Hotspur. I'm an only child and my parents died some time ago. I was always very good at maths at school and my parents said I was going to be an accountant, so, unlike most of the accountants you meet nowadays, I was always earmarked to become an account- ant from the age of about seven or eight! I went to Highgate School. I didn't go to university and after my A Levels went to City of London Polytechnic for a year which gave me an exemption and then I studied for my Chartered Accountancy exams. I qualified when I was twenty-three. I worked for ITT in their special projects division for eighteen months, then joined Courage at Tower Bridge in 1975 as an assistant financial accountant. Two years later I was promoted to chief accountant with Arthur Cooper, which was Courage's Off-Licence division. Then I worked for Mary Quant as financial controller for John Corgi Ltd who made trouser presses. I stayed there for ten years, then was made financial director of Appletiser, which was part of South African Breweries in about 1990. I was with them for about three and a half years. When Appletiser was sold to Coca Cola, I was effectively out of a job during the dodgy times of the early 1990s. I went straight into a job working for a small laminates company to sort out the owner's accounts. After about six months he said thank you very much, so I had about three and a half months off. I'd always been a bit of a train buff as a youngster, no doubt driving my parents mad with my train trips around the country.

I got a phone call in January 1994 from an accountancy agency, Robert Hearth, asking if I would be interested in going to work for British Rail. By this time, although it was quite nice having the time off, I was looking for something permanent. It involved a big reduction in pay for me but I had never worked in the public sector before so I agreed and they put my name forward for both the Chiltern and Thames Train operating units. They were handling both jobs as they were being split at the time. I believe the shortlist they sent Adrian contained about twelve names. The day before my interview with Adrian, I went to the library and studied as much as I could about rail privatisation. I also spoke to a friend, Roger Turner, who became involved later with the management buy-out of the London, Tilbury and Southend. He gave me a few tips on the sort of questions Adrian was likely to ask. So I was reasonably prepared by the time I came to meet Adrian Shooter and I think he was reasonably impressed that I had done my homework and was interested in the job. He phoned me up the next morning and said 'Do you want to come and work for us?' And typical Adrian, he added 'If you do, you can start straight away.'

So I ended up in Eversholt Street with the grey haired Mr Turner and Mr Edgington looking at me and I wondered if I was going to get on with the latter, this Brummie guy, but he became my best friend in the business. While all this was going on I got divorced. I've got three children aged twenty-nine, twenty-four and eleven. It's been an interesting ride and out of all the finance directors I've met in the new railway industry, I'm the only one who has survived to date.

I started with British Rail in February 1994. We had this first get together which I shall never forget in March where the finance director of Network SouthEast told us to write out as many cheques as we possibly could because in the public sector you can't carry forward your borrowing facility into the next financial year. The finance director told us to spend as much as we possibly could on computers, materials, etc. because British Rail had under-utilised its funding for the year. I found the whole process staggering; it was a complete eye-opener. The starting point was 'These were your costs last year; you've got to reduce them by 10 per cent.' As most of the costs in this industry are fixed anyway, this was complete nonsense.

One person whose role in this story needs emphasising is John Nelson, because John had a major role from the start of Chiltern Railways and its successful growth to where it is now. John has sat as a non-executive director on our Board since I suggested it to Adrian early on. As a specific example of why John was so important to us, when we were part of Network SouthEast there were only two of the ten TOUs which were 'growth' businesses. Thameslink was one and Chiltern was perceived as the other. John allowed us the flexibility to get around the annual 10 per cent cost cuts. We just said look, we can't do this, we're expanding the business – South Central may be able to but Chiltern certainly can't. What we needed to do is to stimulate the business and to grow it. John took a relaxed view on that and said, 'Okay, we'll look at your net position; costs against revenue and not just at the cost line only.' It was really from that point that John encouraged Adrian to stimulate and drive the benefits the initial investment programme had given. When we took the business over from the Thames guys, their view was 'Chiltern? No growth, you'll stand still.' By contrast, Adrian's view was, of course, completely different and he was supported in that. If John Nelson hadn't given us support with this flexibility then we wouldn't have the business we have today.

Let me remind you of the process we went through with the management buy-out. There were a number of issues. While doing the day job, we were drafting the business plan which was essentially inviting someone else to come and take our jobs. On a Saturday or Sunday, the door bell would go at some God-forsaken hour and there would be piles of papers and long form reports and invitations to tender; lots of legal documentation lying on our mats brought by courier and you had to ensure that the text was right. So you start off with the registration of interest by companies and then you had to draft these ten long form reports, which were a complete history of Chiltern's business since 1994. You had to go through and check all this blooming stuff while at the same time putting together our own business plan, and running our own business.

The personal pressure was quite simply that if you're doing a 'sealed envelope bid' and you can't re-open it you've got your whole livelihood and your family's livelihood on the line. We knew that if we lost out, none of us would have been employed by the next owners, because they were cost-cutters. They were there to slash costs as the SRA or rather OPRAF.

The pressures may have contributed to my divorce. My wife wasn't working and was at home with my very young daughter and I would be locked away reading all these papers, coming home late at night and I still wanted to have outside friends, as well as seeing my two boys by my first marriage. I had a focus in my life, something to strive for, and we sadly drifted apart. None of the other directors had a young family so they didn't have the pressure of having an under five year old, which made it tougher for my partner. Several of the wives of the other directors also had their own careers as well as older children, which may have made it slightly less stressful for them to cope with while their husbands were putting in these exceptionally long hours.

In terms of our financial commitments, most of us were able to re-mortgage our homes to raise the required capital. If things had gone pear-shaped, the only person who would have been seriously hurt would have been Owen Edgington, who effectively put in his life savings. He was the one who took the really big risk. Happily, he's now sitting on cloud nine in terms of how the thing worked out.

A lighter episode concerned red wine! We'd submitted our indicative offer and were in the offices of Cameron McKenna and told we'd pre-qualified so we'd got over the first stage. But when we'd submitted our indicative bid, we wanted a fifteen-year franchise – LTS got fifteen years, so we wanted fifteen. We knew we couldn't match the other two bidders; there was no way we could beat the French or Stagecoach when it came to cost-cutting, they were on a different plane from us. The only way we could compete with them was by growing the business and by really going for an expansive bid. We played a game – we submitted two bids, we submitted a seven-year bid alongside a 'non-compliant' fifteen-year second bid. While we were at Cameron McKenna we were told we would get a phone call back. The chap who did our financial modelling took the phone call from OPRAF and came back into the office to say that OPRAF had turned down our fifteen-year option.

The gloom set in and we all felt we could almost pack our bags then and there because we had no chance of being able to take the amount of costs out of the business that we would need to. And since it was only a seven-year franchise there was only a minimal amount of investment we could complete in the time. So Alex Turner, ever conscious of the relevance of good wine to serious strategic thinking said, 'Don't worry chaps, how would you like a glass of wine?' Richard Price, the partner looking after us, obligingly produced half a dozen bottles of the nicest claret you could imagine; this was about lunch time. Adrian promptly declared us all 'off duty' and we sat down and just drank red wine and ate lovely expensive sandwiches! And we brainstormed and decided how we were going to respond to this and we decided to do the franchise bid as though it was a fifteen-year franchise and we would put quite a bit of investment and commitment into it, as though this was a stage towards a fifteen-year term. So we basically ignored it on the assumption we would have the next eight years or whatever, so that's what we did and that's why Chiltern has been so successful because we never acknowledged it as a seven-year franchise [the initial franchise being for seven years]. We went right through from the word go for the investment-led strategy and customer satisfaction. That was a turning point for us.

We had Steer Davies Gleave's people working for us on the revenue numbers. These guys looked at the old British Rail figures and financial models of growth, 3 per cent and all that sort of rubbish. We said we don't believe it, this is all twaddle, this is Chiltern, and this isn't British Rail in terms of growing revenue numbers. In fact in the end we jacked up the revenue numbers over seven years by £60 million above the level these SDG people had got, so when we went in with a franchise bid, we were obviously at a higher cost than the other bidders, but we must have had a much higher revenue line. As it happens, the revenue we actually generated was much higher than even we put in the bid: 15–16 per cent a year growth was what we got. We were helped by the strength of the economy of course but it was a bold strategy and it worked. So never be a defeated buyer, just be clear of your objectives, your strategy, what your route to achieving that strategy is and be very clear in your vision. Adrian wanted ours to be the best passenger railway in the UK. Some of us came from the private sector where we were used to dealing with high-quality products and so we were all singing from the same hymn sheet.

We were not the cheapest in terms of costs but we definitely took a bold strategy and continued throughout to invest in the business. We could certainly have made more profit. There's no doubt we could have done what Thames did for instance and not put any bit of investment in. When we were getting to the climax, I was very worried, I'd been out of work twice and in 1996 I was forty-six. When we won it was a huge relief. None of us were thinking in terms of what the spoils would be at the end. From a personal point of view, I was just happy to be in a job and realised that in the private sector I would have more freedom in terms of what we did.

One funny thing happened after we'd won. We all had to take a medical for the life cover and I was the only one of the four who failed the medical, and I'm the only one who actually did any sport! I'm quite athletic. I used to play a lot of football, cricket, tennis and squash. While we were going through this bidding process you put weight on and you don't exercise, you don't have a proper balance in your life. I was diagnosed with diabetes; otherwise I would never have known. The irony is that Edgington smokes thirty or forty cigarettes and drinks a couple of bottles of wine a day and got through it. Alex doesn't do any exercise and is always totally stressed out and he got through his medical as well; Adrian, well he just works all the time anyway!

Tony Allen, 13 August 2003

CHAPTER 16

MY RAILWAY JOURNEY: THE COMPANY CHAIRMAN'S STORY

Sir Richard Morris

In 1995 I met a friend, Sir Hugh Ford – who was Pro-Rector of Imperial College and Professor of both Civil Engineering and Mechanical Engineering – whom I had got to know through the Fellowship of Engineering, now known as the Royal Academy of Engineers. He has had life-long association with railway engineering and through his membership of the British Rail Research Board had known Adrian Shooter over a number of years. Adrian had told him about the proposed Chiltern Rail franchise of which he was currently the British Rail managing director. The route of Chiltern Railways had been modernised over the early 1990s and Adrian had built a strong management team round him who were working on a proposal for a management bid for the franchise, but they needed a chairman.

I met Sir Hugh and Adrian over lunch at the Athenaeum and Adrian explained the franchise process and the proposal for the Chiltern franchise and asked if I would be interested in being part-time chairman, to which I replied positively. This led to a lunch with the management team at a hotel in Aston Clinton soon after. My last interview for a job had been in 1952 before I joined Courtaulds and every job since then had come my way by events and invitation, so I was not attuned to being interviewed for the job but quite used to meeting future employers/colleagues who, for one reason or another, had selected/invited me to join them, so it was an interesting lunch!

Sir Richard and Lady Morris with Adrian Shooter on the special steam train marking Sir Richard's retirement as chairman of Chiltern Railways.

There were four key directors of the Chiltern line – Adrian himself – an experienced manager and engineer of British Rail, a powerful leader with a broad knowledge and experience and an infectious enthusiasm for the railway business and especially Chiltern. His operations director was Owen Edgington, who had risen through the ranks from driver to his present well-deserved position. He knew and understood the British Rail system, its rules and regulations, as well as many of the operators on a personal basis, including key players among the trade unions. He was a competent and safe pair of hands who led his drivers from the front. The drivers are the backbone of the railway on whose shoulders so much rests – safe working, communicating with the passengers and handling situations in conjunction with station staff, controllers and signal personnel. As the railway system as a whole has become busier and new rolling stock brought in, their availability has been a challenge and the continuous training of new drivers, both male and female, has demanded great attention from the operations director and my first impression of Owen was proved correct, and he brought on his successor ready for his retirement after three years or so of the franchise.

Tony Allen was the finance director brought in from outside the railway industry by Adrian, who proved to be a first class manager of the financial detail of the railway. This role fitted him like a glove but as the business grew and its ownership moved towards John Laing Group plc it was clear the more corporate structure into which M40 Trains (as we originally named the Chiltern franchise holding company) had to fit required different skills and it was much to everyone's credit that in the restructuring of M40 into Laing Rail, with its main operating subsidiary Chiltern Railways, that we were able to retain Tony as finance director of Chiltern Railways functionally responsibile to a new post of Finance Director Laing Rail.

The key role of marketing director was filled by Alex Turner, who was also recruited into the team by Adrian from outside the industry. A professional in every sense, he had a real intellectual understanding of the place and responsibility of marketing in the modern railway. He was analytical and questioned everything, sometimes a touch tactlessly. He worked extremely hard in the early years and laid sound foundations for the company's strategy and plans. He decided after three years to retire from full-time employment and work as a consultant in which role he has continued successfully to work for both Laing Rail and other train operating companies – I suspect a role he enjoys more than being responsible for just one business and a large direct staff.

The lunch was enjoyable (as far as I was concerned) and I approached it on the basis I was going to be their part-time chairman – there were one or two amusing exchanges especially with Alex! But I came away very impressed by the cohesion of the team and their focus on the twin objectives of winning the franchise and being one of the best railways in the business. It was a happy day for me when Adrian confirmed their invitation for me to join them in the run-up to the franchise bid. It was an exciting job – unpaid unless we won but the railway staff involved had to work in the evenings and weekends preparing the bid. Our legal team from McKenna's, led by Richard Price, were excellent, as were Grant Thornton our accountants both of whom were on a contract that only paid them if we won the franchise.

It took us nearly a year working together to land the franchise. It involved reading some very heavy contractual documents, which from my days with Brown and Root, I was well used to. It was a steep learning curve to understand the structure of the new railway franchise system and the costs, sales and accounting structure. In retrospect it was a very complex structure with the split between the TOC franchise holders; Network Rail responsible for the track, stations and signalling and their maintenance; and the train-leasing companies, who owned the rolling stock and leased them to the TOCs. The new system was developed by the Conservative Government (as their long term in Government was coming to an end), the Civil Service, merchant bankers, consultants, lawyers and accountants – with the result one would expect from such a combination of interested parties!

Chiltern was fortunate in having a number of quite excellent young managers/executives especially during the actual bidding process initially and later when we bid for the twenty-year franchise renewal (the only one awarded). One key player was Mark Beckett, a very able young man who knew every detail and negotiated with the OPRAF and later SRA with great success. We were able to give him some senior management experience running Chiltern as general manager but had to cut it short when the franchise renewal bid came along. The railway has so many facets and it is essential to have people of Mark's ability to apply their experienced brain power to whatever is the issue of the hour. His good influence has been significant throughout my time as chairman.

There were others, Cath Proctor who was one of Alex Turner's key staff, and succeeded him, as well as being responsible for all station staff. A really lively personality who carried forward much of the initial marketing decisions and in particular creating an expanding business between the Birmingham Snow Hill area and Marylebone given the special opportunities created by the modernisation of the West Coast Main Line – the challenge progressively increasing as the Virgin Trains service improves between Euston and Birmingham New Street. She also handled all the customer relations along the railway, which all directors and especially Adrian have led so competently and tactfully. Everyone involved with Laing Rail is customer oriented – without satisfied customers we have no railway and the way in which the regular meetings with customer based on our stations, the consultations with them and the regular newsletters to customers are a model. Cath Proctor was at the heart of our good customer relations notwithstanding the difficulties created by train breakdowns (especially in the early days of our new rolling stock – Class 168s), signal failures, etc. Rapid dissemination of information is key, coupled with appropriate action where necessary – taxis, buses or whatever.

Our line runs through a wealthy commuter area and it was a bold decision to discontinue first class and have a single class railway on the basis that all customers are entitled to first class travel and this was the basis of the design of the latest rolling stock.

This new rolling stock was ordered from Adtranz at Derby in 1997. At that time they were nearly out of work, no train orders had been placed for 1,064 days and we agreed a design that was a significant improvement on our existing Class 165 diesel trains – in the event they proved a significant and expensive headache. Part of the problem of course was that the former highly skilled workforce at Derby had mostly been made redundant.

The faults we suffered appeared to centre on electronic systems not interfacing with each other appropriately – it took a great deal of effort by Adrian and the team, including Andy Hamilton, to overcome all the problems. I had never come across in my fifty years in industry such incompetence, such prevarication or lack of energy among our suppliers – they have since changed ownership several times and now Bombardier owns the company. Part of the solution eventually was to take maintenance back in house at our Aylesbury depot under Andy Hamilton our fleet manager. We certainly paid the price of being first!

In part it is a problem created by the franchise system – each one allowed to specify its requirements instead of industry standards with powerful suppliers capable of delivering first class trains that meet the required standards and have an economic and well-supported life cycle. The good maintenance of trains is an essential part of a top rate service for customers – reliable, clean, serviced trains are essential coupled with systematic maintenance of engines and rolling stock. It is not an easy task when every train and every carriage is needed to serve our travelling customers. It is a question of organisation and system, which took some time to establish, but with significant expansion of Aylesbury and a new workshop at Wembley I believe we have provided the infrastructure to provide the service required plus more rolling stock.

One of the early decisions was how we were going to ensure we had both financial strength and engineering project capability. I had worked for Barclays as their industrial adviser and went to talk to them about who we should invite to take shares in M40 Trains – in the end 3i became our financial partner and proved a good decision in that they were interested, supportive and helpful. In addition we went to John Laing plc to bring project management and engineering experience and they also proved helpful and supportive. Eventually they bought out Alex Turner and Owen Edgington and also bought 50 per cent of the shares of Adrian, Tony and myself as well as taking over 3i's shares.

Laing went through a difficult period involving a large loss on the Cardiff Rugby Stadium, eventually leading to the appointment of a new chairman from outside the company, and Andy Friend, who had joined them earlier to lead the changes necessary in the company's spectrum of activities – he subsequently became managing director of the group but thankfully remained a member of the Laing Rail Board thereby linking the parent company closely to their investment in the rail business. This proved of great value and the Laing Rail team were much encouraged by Andy to think strategically, which led to the robust and successful bid for the new twenty-year franchise for Chiltern and a strategic development of Laing's rail interest based on the success of the Chiltern franchise.

Throughout my seven years working as chairman we could not have had better partners or owners – they by and large left us to get on with the job giving help and advice when appropriate and needed. The results of M40 Trains in terms of profitability were good, not spectacular, as we were not one of the earliest franchises to be awarded by OPRAF and they had learnt lessons from the earlier franchises; also we were intent on reducing our subsidy from OPRAF and later SRA to the minimum over the seven-year franchise period which gave us the incentive to operate efficiently and grow the business through additional rolling stock and higher passenger loadings. We also worked hard with the support of Network Rail to modernise our London terminus – Marylebone – up to date. It must rank as a one of our successes – it welcomes our customers and genuinely seeks to meet their needs in a modern piazza style.

The need for modernisation of other stations has proceeded and the provision of a new station at Warwick Parkway was an early investment by M40 Trains – who own the new station. Also it was greatly assisted by the Laing engineers and project manager who developed the patented platform design, which enabled us to install the new station (and other platform extensions) significantly cheaper and quicker than the normal railway methods. It also involved fewer line possessions during the engineering work – the design reminded me of my days as chairman of British Lego in the 1960s.

Further modernisation applied in particular to the thirty or so miles of single track going south between Aynho Junction and Princes Risborough (a legacy of Beeching). Tackling this was an essential improvement to enable an efficient and marketable service between Marylebone and Birmingham Snow Hill. This was tackled in two separate projects – the first was executed by Railtrack and was a nightmare, with their layers of management and bureaucracy with its attendant lack of real project management. The second project we ran ourselves working closely with the Network Rail Birmingham team – we completed it very successfully at less cost per mile and significantly less frustration.

Following the close relationship between Adrian and the Japanese Central Railway our staff (including me) were able to see the Japanese rail culture in action – impressive to say the least. Many aspects and ideas have been brought back from Japan and in particular the Chiltern Integrated Control Centre with every operational aspect either present in the purpose built centre at Banbury or linked to it with effective direct communications. This was a cultural change and essential for rapid handling of situations that arise in the day-to-day running of the railway.

The secret of success of any business depends on people – be they satisfied customers or competent management and staff in depth. This was addressed very positively throughout my time and before it with the result that Chiltern has capability to run both an effective and successful business and also develop new projects. I believe the company's future success is assured as a result of the steady recruitment of well qualified young managers. Chiltern is successful and deserves to continue to be so, led by Adrian Shooter and his team.

Sir Richard Morris, Breadsall, Derbyshire, December 2003

(Note: sadly, Sir Richard Morris died on 1 July 2008.)

CHAPTER 17

'TEN YEARS AS A RAILWAYMAN'

Cath Proctor, Managing Director

Born in Singapore in 1969, the first ten years of my life were spent in the sunshine and sandy beaches of a nearby small tropical island, going to school by boat. My father was originally in the army and then in the oil business. When I was only eleven months old my younger sister was born and I was then handed to my father who was told, 'Look after this one while I look after the baby', and I think it's what has made me the kind of person I am, deemed to be an adult at eleven months! Then when I was about ten years old we moved as a family lock stock and barrel to Aberdeen in the north of Scotland. One couldn't really have chosen a more different location, and the environment always seemed very cold, very dark, very windy and of course, very wet!

After completing school with the Scottish equivalent of A Levels, I took a break from exams and lessons, packed my bags and spent some months travelling the world. I've always had quite a lot of itchy feet about me. Then I was persuaded that if you wanted to get on in life, you had to get a qualification and go for it. Consequently I enrolled and spent the next five years doing Business Studies at the local Robert Gordon Business School. This included a year out working for a division of Thorn EMI as a training officer, living in Edinburgh, working in Stirling, just growing up and having a whale of a time! It also gave me a great deal of confidence and I started to work out what I wanted from my life, the values that I have about people and business and all those critically important things.

When I left college, I wanted a career managing people and accordingly applied for three management training programmes; ICI, British Steel and the third was British Rail. Although at the time British Rail's reputation was poor, its training programme was considered one of the best in the country, primarily because they invested so much in you. Also I wanted to go into what was a 'heavy' type industry, because it tends to attract the sort of colourful characters that I like to be around. I need to do something that I believe is important to the society and the country. There is something magical about being part of something that really does things that matter to your customers, regardless of whether or not people criticise you. Travel was something I always enjoyed so I was really pleased when I got into British Rail. The railway industry is an exciting world to be in. It's nice to be with customers who are going places and it is good to be part of that and to make a difference.

So I remember going for my initial interview in Scotland for the management training programme. To get onto it was quite a special thing as there were something like 15,000 applications nationally and fifteen places. I went to an assessment centre for two days; group assessment, individual assessment, personality assessment and among the many very interesting characters I met there was a man called Cedric Knott. Cedric Knott was then the marketing director of Network SouthEast with a reputation as a man with extremely high standards, great passion and pretty much feared by most of the people who came in contact with him. He has always had a special place in my heart, because I remember at the end of my assessment centre period I was called in to see him and he pulled his half-moon glasses to the end of his nose, crossed his legs and looked at me and said, 'Miss Proctor, I have absolutely no doubt whatsoever you could manage in British Rail, but could British Rail manage you?'

The very next day I got a call to tell me that I had been appointed as one of the management trainees with Network SouthEast, Thames and Chiltern, based at Reading under David Dodd. I was literally given one week's notice and Sunday night exactly a week later I was on Aberdeen station about to board a sleeper train with a couple of bags full of clothes, nowhere to live, and I just went for it. It always makes me chuckle because the photograph on my staff pass is still the same photograph that I took that night in a photo booth on Aberdeen concourse! That was how my railway career began in 1992, incidentally a year after Steve Murphy.

The next morning I found a bed and breakfast in Reading, which scared the hell out of me because, it being the only thing I could afford at the time, it had four bolts on the inside of the door! And I put my rather sorry bags of clothes together with some suits I'd made myself in the bedroom and off I went for my first real day's work. It was quite an exciting start really and it was a bit of a leap of faith.

The training programme lasted nine to ten months and the idea of the programme was to fast-track you through the industry. Consequently, I did virtually every job in the industry, from shifting ballast during a night shift on the tracks, to selling tickets, working in an enquiry bureau, selling sandwiches, working in a control centre, etc. I actually had to signal trains in signal boxes across the country. Many of the departments I worked in were very competitive and liked to blame other departments when things went wrong, although the reality was that they were absolutely dependent upon each other to make things work. So, altogether, I had a really fun time although it was not always happy because there were parts of the industry, particularly within Network SouthEast around London, with a huge void between managers and the staff, particularly on what are now the Connex and South Western Trains areas. I remember entering driver mess rooms with 200 drivers and because I was wearing a suit, the whole room would go silent as I walked in. They would just stare at you! It was a culture based upon power, control and intimidation. During this time I did often wonder whether this was a place where I wanted to stay. Managers who could inspire me and give me confidence that there was the will and competence to change the industry, sadly, were very scarce.

My first real job after finishing my training was with Thames and Chiltern as duty station manager at Oxford station, including Banbury. I was in charge of the passenger environment on the station, the toilets which were the bane of the passengers' and my life, and generally learning how one runs a station.

The stations were very different then and the first day I arrived at Banbury, I actually showed up on a Sunday, knowing that they were all expecting me on a Monday, in order that I could find out what exactly was going on. What I found was a lady on the platform selling eggs to the local community and when I couldn't gain access to the ticket office, I went off to find some keys and came back and found the entire staff cooking themselves Sunday lunch in the kitchen at the back! The ticket office was closed so I knew at that stage there were going to have to be some changes!

The Chiltern route was, at that time, still considered very much a branch line and while at Venture House in Reading, I hardly knew it really existed. It was a very small route, with one person, Donald Wilson, later Marylebone station master, who dealt with all the correspondence.

But I joined the railway because I believed that the railways had a very strong and positive future in this country, albeit defined in what you deliver for your customers. The values that Chiltern have now were the values at the start. It's about getting the simple things right, it's about always making sure our railway is safe and that we never undermine that. So we always stay in touch with our customers and they change, every year they change, they grow older, they change their expectations, new younger customers come along and we continue to grow; we grow 10–15 per cent each year. That's a lot of new people we have to stay in touch with. We need to put them at the forefront of everything that we do; we need to make sure that their ideas drive the change and evolve within the company. And finally, from a management perspective, it's not just customers, it's also about staff. This railway is very much at the heart of the communities it serves and we have grown and survived as much because of the encouragement and support we've had within and outside the company as anything else. There's a huge amount of commitment and goodwill towards the railway and everybody wants to see it succeed and everybody feels it's theirs! So I've always felt that the management team at Chiltern were very much custodians of the community's railway.

My initial interview for Chiltern Railways was in what I called Euston Towers, where I met two of the most influential people in my career, Adrian Shooter and Alex Turner. The place where we met was awful and I remember sitting outside the waiting area ready to go in having just met Julie Abbott, Adrian's first PA, and I was very nervous because I desperately wanted the job. I was going for the post of area manager for the south, which included being station manager at Marylebone and all stations as far out as Beaconsfield. Adrian was overrunning his previous interview and I had to sit for an hour while he interviewed a man with silver hair wearing a navy blue suit looking very much a City type. I just sat there wondering what position that person was coming for. By the time Adrian called me in I was drowning in adrenaline and could barely even speak my name. I was interviewed by both Owen Edgington and Adrian Shooter. It was the first time I had ever met Adrian and I thought what a fearsome man he was! Enormous stature, enormous hands and he had glasses on the end of his nose. He looked from where I was sitting about 10ft tall and he sat back from the table and questioned me over his glasses. I could tell this was a man who had been given the rare opportunity of picking his entire management team from scratch. So I was put through my paces and at the end of the interview he said to me, 'I've been quite impressed with the interview today, and I am perhaps going to offer you the job that you want. But if you want this job, you have to demonstrate to me that you can in fact sell and you can in fact persuade people to do things they haven't done before. You see that silver haired gentleman out in reception? His name is Alex Turner and I am considering making him my marketing director. However, Alex has some concerns about whether he wants to join and I am only going to appoint you if you can persuade him to join. Off you go, you've got thirty minutes!'

I went out and met Alex Turner and started to have a conversation before he went back in to see Adrian. I didn't know the conclusion of the conversation but I did know I had been appointed area manager because I got a telephone call when I was home in Aberdeen. I was waiting for a bus at the time and my mother came out very excited in her dressing gown and slippers, much to my embarrassment, running along the road shouting: 'Catherine, Catherine, that man's on the phone! Come and take the call.' So I ran back and Adrian said to me over the phone: 'Hello Catherine, I'd like you to start on 27 February. Your salary will be such and such and I'll see you then.' I put the phone down and thought, hey, that's unusual, isn't he supposed to ask me if I want the job? I was basically being instructed that I had got the job and I was to attend on my first day's work! And that was pretty much how my relationship with Adrian started. I have to say, nothing has changed.

At our first management team meeting in February or March I was of course looking for that silver haired gentleman. There must have been about twenty to twenty-five of us at the time, the whole management team, of which very few remain. And there he was! He looked at me and winked and I winked at him and we both knew exactly what had happened. To this day, I think he blames me for him joining Chiltern!

What was remarkable about Chiltern's management team is that the values we have now were the ones that we started with. It's very tempting in an industry which is probably at its lowest point, and on its way up, to get distracted by so many things which are exciting or sexy or headline grabbing. But I think one of the things that Chiltern has always done is remain very true to its values and never got distracted. And I think the most successful businesses right across the world, do what their customers originally wanted very well every time. I'm very proud of the company for doing that because it's very easy, under pressure whether from politicians or customers, to deviate, but we never ever have, and I think that makes us strong.

The next few years were an absolute rollercoaster. We started out in 1994 with a very firm belief that this 'little branch line,' as Network SouthEast had named us, was going to be phenomenally successful and that when the franchise came to be let, we were going to win it. Unlike some other railway companies, we always believed the future of the business depended upon us being able to grow the passenger numbers and consequently grow the revenue, as opposed to slashing the costs, which is what many others believed they had to do. And we watched other industry managers bury their heads in the sand about whether privatisation was ever going to happen. We believed it was – we believed it was the right thing, for both business and customers.

In terms of the highs and lows of the last ten years, the moments that mattered most to me are really the stories of the people and some of the things that Chiltern have managed to do that people always said we couldn't. We've done so many things; I can remember one of the proudest was ordering the new Clubman trains. That was wonderful. I remember standing with Adrian at Derby and we were preparing to make the announcement to the work force at Derby that we had signed with Adtranz, the first order for new trains in the country for nearly four years. By that point in my career I had done a lot of jobs for Chiltern but was then managing the image and communications and so I got to know Adrian at a very early stage. He is a very accomplished public speaker but this was the first time I had ever seen him with a lump in his throat, and actually a little nervous about what he was going to do and say. He said to me, 'Cath, I just want to take five minutes before we go on. Come for a walk with me.' So we went for a walk around the depot and he said, 'I don't know what I am going to say.' I replied: 'Well, what do you want to say?'

'I want to tell them that this is a very important day, because it is about re-starting the manufacturing of rolling stock in this country after a famine. It's about people who thought their careers had gone for the rest of their lives getting another opportunity to bring their experience and skills back into the work place. It's about the first real step across this industry investing in new trains, taking a risk, making a real difference to passengers. That's what I want to say.'

So I said: 'Well, simply say that!'

It was probably one of a handful of public events we have been through together where I had a tear in my eye that day, because Chiltern, this small company, was brave enough to make a huge investment when no one else was, and this was with people's re-mortgaged houses on the line. There was no pot of gold that people were going into, it was money that in those days was created by them through investment and we kick-started something that is now so big. And the trains that were designed for our little railway are now all over the country. That was a really important moment in my career and I am very proud to have been part of that.

I am always proud of the staff who work for Chiltern. Having been at the front line and done most of those jobs in good times and bad, I learnt a long time ago that people put their hearts into the jobs, that it takes a great deal of courage when you are a guard on a train or on a station and something goes wrong and you have three or four hundred people shouting at you and you have no control over what is going on. To actually turn that situation into something that creates praise letters, letters of thanks, takes enormous courage, great talent and a lot of heart. And my staff have that wherever they are so I am constantly impressed by them.

One time when Chiltern stood head and shoulders above any of the big boys was just after the dreadful Ladbroke Grove crash which, contrary to the press, affected the whole industry. We all feel pain, real pain, at the deaths and injuries that happen as the result of an event like that. When the repercussions of that and Hatfield hit the industry, which then started to go into a dive in terms of morale, performance and everything, I remember sitting in a meeting with the commercial directors of all the other train companies. They were telling me how many thousands of customer complaints they had to answer, how their staff sickness was going through the roof because no one was coming in to work, how they could barely pull it together to operate a train service. I said that because they had screwed up all the journeys for all those people, they should take a leap of faith, write to every single one of them and give them a refund of forty pounds, fifty pounds, whatever and apologise and explain the situation and then start again and release their resources to run their railway. But of course they didn't, people didn't have replies, more complaints would have come and they didn't manage that either.

The point of that is our staff sickness reduced during that time! In a time of crisis, all of our staff came into work for weeks and weeks, even though Chiltern had speed restrictions we made the decision to run our full timetable although it caused a lot of pain to my staff, despite getting more complaints than many of them will have ever experienced, they came into work every day with a smile on their face. That was just such a moment I was very proud of. We were all working very long hours to keep the trains running, to keep things going and our ten or eleven years have been littered with stories like that.

Like many talented people, Alex Turner could be a very difficult person to work for. Steve Murphy and I always say we were brought up in the Alex Turner boot camp! Frankly, many people would have walked out on him very early on. But despite that, what was great about Alex was that he had these lapses of confidence because he desperately wanted to get it right. And he believed it so much in his heart; if something matters you have doubts occasionally don't you? And that's what he was like. You have to have the adrenalin, you have to think about it, it has to matter to you and it did to him. I can tell you there were many occasions when my resignation letter was going to be handed in! But Alex taught me a hell of a lot. When things got tough, it was Adrian Shooter's support and faith in us along with his wish to keep Steve Murphy and I within the industry that held us all together.

Alex taught me a huge amount, it was just his energy, his ability to say exactly what he means regardless of the consequence, the total commitment to put passengers first, the ability to fight wars over things that to some would be so small but he knew were very important to the customers, or the business, or staff, to take other operators on over service changes that caused huge headaches in the early days. To rip apart a timetable and start again took an enormous amount of courage because it is a very complicated thing. And when I look back over my time with Alex, I know that I had more good times than bad and along the way we've shared some pretty amazing experiences together!

The sale of the shares was another interesting time for Chiltern. Throughout that episode I was the Chiltern PR adviser writing the messages to staff, passengers and press, so I was quite close to Adrian Shooter and the other directors when the media were giving them a hard and frankly hurtful time with their 'fat cats' accusations. But Adrian was an inspiring leader and all employees respect him. We have always totally agreed that in good times or bad, it is essential to always be open, to always go out on the front foot and tell your story honestly. Of course Adrian didn't sell all his shares. He kept a stake in the business and that was important to him. But something which I think is a real test of the man underneath the persona is the decision Adrian made to share some of the money that he got with all the employees in the business. But he did it in a typically very personal and private way and therefore not many people know of this to this day. All the other directors, being very different characters, reacted in various ways. They were in it for different reasons. I know Adrian found it a sensitive and difficult time, but Adrian is still associated with the company that he loves. Alex Turner had had enough, at the time it was telling on his health and it was time for him to move on. Owen went off and enjoyed his life! He had started as a train driver and never for a moment probably imagined that he would be able to enjoy such a quality of life change. Tony Allen is still with us as finance director. He is still the wonderful bundle of fun and talent he always was!

My own vision for the future of Chiltern? I can't come out with some amazing new perception that everyone else has overlooked! My belief is that its destiny is within its own hands and there is no limit to what it can achieve. I've been told so many times over the years that Chiltern has reached its high, 'there are no more customers, there's little point in investing in more car parks or trains, and you've had the fruits of your labour.' That's just utter nonsense! The Chiltern story proves that railways can grow and be successful, provided they focus on the job in hand and don't try to be something they are not. We are not airlines, we are not in a glamorous business. We're in the business of moving people safely, comfortably and on time for a decent price, on a journey they want to make. And that won't change in the future. In so many ways, Chiltern Railways will continue to be the Chiltern of the last ten years; I think that is absolutely right. That is exactly what our customers want. There are things, however, that we need to refresh and review to ensure we are constantly in touch with our customers. The new trains need more life putting into them. Do we need to offer new services on our trains? Are we still putting enough into the detail of our stations? Why aren't we making more use of technological advances, smart cards, ticketless travel the official way, the use of the internet to help keep things alive and fresh? All of these help us but it is all about the same thing, the same principal values. That's the strategy that I completely buy into and it's the one I intend to continue to deliver, until evidence convinces me otherwise!

From my father I have inherited a fiery and passionate nature. We both believe strongly in what we do, expect extremely high standards and are not frightened of insisting that these are delivered. I always used to laugh with Adrian and say you know I am never ever going to survive twenty years in this industry without being fired! So we used to laugh and I said to him that the only problem was I would really like to get a gold watch because my grandfather was a signalman in Wakefield in Yorkshire and he had a gold watch for completing his twenty years' service with the industry. I said to Adrian, 'Do you think I can have my gold watch early?' I said it as a joke, and he said, 'Okay.' So we had a standing joke that when I got to ten years it would be the same as twenty years. So on my ten-year anniversary we jointly hosted a barbecue and he presented me with a gold watch with the inscription which is now well known, 'in lieu of twenty years' in case I didn't make it!

Cath Proctor, 6 November 2004

Note: Cath Proctor's many contributions to Chiltern's success story include major inputs to the interior design of the new Clubman trains; the design and overall preparation of the refurbished Moor Street station; launching a series of very effective TV ads that were central to making Chiltern a serious competitor to Virgin for the London–Birmingham market; a significant role in the development of Marylebone station into the pleasant environment it is today; inspiring a very effective target-driven approach to booking office sales at all stations; Post-Hatfield when Chiltern, despite all the difficulties with loads of TSRs, continued running their full timetable, Cath Proctor led by example from the front working very long hours alongside the station and operating staff, all remaining at their posts very late each day until all the passengers were safely home. In addition, Proctor also won numerous awards from the marketing and advertising industry and was instrumental in helping Chiltern achieve the series of National Operator of the Year awards won during the last decade.

In 2004 Cath Proctor became managing director of Chiltern upon Steve Murphy's move to Ireland and helped steer Chiltern's successful recovery from the devastating effects of the 2005 Gerrards Cross tunnel collapse, the 7/7 bombings and the Wembley fire. By 2007 her itchy feet got the better of her and she left Chiltern to travel and work on a freelance basis.

She had served fifteen years as a railwayman!

CHAPTER 18

THE PAS' STORIES

Julie Abbott, Merryl Potts and Lesley Knight

Julie Abbott (1994–1996, Alias No. 1 Rottweiler)

The early days

Before joining Chiltern Railways I was already working for British Rail at Derby in their Central Procurement function. With an impending relocation to London I was challenged with the task of looking for a new job and decided to look internally for a suitable vacancy. Back in those days British Rail circulated regular internal vacancy notices and on scanning the pages one day I noticed a job advertised as PA to the managing director of Chiltern Railways. I was immediately drawn to the vacancy as it described Chiltern as a newly formed TOC, which I thought sounded exciting and challenging. I was not to be disappointed!

Following an interview and a series of various tests, I was then invited for an interview with the new managing director Adrian Shooter and his production director, Owen Edgington. Adrian's reputation for being tough but fair to work for was already known around the industry so I had some prior knowledge of him. As there were more than twenty applicants I took along a presentation of my previous work. I was very determined to sell myself well and be the one chosen for the job! It paid off, although I am not sure if it was the presentation that impressed them or my sheer determination to get the job! But I received a telephone call at 'the crack of dawn' the following morning (an Adrian trait) to offer me the position. I was later told by the then personnel manager that Adrian had in fact already decided that I would be his new PA the first time he met me, along with all the candidates. If this was the case he never let it show and made sure he put me through my paces!

There it was then; I was officially Adrian Shooter's PA.

Just before Christmas in 1993 I was invited down to London to meet John Nelson, then managing director for Network SouthEast. At that time Chiltern was a constituent of the joint Thames and Chiltern Division, until they separated at privatisation. Following a pleasant buffet lunch I was presented with a beautiful bouquet of flowers and Adrian made a speech welcoming me to his new company. This increased my enthusiasm for the new job, which was just as well as later that day I got an unexpected taster when upon returning with Adrian to his office at Euston House he found that his temporary PA had not turned up for work and he asked me to stay a couple of hours to make a few 'phone calls and type some letters. I eventually left London at 7.00 p.m. to catch my train back to Derby!

4 January 1994 was my first official day working for Chiltern, still operating from Euston House. I was still commuting from Derby and did so for a couple more months. This I found a particular strain, as I was up at 5.00 a.m. and didn't get home until 9.00 p.m. in the evening.

To say I was 'in at the deep end' from the start would be an understatement; before I had even got my coat off Adrian had a list of demands as long as your arm, from obtaining phone calls to making coffee! Being a new company the management team had not yet been appointed, except for the directors of marketing and operations. The finance director was appointed later and I had some involvement with that one. In the early days my role was very much like a project manager, taking on many tasks, which involved anything from recruitment to procurement. As new managers came on board I ensured that they had the necessary desk, computer, telephone and secretarial back-up. As more and more managers joined the company this became harder to do on my own and later I recruited a small team of secretaries to assist me.

As Adrian's PA at that particular time I found him extremely demanding and the role very stressful at times with no room for error. This was perfectly understandable as Adrian had the task of setting up a 'new business' with a 'new team' and great responsibility; I had to be there for him every step of the way. I had to read and where appropriate, action his post, take calls and diary meetings for him, arrange conferences and foreign visits as well as look after the 'top team' (as they were known in those days). On top of all this, additional pressures, both work related as well as domestic, built up among the senior management team as they got more deeply involved with their management buy-out bid. This meant extra work for me as I often joined them in meetings and conferences and later when I was often required to accompany them on away days, as well as preparing confidential papers. I was also the office manager looking after HQ's stationery requirements, maintenance, landlord liaison, postage, etc., as well as managing a team of secretaries. All in all a very busy job, and, looking back on it, a very tough time.

Move to Aylesbury

Two months into my role the team moved to Aylesbury, which was to become Chiltern's headquarters for the foreseeable future. Adrian was particularly keen that I personally managed this whole process and I agreed to take on the task on the proviso that I could temporarily step down from my own position as his PA. He eventually reluctantly agreed to this and a new agency PA was appointed to take up my position; unfortunately she was a very determined lady, who was quite used to doing things her own way. As you can imagine, this did not fit well with Adrian and he badgered me daily to hurry up the move and come back to him! For me this was one of my greatest early achievements in the role as I personally project managed the move. This involved negotiating lease terms for the office building with the landlord, space planning, instructing and overseeing contractors' refurbishment works, purchasing all office furniture, computers and signage.

I was given a total budget of about £30,000 for the move. This sum had to stretch over the whole redecorating and refurbishment, including all the furniture and fittings as well as computers, photocopiers and all the other office furniture. As we needed thirty computers and a server the money was clearly inadequate. For a while I was stymied but then remembered seeing a pile of old computers dumped in a basement at Euston House! I quickly used my contacts and was invited to help myself to the best; not easy as they all looked rather dirty and discoloured. But the deal was done, a van brought them to Aylesbury and I spent most of a weekend setting up the desks, plugging in the computers, cleaning them and generally making the place look business-like for the staff's first day on the Monday morning. Adrian said he wanted all the computers in place and everything looking ready for the Monday morning. It did! It certainly looked right, but at the time he never knew some of the computers didn't work. Of course, come Monday morning, I got loads of complaints from the staff about their computers particularly from the finance department because their high-tech software wouldn't run on such antiquated equipment! Nevertheless, we had started.

The first year at Chiltern was very exciting, albeit hectic at times. The 'top team' was now in place, with the final appointment of the personnel director, Caroline James. We had also recruited most of the management team and knuckled down to prepare for shadow franchising. There was a buoyant atmosphere and everyone was so enthusiastic and motivated. I have to say ten years on that same enthusiasm and drive to make the Chiltern business a success still exists today.

After eighteen months I felt that my job was done in assisting Adrian with the formation of the company and although I enjoyed working for him personally, I wanted to move on and try something else. With Adrian's full support I took up a brief position with Chiltern Procurement as a buyer. In 1996 I left to have a baby and while on maternity leave Adrian called me and asked me to come and see him. He offered me a new job as property manager, which he thought might help fit in around my new responsibilities of motherhood. Property was at that time outsourced to the then British Rail Property Board and I eagerly took up the challenge to bring it in house and manage it. Adrian made a commitment allowing me to work from home, which I have done ever since!

My spell at Chiltern is the longest I have ever worked for a company and I am proud to say that I enjoy every minute of it. The employees are what make this company so great and such a pleasant place to work. There is a real family atmosphere with everyone sharing the same enthusiasm and commitment, underscored by strong and visionary leadership.

Merryl Potts (1995–1997, Alias No.2 Rottweiler)

The 'mid-way' PA!

At the tail end of 1995, I was working in Aylesbury but looking for a role that would stretch me just that little bit further. I heard of a job for a managing director of a 'forward-thinking' company that had just moved into the private sector, where the present PA was being given the opportunity to 'spread her wings' – what an enlightened view I thought – sounds like the sort of place I would like to work, hence my application to join the Chiltern Railways team.

My interview, which was held in Western House, is where I met Julie for the first time. She explained that this was a 'special job' for a 'special person' – looking after their managing director was no easy feat but would necessitate juggling the office management of Western House at the same time. Just the challenge for me I thought! I returned a couple of days later to meet 'the main man' and his presence filled the room, never mind his stature! I have to say, it was more a talk than an interview and the topic of conversation was varied. It was really a taster of how varied Adrian's working life was, from meetings at Little Kimble and Saunderton stations to Board meetings in the City, to overseas trips to visit Japanese Railways (yes, we have all organised that one!).

My first two weeks, like Lesley after me, were spent organising a two-week self-induction where I was to 'get out, meet the team and report back on how I found the company'. Well, I soon realised that Chiltern's punctuality figures were something to be noted – I had been caught up in a meeting with some of the London team in the offices above Marylebone station and as I rushed on to the platform, I realised I was going to miss my next rendezvous on the 11.18 a.m. departure because it left on time! That was Chiltern all over, I am pleased to say – full of surprises but with very high standards.

The next eighteen months flew by with a wonderfully taxing diary to try and organise, as well as watching the company evolve into a market leader with a great team of people at both its helm and in the engine room!

In mid-1997 I remember being at a company conference passing a comment to a visiting TOC's managing director that I would like to try something new and that sales interested me. But where would you find a company in this day and age that would let you try something new just because you believed you could do it without having a proven track record? Well once again Adrian was that enlightened thinker and he soon offered me the opportunity to rebuild Chiltern's business travel section (just as the new Clubman service was coming on line). And the rest is history – Julie and I were tasked with finding my replacement before I could relinquish my PA duties – we sifted through many CVs and interviewed those who looked good on paper but in person, Lesley was our lady and thankfully, Adrian agreed!

Lesley Knight (1997–to date)

A new beginning

Unbeknown to me Adrian always stipulated that he would only allow his past PAs to move on providing they recruited their successor! Hence my first meeting and introduction to Chiltern Railways was not with Adrian Shooter but a gruelling, though also fun, couple of hours with ex-Rottweillers Julie and Merryl.

They were very committed to the task and used their four years' collective experience to find someone with the personality and business acumen who would complement and fit in with Adrian's stringent requirements. After all they weren't just interviewing for any old managing director!

After that I was handed to the personnel manager and asked to carry out a number of tests, presumably to confirm that I had a brain! That evening Merryl called me at home and asked me to come in for a second interview with Adrian. She spoke at some length, and at the time I was puzzled at why she was so persistent and persuasive. I later discovered that she and Julie were concerned lest their graphic descriptions of a typical day in the life of the managing director's PA might have put me off!

Like most people on meeting Adrian Shooter for the first time, I had an immediate sense of a physically commanding presence with personality and professional manner to match. Despite this initial challenge, as the interview progressed I felt reassured that I would enjoy working with this person. The initial topic was to discuss the company's mission statement and the reasons why I thought it suited the Chiltern business. My response was met with a smile of approval and after several more questions about my employment history, Adrian and I shook hands. As I turned to leave the office, I noted Julie and Merryl gazing through the window with beaming smiles. Later, when Merryl phoned me at home to confirm my appointment, I realised the significance of that handshake as confirmation that the 'big man' was happy. So I joined 'the league of Rottweilers'!

My first week was a somewhat frenetic planned tour of Chiltern Railways, visiting most of its parts and meeting almost all the staff. I had to follow this by writing a detailed report on my findings and what improvements could be made within the business. This was obviously approved of as I was allowed to come back the following week.

Ready to get to grips with my PA role I came in on Monday morning all set to go. I had barely removed my coat when I was summoned by Adrian into his office – armed with notepad, pen and diary I eagerly waited for his instructions. I was instead handed a very thick book, which I soon discovered was ... the National Rail timetable! My mind very quickly took me back to my first interview with Julie and Merryl and what at the time seemed a curious question when they had asked me, 'Have you ever come across a National Rail timetable and if so can you read one!' Was this a joke? Of course not! Adrian was deadly serious, after a quick lesson, he set me the task of planning a journey from Glasgow Central via Hull, changing at Liverpool and onto the Isle of Wight, with a dog in tow! The journey details were to be on his desk within ten minutes. This was to be the first test of many.

The great thing about working for Adrian is that one never knows what challenges will occur next! One result of this is that, paradoxically, one soon begins to discover just how private a person Adrian is away from work and, for a man who can get his head around the most complex technical problems while running a railway, he is surprisingly vulnerable when it comes to computers, mobile phones and even tying a black bow tie!

This was particularly impressed upon me when Adrian called me in one Monday afternoon (he's often at Aylesbury on Monday's, it's his 'catching up day' and also his day for setting me little tasks and challenges!) and greeted me with 'Lesley, I have a little job for you.' (always a bad omen!) 'I have a new mobile phone.' He then showed me a very pretty and very small delicate pale blue phone, which of course in Adrian's hand looked even smaller.

'Oh, that's very nice' I said, wondering at the same time how on earth his substantial fingers would manage to press the minuscule buttons!

'Well, I'd like you to know it a little better!'

'Ok, what's that?'

'I've got to enter everyone's name and phone number into it, so I'd like you to take it away with you. Here's the instruction booklet and if you could read that and come back in an hour or so, we will sit down for the afternoon and load and record all the names and numbers onto the 'phone.'

That was fine except it was also nerve-wracking for me as I'm not too au fait with latest mobile phone technology myself. Nevertheless, I thought, 'Great, I can load it all on, type all the numbers in', but no, he wanted to be able to sit there and hold this phone, it had a wonderful new mechanism whereby all you did was just say the name of the person you wanted to call into the phone. But that meant I had then to come into Adrian's office, sit for two hours, having only just read the manual on how this new phone worked, so that I could type the number in and hand the phone to Adrian so he in turn could speak the number, it being voice recognition. So I sat there for two hours, prompting him with 'now Adrian, now' at which he would call out, for example, 'Cath, mobile,' or 'Cath, home' and we went through this for two hours until he'd got all the executive and other important numbers in the 'phone. Quite a pressurised afternoon!

A couple of days later I detected intimations of a certain kind of frustration coming from Adrian's office, punctuated by loud cries of 'Mark, mobile, Mark, mobile!' repeated again and again. We got that sorted and at the conclusion of the next executive meeting he was able to show off his new toy by setting off their mobile phones one by one after simply calling their names!

Recently, a huge catering pack of Uncle Ben's Rice was delivered to the Aylesbury office addressed to Adrian Shooter. After I'd opened it and discovered what it was, I went to Adrian and asked what he wanted doing with it?

'Well Lesley, you'd better see if there's a needy person within the office who likes eating an abundance of rice!'

That was okay because I knew there was one guy who is a vegetarian so I asked him. 'Yes, that's great, I'll have it, thanks.' One week later I got a call from Uncle Ben's Rice to ask what Adrian Shooter thought of it. I explained that he had given it to a member of staff because he did not require a catering pack of rice. The person the other end of the phone sounded puzzled.

'Why not? We understand he is the chef and does all the cooking for the company!'

Adrian looked thoughtful when this dialogue was reported back to him and wryly observed he didn't think his duties as company chairman stretched quite that far!

In 2004 Adrian opened own private garden railway, which created some interest in the media since the beautifully restored little locomotive came from the Darjeeling Himalayan Railway in India. I was standing there on opening day reflecting on all the rules and regulations that I'd typed up to ensure its safe operation, when one of the people who had been involved with restoring the engine came over and thanked me for the wheel-sets I'd made for him out of card. He said they were wonderful, perfect and exactly the right size and worked really well! For a moment I was nonplussed until I remembered Adrian coming up to me early one morning at Marylebone – and again this was a job that had to be done instantaneously – and drew on a piece of white paper this shape with just the measurements on it and said:

'Right, Lesley, I'd like you to go away and make me four of those, two like this and two like that, out of card. They will be collected within the hour and they are going off to be used as the template for my wheel sets.'

This wasn't easy, especially as we were at Marylebone at the time where it is not always easy to lay one's hands on what one needs, but eventually I found some cardboard, not quite the correct size or thickness, but with the aid of Sellotape I cut out the wheel-sets and off they went. Just another example of the unexpected things one has to do in a very short space of time!

Naturally, just as Adrian's role has evolved during my six years in post, so has the nature of my little challenges! He became chairman of both parent company Laing Rail as well as being chairman of Chiltern Railways. By 2009 he was executive chairman as Chiltern starts a new chapter as part of DB. He now has a much higher profile within the rail industry both in the UK and internationally. Managing all these often conflicting commitments and keeping his diary straight on a day-to-day basis is now a full-time task in itself and I am thankful for my own administrative assistant and many other colleagues. Along with all the numerous Board and committee meetings, we have such things as the UK–Japanese Railways exchange programme which involves many

Lesley Knight unveiling
the nameplate on
Chiltern's latest
locomotive, Aylesbury
depot, October 2009.
(Chiltern Railways)

complicated travel schedules and programmes of visits for our Japanese guests. And when at my
initial interview I'd been asked if I spoke Japanese and liked sushi I thought they had been joking!

Chiltern Railways itself continued to grow under the leadership of Cath Proctor while she
was managing director but sadly, she eventually felt a need to move on, as did Mark Beckett. We
continue to grow as part of Deutsche Bahn and now employ three times the number of staff than
when I first arrived. During my time its forward-thinking strategies have taken it from strength to
strength – it has earned many accolades and although my life seems ever more hectic, I have truly
enjoyed the last twelve years. The impressions I gained during that first induction week of the
enthusiasm, hard work and sheer professional commitment of staff at all levels has not changed and
I feel proud to be part of the team.

CHAPTER 19

THE DRIVER'S STORY

David Newell

My motivation was just a love of railways which was not surprising as I came from a railway family. For example, when I was just six or seven years old, and I was living near Upminster in Essex in 1958, one summer's evening I went for a walk across the park and wound up in the car park of Roomes department store watching a steam engine sitting by a ground shunt signal. This steam engine wasn't going to move; I wasn't going to move! Eventually I came home just as it was getting dark. I'd always wanted to be a train driver and I remember coming home, although by this time my mother was in tears and all the neighbours were getting their cars out to come and look for me. I was really in trouble! By a coincidence, one of the neighbours who was out looking for me is now chairman of a businessmen's club in Hornchurch, for whom I occasionally do talks and takes great delight in telling this story.

But the mould was set. I wanted to come on the railways and I joined British Rail on 3 January 1972, passed for driving June 1975 and I learned all the routes in East Anglia I was allowed to go on, because at the time I was a junior driver. If you knew the traction and signed for the route you did it, so I was going to Liverpool Street, Kings Lynn, March, Norwich, Bury St Edmunds, Harwich and all the London area. It was all diesel or electric by then but bear in mind that steam was still fresh in the memory. Steam had finished on British Rail in 1968 so I missed steam by four years.

I had some really good men looking after me and if you showed an interest they pushed you in the right direction. I was taught to drive and it went on from there. Then along came sectorisation in British Rail and I elected to stay with what became known as Network SouthEast. Once again I was having a good life. I was going to Liverpool Street, Kings Lynn, Ipswich, Harwich, Clacton, Walton on the Naze and suburban work in all the London area.

Then privatisation loomed up and the work was divided up so you either had to go to a Great Eastern depot, which in my case would have been Ilford and Gidea Park, or I could have gone to a West Anglia depot though half of them were shut by then, so I thought, well, I'd already had a move into the top link, known as the Norwich link, which is now the London base of Anglia Railways. But at that time there was talk that it was not going to exist any more with the possibility of redundancies so it might not have been so secure.

Therefore I looked around at other London depots and came to Marylebone one day, was shown around by the supervisor and just fell in love with the place. That was in 1993. There was an atmosphere, there was a buzz, and it was a smaller railway; everybody seemed to know everybody else. There was a happy atmosphere on Chiltern Railways, then part of British Rail London Midland Region, and a sense of independence. There was 222 Marylebone Road, British Rail Board Headquarters, affectionately known as the Kremlin, just across the road, but here was a railway more or less pleasing itself what it did. I thought I can't wait to get here!

So I put in for a move – that was 1993, after the Chiltern line modernisation was complete. Off peak we had an hourly service to High Wycombe, an hourly service to Banbury and a branch line shuttle between Princes Risborough and Aylesbury. Down what we call 'The Met' which is Marylebone, Harrow, Amersham, Aylesbury, we had a half-hourly off-peak service. We had modernised with thirty-nine class 165 Turbo trains. The thing that did annoy me was Roger MacDonald and Thames Trains walking off with 165s numbers 001, 002, 003, 004, 005, 006 and 007. We got 006 and 007 back but for some reason 007 had to remain with the Thames logo on the side. So in effect they purloined five trains we badly needed. .

But all in all it was a very enjoyable place to be. I remember learning the traction at Old Oak depot with John Davidge the traction inspector who taught me the 165s and then I had a period of route learning. I remember getting to Princes Risborough one day and there was a line off to the left and I thought 'Where does that go?' So I thought I'd better go and have a look. It was a half mile long siding down to Thame Junction. Being a railway enthusiast I researched the history and realised that one way went to Thame and Oxford and the left went to Aston Rowant and Watlington. I walked around there and got a thorough soaking for my troubles because the heavens opened so I then came back and decided to learn Princes Risborough to Aylesbury and I went backwards and forwards through Monks Risborough and Little Kimble and from that decided then I was concentrating on Marylebone to Princes Risborough and Thame Junction to Aylesbury and also the Met. I learned the route to Banbury after that and I remember going in front of an inspector, Alfie Bryant, who came back as a driver, being asked questions on the route; he wanted to know the turn-back points, as well as the speed restrictions, signals, etc. Then came the day when I was to be turned loose on the Chiltern Railways public!

Now I have to tell you that coming from where I did before, on the Liverpool Street Division as was, this was a total physical and mental culture shock. For a start, I couldn't get my head around this railway. Liverpool Street to Gidea Park is fourteen miles. There were about eighty signals. Amersham to Aylesbury is also about fourteen miles; just three signals and one is the distant signal that protects the station at Aylesbury. Coming out of Liverpool Street through Romford and up Brentwood Bank is virtually dead straight. On our Chiltern line we don't stay level for very long and we twist and curve around all over the place. The kind of passengers we carry and the public you are meeting are different. I have met and still know some of the passengers on the Romford and Emerson Park and of course I live amongst them now, but on this line people would talk to you; the pace of life seemed to be slower. Commuters will come up and say, 'We like travelling on your train driver, we can guarantee a seat!' They express appreciation of polite drivers making public address announcements and of course the new trains. The Chiltern Railways' mission statement – telling other people of the good service so they will pass it on to others, and thereby growing our business by word of mouth – is working.

So, after getting used to the idea, it was on 7 March 1994, yours truly gets two 165s coupled together on the 17:12 to Aylesbury via Amersham. Although I'd been driving trains all these years, I was nervous, of course I was; I'd signed the route, I was on a completely different railway, and this was it, you're on your own, you're in command, you're going! Away we went; I had a trouble-free trip there and back and for the rest of the diagram. I do enjoy it and get a kick out of it even now.

When I first went to Marylebone, it felt interesting and I thought I'd like to be part of this. At the time, Adrian Shooter had just arrived and was in charge, but Chiltern was still part of British Rail Network SouthEast and under the overall control of managing director, John Nelson. I'd first come across John Nelson some time before this, when he was observing what I was up to at Ipswich one day with a Great Eastern train when we got a signals delay and I was keeping the public up to date and finding out what was going on. Of course, I didn't know who he was then and possibly he didn't know who I was but I've since met him at the Chiltern Railways annual staff barbecue.

Bearing in mind that although Chiltern Railways was a separate entity and we more or less pleased ourselves what we did south of Aynho Junction, even further north the impression was that we were a railway that was different. I'm not spinning any yarn here, I sincerely mean this, and I'll digress to illustrate the point. I travel widely around the country and, like any railway person, I will be prepared to offer help in an appropriate situation. For example, at York one day, to say something like, 'I'm an off-duty Chiltern Railways driver, could you please make sure this disabled lady gets her connection to Malton?' you're likely to get the reply: 'Oh, Chiltern Railways, yes certainly I'll do that for you, no problem.'

One of my most striking memories of this was one day when I was in Scotland visiting an aunt of mine, Dad's sister-in-law. Usually I stay with a cousin, I call her my big sister, Marion at West Kilbride, but I decided this time I was going to stay in a hotel and go and visit the relations from there.

I was at Ardrossan South Beach, my train was half an hour late because of a track-circuit failure and there were 150 Glaswegians on the platform and they're having a go at the driver, because they were all trying to go to Stranraer harbour for the boat to Northern Ireland and had been put on the wrong train. As I walked past I thought 'No, you can't do it!' So I went back, got my pass out, introduced myself to the driver and asked if I could help. He said 'I don't know what to do with these people!'

So I shouted to all the people, 'Ladies and gentlemen, please stand well back from the platform edge, the train is moving.' 'Oh thanks pal, thanks, I can go!' so he shut the doors and drove off to Largs.

I put my orange vest on and went down to the signal post phone and rang the box and a voice said, 'Aye?'

I said, 'Is that the power box supervisor please?'

'Who are you?'

'I'm train driver David Newell, Chiltern Railways, London Marylebone, Schools Safety Adviser and I'm on holiday, but you've got big problems up here! I've got a high-visibility vest on so it's alright.'

He said, 'Are you all right with the public?'

'I've been told I'm all right with the public! What do you want me to do?'

'Can you look after the passengers? The Ardrossan Town driver has already said that instead of having a meal break he's going to come back "all stations" to Kilwinning and the Stranraer boat train will stop specially at Kilwinning to pick all these people up.'

And I said, 'Box supervisor, I'm asking you, and I'm asking you now, you're not lying are you?'

He said, 'What kind of question is that?'

I said, 'because when this train to Glasgow gets back here from Ardrossan Town, if that Stranraer boat train does not stop at Kilwinning, they'll take Kilwinning station apart, the train and the driver with it!'

And he said 'No son, I can guarantee that train will stop!'

'All right, then I'll tell them.' Now first of all I'd left my bag with some Scots I'd got talking to and it only turned out they'd got relations in Hornchurch where I live now, how about that for a small world! So the other train comes in and I'm waiting for the driver who said: 'Who the hell are you, you're English?'

I said, 'I'm on holiday, and all these people are okay' and all the people on the platform were saying, and I love this bit, 'Who are you, where are you from?'

I said, 'Chiltern Railways, London Marylebone, you must have heard of us! We are The Railway out of London!'

'Oh yes, we saw something about you on the news.'

To cut a long story short, they all loaded on the train, all waving and saying, 'Cheerio and thank you very much' and I went to the hotel just twenty-five minutes later than I would have done.

You see, there's one thing about this railway, it lets you be the individual you want to be. I've been told that the work I do in schools with retired driver, Michael Benson, gets across well to the children. We're known as Batman and Robin, although we don't tell them that until we've got them in front of us. We teach from reception up to nineteen year olds, so we usually stop the Batman and Robin routine by the time they are about thirteen. But it works and we indirectly market Chiltern Railways, as well as teach railway safety. On another visit to my cousin in Scotland I was persuaded to do a session at her daughter's primary school for which of course I had to square it first with the ScotRail marketing manager.

Along with other colleagues such as Mike and Mrs Cooper from the retail side we also run stalls at summer fairs at places like Princes Risborough and Bledlow. Also Dave, the regular bus driver is there with the Chinnor Link bus so we are selling ourselves in the community. Alex Turner and Adrian wanted this railway to go as a community railway and let's face it, that's what it is. So I am quite prepared to walk down Banbury High Street and wear the uniform and people will look at you and say 'Oh, Chiltern' and when you are away from your own railway, you are still held in high esteem as if you are a railway that knows what it is doing and going somewhere. Other companies may not have the same rapport with the public. We certainly have and it gives me a buzz. I really do just love going to work every day!

My satisfaction with working on the railways probably has something to do with the fact that it's a single right of way, it's a disciplined environment, you are serving the community, you are serving real people, and if you are carrying freight you are serving real business. From the driver's point of view you are your own master, provided you work within the parameters you are set. People come to you to travel to where they need to go and you are performing a service to the community. Although I like my train full of passengers, whether full or lightly loaded I am happy to run all day to provide a service for the public. People have a choice and it's crucial to offer a safe, disciplined, regular travel environment to encourage people to use the trains when they need to travel.

From my point of view it's the independence, it's the discipline, it's the people you meet, and it's just the buzz you get. This buzz, if I could bottle it, I would!

David Newell, 2004

(David Newell continues to enjoy driving on Chiltern Railways.)

CHAPTER 20

THE SCHOOL SAFETY OFFICER'S STORY

Driver Mick Benson

I was born and grew up at Berwick on Tweed. My step-father got me on to the railway for the simple reason that he was a gaffer, an inspector on the railways up north. At the time I was learning to be a policeman but had an accident. The money the railway cleaners were getting was a lot more than I was getting at the police academy, so I transferred to the railway.

I was sent down from up home in Tweedmouth to Newport in Middlesborough and I was cleaning engines down there and firing at the same time. After about two and a half years I was made a fireman and I was firing on Q6s, J26s, J39s, B1s, K1s, K3s, L1s,V2s,A1s,A3s, all these North Eastern engines at Newport going up to Leeds. Then we were put on to testing the Garrett for six months, which was built at Eaglescliffe near Stockton on Tees and we used to give it a run out. Then I was made redundant at Newport and moved to Thornaby, because five different loco sheds of Saltburn, Middlesborough, Haverton Hill, Newport and Redcar were all closed down. Most of the work up there at the time was with the steel companies, running steel, iron ore and the likes to the smelting works, and all the engines went into the one big shed at Thornaby. I was made redundant on the Saturday at Newport and started at 00:01 the following morning at Thornaby loco shed next door. I was one of the first men to start work at the new shed, worked there for about two or three years then moved on redundancy again to Sowerby Bridge and the passenger trains to Leeds, Liverpool, Manchester and Todmorden and Blackpool.

While at Sowerby Bridge, I suffered burns in a blow-back on a steam engine. The medical officer advised me to move because every time I went over the line where it happened, I was getting nervous. So I moved to Consett, Co. Durham, living at Railway Cottages, Langley Park, one of the old stations that were closed along the line from Consett to Darlington. I worked from there with Q6s and 9Fs. We used to work two 9Fs on the iron ore trains from Tyne Dock, one on the front and we would stop at a yard on a certain point along the line and we would have another 9F come up on the back of us. We only had nine wagons and we were guaranteed the road from the bottom of the bank right up to the gantry at Consett iron works, because if we had stopped we would never have got started again! It used to take a lot of power just for those nine wagons. We would get them on the gantry at Consett and just flick a lever and they were all unloaded automatically, the power coming from the Westinghouse steam pump on the engine. The iron ore would go straight out down into the pit underneath. By the time you got to the far end and stopped, you'd nearly emptied all the iron ore. You just closed the doors and the engine would back out and you'd go on your way.

Then I came to Old Oak Common. That was a culture shock. It took me years to get used to living in London. To start with I lived in the hostel. Then after a year I got a house and my wife and children moved down. Many of the loco men were old Great Western men and my first driver was 'Cannon Ball' Stacey, an ex-marine from Plymouth. With my seniority I went straight into the Top Link and I was on the double home working to Plymouth. I also worked the 'Bristolian', by then mostly diesel hydraulics. Sometimes I would get a steam engine, a 'Castle' or a 'Hall' class. All the 'Kings' had been taken out of service by then and a few were on the private railways. I once fired a 'King' but didn't like it.

When I first started firing on the 'Western' I got the biggest shock of my life to see their firing shovel. It was a lot different to a North Eastern shovel. But it all comes back. Then I was taken off the good bits, main line working, because drivers that were passed for steam were getting a bit short and I had to start doing driving turns, as a passed fireman, up and down pilot working from Old Oak Common to Paddington with the coaches. My mate wasn't very happy with that because we used to work as a team, one of us would drive down to Plymouth and one of us would drive back. It used to work lovely but if I was taken off, my mate would have to do the driving both ways.

Comparing North Eastern with Great Western engines, I drove 'Castles' and 'Halls'. The Great Western engines were good engines but they were a bit heavy on coal. They used to use what we called steam coal, whereas up north we had a coal that was a lot harder. The Western engines used to burn a large amount of coal and if you didn't watch the clinker it could be very hard on the fireman's back. Once you've driven a steam engine they're basically all the same, just a different layout and driving position. You got to know different steam engines because you could have a good one, you could have a bad one and you could have a right damn rotter! If you went on and you were told that that was the engine you had, that spoilt your day for a start. Every engine had its characteristics. Nowadays you get on the trains and they're all the same. The things that I miss on the railways are the steam. The last steam engine that I ever drove was when I was just over sixty-four on a day out with a friend on the Severn Valley Railway and it brought everything back to me. I thoroughly enjoyed it. There's nothing like the smell of smoke and steam. It's a lovely smell.

From Old Oak Common, I came to do a spell on the Southern. I was going to be made a driver at Old Oak Common and I was going to be stuck on the 'Pilots' for a good few years and I didn't fancy that so I took the job at Wallington, between West Croydon and Sutton on the Southern, driving electrics on the third rail. Then I was moved from Wallington to London Bridge and had three years at London Bridge working to Brighton, Eastbourne, Hastings, down to Bognor Regis and Littlehampton.

Today, as a retired driver, I teach child safety on the railways. I've been doing it for nigh thirty years. I like to think that I'm saving a life; that gets through to the children that play on the railway because nowadays the trains you can't hear them, not like the old steam engines, and if you're playing on the railways nowadays, the speed of the trains means they will come on top of you in no time and there's no chance a child can get away from it.

My work with child safety on the railways all started when I was still up north. I was doing my turn as a fireman with my driver in the early days. We went down the line one day with a diesel, doing about seventy miles an hour and a group of five children was playing on the track. We killed four and the fifth has been in a wheelchair for the rest of his days. I always said after that that was something I would have to live with that for the rest of my life and I didn't fancy my mates, friends and that getting it but I was given the opportunity to help the children in school. I would do half a day's work, about four or five hours, then spend the other half talking to the children in the schools around the north about the railways. I made a bit of a career out of it, I loved doing it. I find I can get through to about 75 per cent of the children. That other 25 per cent, no matter how hard I try, I can't. But it eventually does. Perhaps three years later, at the same school, those children who were the least attentive previously can now be the first to shoot their hands up and be shouting and screaming to answer the question. I have loved doing it because, to me, you can't put a price on a child's head.

I met up with David Newell when he first came over from Stratford and worked with me at Marylebone. I had recently transferred from the Southern because I was then living at St John's Wood and was getting fed up with the travelling across London just to get to work. I still had a few years left. When I came to Marylebone it was still under British Rail. It was classed as the Chiltern line then after privatisation it was Chiltern Railways but even in British Rail days it was always more like a family concern. Aylesbury, Marylebone, Banbury at first then we started to go back to Birmingham.

I've got lots of friends on the railway. It's amazing how things come around in circles; because I used to run trains as a passed fireman, from Paddington to Bicester, Banbury and Birmingham Snow Hill which was the old station in them days, through to Wolverhampton, through to Shrewsbury, it was all double track then. When I came back from the Southern to Marylebone and started working down that track again, a lot of it was then single track. I worked on that line when it was double track, single track then double track now that it's a proper railway once more! It's one of the best railway companies. All the passengers have praise for it.

David Newell and I went into the classrooms together. We found you get on a lot better with the children if you don't pretend to be superior. Starting off we introduced ourselves by our names, Mr Newell and Mr Benson, but after a while we asked the children if they would like to call us by our nicknames, Batman and Robin. That's how most of the children in Oxfordshire and Buckinghamshire knew us. One of the nice things is when teenagers whom we taught some years before would come up and thank us for what they learnt, a marvellous feeling.

We would talk about electricity, both overhead and third rail, about crossings and the need to think to take the same precautions as in the Highway Code for crossing a road; look, listen, look again and walk across rather than run to reduce the risk of slipping. After all, if you fall over, the next person to find you could well be the train driver. If you drop something, leave it, carry on, and don't stop to pick it up. Then we'd play a little game and get two children out; twins are best if there are some in the class, as one twin will always go to aid the other twin. We'd also involve the teacher and sketch a scenario where one of the children, who is a little devil, just as I was, climbs over the bank and runs down on to the railway line. We'd ask what the teacher would do and invariably the teacher would say they'd go down to try and assist the child on the line. We'd then ask the other child what they would do. If it was a twin they would also say they would go to help. What we hadn't reminded them was that the line was third rail electric so both the child and teacher on the line could well be electrocuted. What should be done first is to dial 999 and ask for help. I wouldn't tell them the answer, I wanted them to realise for themselves that they had to get help. How do they get help? They telephone 999. I'd also get them to work out what to do if the telephone is out of order, to look around and look out for a house with telephone wires going into it and get the people in the house to make the call for them, warning them not to go into a stranger's house on their own. 'Stranger = danger, etc.'

After third rail, we would deal with overhead wire electrification at 25,000 volts and tell the children how they don't even have to touch the wire, they've only got to get within nine or ten feet of it and the electricity can jump and kill you. The third rail is direct current and will hold you like a magnet and no matter how much you pull you will never get away from it. It's very dangerous stuff and if parents aren't keeping an eye on what their children are doing and they are wandering around and getting on the railway, they can get killed.

Chiltern Railways is the only train operating company putting money into railway safety lessons in schools. Network Rail do some work but with Dave and me have been able to give the driver's point of view, which seems to carry more weight with the children than someone just out of the office, and Adrian Shooter, the Chiltern Railways chairman, is all for railway safety.

Mick Benson, February 2004

(Sadly, as the finishing touches being put on this book, Mick Benson passed away on 3 April 2010.)

CHAPTER 21

THE STATION MASTER'S STORY

Donald Wilson

I was born, brought up and attended school in
Wimbledon, south-west London. After A Levels I went
to work, having opted out of university. I was a bit lazy
you see. My mother wanted me to be an accountant but
it didn't appeal. But I liked French so I got a job as an
office junior in a French company just two blocks away
in Crawford Street. They specialised in floor coverings
with factories in France at Lyon and also in Ireland and
other places. After twenty-odd years, there I was the
supplies manager dealing with things like warehous-
ing and distribution, transport, customer service, special
orders and all that sort of thing. There was a variety of
work including using my French-speaking in the factory every day. So that was my background until the
company was taken over and absorbed into part of BP
in 1987. My boss retired and a new boss came in who
didn't like about half a dozen of us, and basically I got
a cheque with lots of noughts on, which I then photo-
graphed and promptly had a year off and went travelling.
This was spring 1988. So I then had my gap year trav-

elling with a friend in South America. We went to Buenos Aires for three months and around
Argentina, Paraguay, all over the place, then Brazil. When I came back I went off to India, Pakistan
and the Khyber Pass.

When I returned that October I spotted an advertisement for a part-time station announcer
at Marylebone station, 3.30–7.00 p.m. I thought this is a nice cushy number! It sounded interesting. Meanwhile, the company I had worked for, as part of their pay off, had got a firm of
head-hunters sending me details of all these high-powered jobs for which they wished me to
go for interview. I said, 'Oh no, I'm just taking it easy at the moment.' and went for this part-
time job just really for interest. I'd always had an interest in railways ever since I was put on the
footplate of a steam engine at the tender age of six, so basically, I thought this would be a fun job
to do, part time, and spend the rest of the time doing up the property in which I had invested
my money. Then British Rail wanted to make the job full time and I didn't want to go full time
doing station announcements. It was only fun until something went wrong. In those days we had
the old trains, no radios and manual signal boxes. Everything was different and we only had half
the number of passengers we have now. By 7 p.m. the place was dead and you could hear the
birds singing in the roof during the summer.

Then my parents became ill so I went home and looked after them. British Rail sent me to Reading to work in customer services, where I personally looked after all the Chiltern letters. They gave me a laptop so I could work from home and just went to Reading twice a week, combining the work with looking after my parents. Rail privatisation was then announced and the company was split away from Thames in 1994.

I chose to go to Chiltern, so I went up to the office in Aylesbury, doing exactly the same thing as before. Then the job here as station manager was advertised in September of 1994. Cath Proctor was my predecessor whom I'd first known as a management trainee at Reading. She was station manager here in 1994 and I took over from her when she went to sales and marketing. When I started here in November of 1994 it was really a quiet railway and nothing like the hectic place it is now. My memories of starting here include sitting in what was then the announcer's spot and drinking more cups of tea than ever before in my life. We also had a cleaning lady, who used to sit in here and only went out to clean the toilets when someone came and complained! We had another chap, a porter whose job it was to light the oil lamps for the signals. His other job was to help the disabled but every time a disabled person came, he didn't want to know, so I used to go out and help them and all that kind of thing used to go on. In a way it was all quite funny and gave me a tremendous insight and of course endless stories about the railway.

As the railway grew so did my interest and I developed a small team. At first we had no separate ticket office of our own and all our tickets were sold by London Underground on a commission basis. This was because the station was earmarked for closure in 1985 but the change in its fortunes caused investment to happen. Of course, as soon as we began to build up the business it was getting almost impossible to control the passengers without our own office; the Underground had huge great queues at their window, so we quickly had two ticket machines put in. Then I managed to persuade Adrian that we should have what was referred to as a 'carbuncle' on the concourse, a PortaKabin, for our own ticket office and it started to take phenomenal amounts of money. Then we realised just how much we really had been losing out.

I also began to have a different vision for the job – in the rush hour we should be out there to help people because, if there had been a problem in the morning, people wouldn't want to stop and talk to you then, as they were on their way to work. But they would speak to you in the evening, so I tried to develop a higher profile. If I hadn't got the answer for the customer I would try to find out and they could come and ask me the next day. The whole idea of that was to save writing letters, which are quite expensive to research and answer, and also I could answer many of their queries immediately. For example, a common question is 'Which is a front train?' when we have to run two trains from the same platform. 'Is it the one I come to first or the one at the far end?' It's the reassurance people want. The regular commuters know where to go but more and more we were bringing in casual passengers and they need reassurance.

We worked very hard at Marylebone building up the team and when we had the new development done we had an office with five ticket windows. Putting in ticket gates helped people, as well as increasing our revenue enormously in that first period. Our sales to Wembley Stadium went up from fifty a week to 300 a week. Sadly, there will always be people who will cheat and in time we became quite cunning at getting hold of them, often with the help of our computer records – for example, when they live in Great Missenden and ask for a 'zones one-to-six' travel card!

Now the most difficult thing in the rush hours is to try and turn the trains around in time. So it's a constant challenge with all the staff, ticket office, station announcers, dispatching staff, and dealing with all the tenants, as well as rubbish disposal, deliveries, parking – all those kinds of things, not forgetting the security and safety of the station. We rent the station from Network Rail, and Marylebone is the only London terminal station which is tenanted.

One of the high spots was the centenary of the station in 1999. We had a centenary luncheon in the Landmark Hotel opposite for 350 guests, which was wonderful. Guest of honour was Edgar Fay QC, the son of Sir Sam Fay the general manager of the Great Central Railway, who at the age of ninety gave a twenty-minute speech without referring to any notes. The another 'high' was September 1994 when Marylebone was awarded the 'best station in the UK' award in the medium category at the National Rail awards at the Grosvenor House hotel. We worked very hard at that. Basically, the whole thing was a matter of housekeeping, keeping the place clean, getting the co-operation of the tenants and generally keeping the place ship-shape and maintaining a welcoming atmosphere. Other highlights included greeting royalty – Princess Margaret's been here. Most recently the Duke of Kent came wanting to travel in an ordinary train. I greeted him at the station front and chatted to him in the train before it left. Seeing as he's also interested in railways he purchased some books at W.H. Smith. Also Jack Straw has been seen here, as has Glenda Jackson and other transport ministers at various times as they are always changing. Barbara Castle used to come through here a lot and always used to call me 'My dear!' when she saw me. I always used to give her my arm and we would walk down to the train together. She was very sweet – a very small lady, but a wonderful speaker. She had a sharp mind even into her nineties.

Among my worst moments I suppose are crowds, particularly football crowds, which are very difficult to manage, also fire alarms and evacuating the station and things like that, which are always a worrying responsibility.

Nowadays the station master has to get involved with everything, rubbish disposal, the lot. One also has to deal with the local residents, the Marylebone Society, Westminster Council, by keeping a profile among the local population so that if anything happens such as concern at the volume of station announcements, they come and talk to me first. Basically, it's trying to be a good neighbour. An important part of that is maintaining good relations with the churches and schools. We do practice safety on the railway for the children and I often have school tours here. Two or three times a year the little tots come around and see the station. I take them into the cab and get them to blow the horn and get them to promise to be train drivers when they grow up. They love all that.

Carol singing at Christmas, organising the Christmas tree, it's all part of it, all non-stop and far too much work really. There is never enough staff. It's a challenge and keeps one's mind active!

In my holidays I travel very widely around the world. For example, recently I went to Peru and right up into the Andes. I am going out to Poland, for a new experience. There one can pay to drive one of the steam trains that are still left as a training experience. I thought I'd better do it before the EU stop it as a dangerous practice! I do a variety of other things, including lectures about the Kent and East Sussex Railway and also the Great Central Railway to various railway groups. Also I do lectures on my travels and write magazine articles. Recently, I've written on Sweden and Norway in the book about *Great Railway Journeys of Europe*. I also do a lot of photography and just love travelling, hoping to do much more of it when I finish work.

Also, for fifteen years I've been a driver on the West Somerset Railway between Minehead and Taunton, driving the old diesel trains which by coincidence in their British Rail days also used to work on the Chiltern line. I was first invited down to help when they were in a very bad way and I've stuck with it. Each year I have eight or ten days when I go down and help them. It's a twenty-mile line, run very professionally. I've gone down occasionally with Adrian Shooter. He used to be the manager of the Bletchley depot where, in times past, these old trains were maintained. Amazingly, at Minehead he saw the numbers on the coaches and knew each one of them individually! It's a very responsible hobby but very relaxing because it's away from London and it's something I enjoy doing. I'm not someone to sit on the beach all day, that's not my scene at all. But I enjoy having children sitting behind me and looking at all the animals, the deer and the pheasants that go past. It's great fun and exciting because the children see a great big wheel in front, which is the parking brake and they say, 'Please sir, what's that?' To which I say 'You tell me! It's not your Dad's car; what do you think the rails do?' They all think then and the parents come and thank you for making the whole thing interesting for them, so I keep myself busy, always charging around the place.

Donald Wilson, March 2004

(Donald Wilson retired in 2007.)

CHAPTER 22

DESIGNING THE CHILTERN CLUBMANS: THE TRAIN DESIGNER'S STORY

Neil Bates, Creactive Design

In the beginning, it was us who approached Chiltern Railways. We wrote to Alex Turner to say we understood Chiltern was in the market to develop some new trains and we thought our skills could be very important because they would be going to a train manufacturer who will want to sell Chiltern a train 'off the shelf' which may not necessarily be the one you want to operate, and that's where we come in. The 'one design fits all' approach doesn't work because the requirements for something that's working say from Leamington to Birmingham or Hatfield into London is going to be quite a different proposition than a vehicle that's running between Birmingham and London.

The demands of the vehicle have to reflect the people that patronise the service. We've got to have a measure of what is important and what makes it attractive to customers. We need to know everything about them. Chiltern are very good at this, they actually know a great deal about their customers; some railway companies don't but these guys do, and when we first started working with them they had a pretty good picture, though not yet complete, from the design perspective.

Turner quite ably took on some research. We did the original qualitative research for the Clubmans but Cath Proctor had subsequent research done by others, usually by Oxford Research. We had to draw from small qualitative groups the kind of 'steers' that as designers we need. Designers tend to feel the need to leave their mark but I don't think that works in trains because if it is obvious to the passenger then the designer has probably missed an opportunity. I believe that the best designed trains are the ones that don't look as though a designer has been anywhere near them! It's just fine; people get on with what they do on trains: eating, sleeping, drinking and reading. I think the worst excesses of design, certainly in public transport, are often there because someone is trying to make a statement of some sort.

Running a railway is quite a difficult enterprise and although I went into fine art, I actually trained in maths, physics and chemistry and did a year of an Open University engineering course, so I understand engineering, but choose not to as I've got engineers around to help me do that. However, running a railway is quite a different matter; safety is an absolute and working alongside career railway people like Adrian Shooter and Andy Hamilton, one realises just how much care and absolute effort goes into that. We turn up as and when we are needed to do the things we do. We dovetail ourselves into the company so that we fit and understand the relationships and the people we have to work with. If we are dealing with an issue of functionality on a train, ergonomics and space, or the ability to read a passenger information display or the ability to reach and hold something safely, then they will take our advice and guidance on it. A lot of practicality and common sense is needed and thankfully most people in railway companies have it in abundance! But at the end of it, most of the important decisions are emotionally driven and you need to quantify that, which is where all this research that's sitting in front of me, the designer, comes in.

Turner broke new ground with his very brave decision to make the new trains one class. Much of the research behind that decision actually took place here in this studio. When we asked the question the research groups said, 'OK, if you are aiming to give one class of travel, that will be Standard Class, won't it?' If this was the previous regime, then that kind of cynical response might be justified. However, this is under new management and we are actually going to position it somewhere in between the two but definitely nearer first class. The reason for that is the length of the journey: if you are going from London to Birmingham you are going to be in that seat for about two hours. There is an interesting anecdote about this. When the seats for this project were being discussed, the word 'comfort' was not in the specification. It just did not exist in a railway specification. Fire performance, smoke, toxicity and all sorts of mechanical stuff was there, but the word 'comfort' wasn't! So we had to categorise seats by ourselves, by whether it was a 'forty-minute seat', a 'two-hour seat', a 'three-hour' seat. We categorised seats in quite a different way because we were coming at it from the passenger's point of view.

The research tells us that of the top five things that the customers feel most strongly about, four of them are to do with seats. So the seat is, without doubt, the single most important thing on the train. The financial directors of railway businesses think in a slightly different way though! When they see a three-car train they want to know how many seats are on it because that's how they determine their ticket price. You can't work that way when you are trying to design an Inter-City product. An Inter-City product has got to have certain things about it that make it Inter-City. On a bay, it's the seat pitch and I can tell you that a Chiltern seat pitch is 1,860mm because that is indelibly printed on my brain! It is an acceptable seat pitch to most Chiltern travellers, although you would rule out unusually large people because you can't design something that suits absolutely everybody. Also, naturally, 50 per cent of passengers are female and some may not be able to reach the floor when in the same seat, which is more uncomfortable. So it is always a compromise. Our percentile ranges are the 5th to the 95th percentile. However, it is biased and the reason for that is very simple: that you have to have something that works for everybody. One of the other direct results of the research was the decision to have two different designs of seat in each carriage. This was also prompted by the fact that Chiltern at that time had an extremely 'high percentile' managing director in Shooter who really found it quite uncomfortable sitting on the seats with sculpted headrests because they hit him in the middle of his back! Having these two types of seats means that people have a choice, and that is something that had never been asked for before.

The focus groups and the rail user groups were all asked to travel on Chiltern services to test two seat types. These were the best designs we could get hold of, so we put them on to an existing Chiltern train and made sure these people used them. One amusing incident was that when we had the focus groups meeting here, Turner wanted to attend. We said 'No, because your presence would influence the proceedings!' We eventually agreed he could come in if he sat quietly and acted as an assistant. To his credit he did and at the end of it he announced who he was to everybody, and on a couple of occasions had to field some pretty direct questioning. With due respect to Turner, he didn't speak out of turn and I actually think he learned quite a lot, not least about us.

The qualitative research on car users in the study was structured to provide consumer input to the product design. Three qualitative focus groups were selected, one group of First Class West Coast passengers, another group of Standard Class West Coast passengers and one group of car users for business trips to London, typically drivers of BMW 3 Series or high-spec. Mondeo-type cars. Very often these people would be involved with small- and medium-sized enterprises, for whom 'value for money' was important. All groups were a mix of male and female. Prior to attending the groups, all respondents were asked to travel on a Chiltern service to London to test two types of seats. The focus groups were all provided with stimulus material in the form of computer-generated images of a range of vehicle interior arrangements along with swatches of fabric and materials, to encourage consumer reactions.

The rail users perceived rail as the natural choice for journeys to central London, although for many other destinations, including the outskirts of London, the car was often the first choice. Those regularly travelling first class on the West Coast Main Line volunteered that they chose first because it offered privacy, a cooked breakfast, space and comfort and, not least, their business was paying the fare! A typical quote was: 'Our head office is in Central London in which case I use the train. If it is on the periphery of London then I would drive.'

Car users said their choice was often dictated by the need to convey equipment; they felt rail was expensive and unreliable and they often enjoyed free parking. However, they did not reject rail completely and confirmed that cars also have their disadvantages. They would like to have a choice, recognising that rail offered both relaxation as well as the opportunity to work. All respondents believed that rail could provide the best option for travel to Central London. To make it attractive, however, factors that would need to be in place included:

- a comfortable seat with adequate leg and shoulder room within a warm stylish environment
- sufficient personal space for work and comfort (tables were perceived as important)
- a clean, reliable service
- some form of catering with the emphasis on quality rather than quantity
- the overall cost needed to be reasonable, although this was less a concern to those who regularly travelled first class

When respondents were questioned about Chiltern, many were either unaware or vague about it, with little knowledge of Chiltern's route, termini, cost or journey time. When those who did use Chiltern were questioned, they felt Marylebone was potentially a strong asset and Solihull was a good alternative to Birmingham International, not least because of parking problems at the latter. There was no particular preference between Birmingham Snow Hill and New Street. The current service (Class 165s with many stops) was not considered appropriate for the journey length; it had more the feel of a commuter, rather than an Inter-City, service.

At this stage, the respondents were introduced to Chiltern's new service propositions with new one-class trains and improved journey times. There was general approval, although the first class respondents were less convinced. Neither were the first class travellers especially sensitive to the projected ticket prices. Nevertheless, overall the respondents were looking for value for money and there was prolonged discussion over the new seats and the classic trade-off between comfort versus cost. Some stated that the comfort level would have to be higher to make the product value for money: 'I want a bargain. £40 sounds good but if it takes longer, if you make me uncomfortable then Inter-City West Coast starts to look good'.

The preferred interior was that chosen for the new Class 168 trains. Correspondents particularly liked the glass screen dividers, the warm inviting look suggesting comfort without appearing ostentatious: 'It looks a bit more expensive, it looks a bit more classy'. The carpeting was particularly welcomed and the tables were felt to be a very important feature with the proposed mix of bay and in-line seating seen as appropriate although prolonged discussion indicated it was difficult to find the right balance.

There was a general expression among the correspondents that the exterior of the new trains was a secondary consideration. However, there was a recognition that the exterior can communicate specific values to do with a sense of speed, cleanliness and service differentiation. In particular, the train front emerged as a key design factor and it was commented that the rather flat front of the Clubmans conveyed the feel of a slow stopping train not a high speed service. When it came to choosing a name for this new class of train, revival of the Blue Pullman name was felt to be inappropriate and oversell, Midlander was felt to be too geographically specific, while Chiltern 100 was not understood, being confused with a local radio station or cigarettes (anything except a parliamentary sinecure apparently!). 'Clubman' was felt to strike the right balance.

An interesting comment made on catering was: 'If you can offer me at-seat catering, I will travel with Chiltern purely and simply because when I go with Virgin, and I get on at Birmingham International, I queue for my coffee and breakfast bun and by the time I've done all this, we're past Coventry and someone has taken my seat. In other words, my choice on Virgin is do I sit or do I eat!'

One of the strongest remarks out of any research we have done was: 'If you can give me Marks and Spencer quality food, a good cup of coffee and a good breakfast bun, I don't care what I pay for it, I'd rather have an extra ten minutes in bed!' Now if you put that together with the earlier comment, you have got the motivation for the Chiltern Railways catering philosophy. It's very simple. The other thing, and this is where Cath Procter has had a major input, is the engendered feeling of 'family-ness', that people care and want to look after you. The people in any railway company who operate the trolley service do not usually rate highly within the company's hierarchy, yet from the customer's point of view they are very important. Like any railway company, Chiltern has a fair turnover of staff, but passengers do get to know them quite well and consequently, these guys do a really important job and Cath knows and respects that. I think one of the things that happens on Chiltern, and it's done by careful management not by luck, is that the people at the 'coalface', the catering and booking office staff, the people talking to the customers, are very, very good.

By understanding the customer we have to come up with the things our client doesn't yet know about. Customer's expectations are always shifting and our main competitor is the car. Cars will never disappear; they will be with us for ever because they are so versatile and flexible. However, they are the second biggest business on the planet after armaments, and railways will always have to compete with them, and unfortunately the railways are not the third biggest business on the planet! So, railways have to compete with the car, but with none of the funding and resources, and therefore really do have to punch harder than their weight. Design can help with this and is probably one of the most underused resources commercially anywhere. Britain is not really different from anywhere else but the value of design truly can make a significant difference to anything, whether it is a bucket, a bowl or a train. If you get the design right, the product should walk off the shelf! There is a great comment here from Oxford Research, December 1999, after the Clubmans had been in service a couple of years:

> Although not a particular focus of this research, it is clear that the Clubman trains are very well rated by both commuters and business passengers alike for their seating, comfort and spaciousness. As such it recommends that these Class 168s should therefore become the template for any new and refurbished train designs.

So what this research is telling us is 'you've got this right guys, don't go changing it! Make the old ones the same'. Well, you can't really make an old one the same as a new one but when we started work on the refurbishment of the old Class 165s we took the family values from the Clubman, put them into the Class 165s but with a 3+2 seating layout, and we have put 'Chiltern-ness' into the old trains.

Regarding external livery, Shooter made it clear he didn't want to waste money repainting existing 165 trains. So if everyone else painted their trains new colours, Shooter would be quite happy for his to stay the same because no other trains would look the same anyway! Actually, Turner gave us quite a firm steer on this based upon the existing Network SouthEast combination of red, white and blue:

> Look, we are like British Airways really, we might run on steel wheels but those are the kind of service values we want. We go through the heartland of commuter territory, Beaconsfield, all those kind of areas, we've got to appeal to those kind of customers and therefore the livery should take that into account. So you can take those kind of core values, the 'Britishness,' the national colours of red, white and blue in that kind of way.

Using groups again we researched various liveries and a clear favourite emerged. Of course, it had to sit next to the old Class 165s that weren't being changed at that time, so the two are complementary. We took the direction which said: 'They can't be the same, so let's put them all comfortably together'. This now even applies to the 'Bubble Car' that runs between Princes Risborough and Aylesbury, strange device though it is. Again, that is a good example of how these guys think. They needed to liberate a Class 165 unit for refurbishment so they put this old unit back into service and made a feature of it! It shows what can be done with a bit of intelligence and imagination.

After being told to get 240 seats onto a three-car train, after two weeks we came back and told Turner we couldn't do it. We explained that his customers had said how long the seat pitch needs to be, and with the train length being 'X' we could therefore only give you 200 seats. That's it! We put the design proposals very quickly into train plans and sent them to Turner. Then we had our first meeting with Shooter who was clearly not happy with this. We said, 'look, this is clearly not what you guys expected, we've not been able to fulfil the brief; we can put 240 seats in if you want, but you don't really need us to do that because that's simple maths, and we can help you with the colour and trim and all that, but if you want us to do a job of work and get it right, you've got to lose forty seats! But if that's what you want to do, and you want to go for 240, here's the work, we're not going to charge you for it.' They clearly thought about it and quickly came back to us and said 'OK! Go along with it.' Turner had clearly fought the corner for us and I think that must have been a fairly formative experience because Shooter had obviously built a business case around 240 seats. It was very difficult to lose 20 per cent of his seats just like that!

A little while ago we were travelling to London with Shooter on one of Virgin's new Voyagers and he actually said to us, 'I think the most important thing we did was to listen to you guys, because I know now we have got it right.' At that time he was pointing to all the things that disappointed him about the Voyager and we added a few of our own. OK, it was all a bit of mutual back-slapping but it was also an acknowledgement that our advice was right. However, the relationship between seats and windows is also a fairly important one for rail users and the fact that you sit down and are confronted with a foot-wide pillar for the rest of your journey is not good, and some of those trains do go on very long journeys. I am not going to comment on the work of others because I don't know the constraints that the design and development team worked on, but I do know that they built them in a bit of a hurry. Incidentally, something that came out of our research was that people hate listening to other people's phone calls, so in the 168s the screens are there to cut down the noise and compartmentalise it into discrete spaces but without compromising on visual security for female travellers which is important, particularly on late night trains.

For the habitual car user, our research clearly emphasised the importance of 'choice', along with the ability to use your time more wisely. There is quite a sizeable business community in Birmingham associated with accountancy, law and finance and one does now see quite a few people travelling between Birmingham and London using their laptops to work on the train, which confirmed our recognition of the importance of deliberately designing a high percentage of seats with tables, with the carriages split into three zones by the door positions. The doors were determined by Shooter and his colleagues who decided that was the best way to get people on and off the trains quickly, endorsed by their experience with the old 165s. The middle part of an individual vehicle is treated almost like an office space: four seats with a table right the way through. Then, at the end of the vehicle, there are more seats in line but with a table so one of the seats can be inverted backwards. The benefit of this is that if the seat is used without the padded headrest then taller people can accommodate themselves at the vehicle ends. Regular users will get to know where they prefer to travel on the vehicle. Four people would not, without some negotiation, find it possible to work together but two people sitting diametrically opposite would be comfortable.

On the emotional side, the red, white and blue theme carries on inside the vehicle. There are deeper, richer reds and darker blues so we are using the vehicles as an opportunity for three-dimensional branding. It's not a very strong or loud proposition but it reinforces what I would call 'Chiltern-ness'. This is important, especially when Chiltern trains are standing alongside those of other companies people can still identify the product and understand what values will be found in the vehicle. They know it will be comfortable, spacious, well appointed, safe, reassuring, and all of the other things that make Chiltern trains 'Chiltern'. Now the same things have been done on the refurbished 165s as well.

Another major Chiltern project was Warwick Parkway. We were brought in deliberately because of our previous work on the trains and when we first got our design direction for a half-timbered railway station, some wondered if we were going to put up Ann Hathaway's cottage! The station building is oak and when it has weathered naturally it will go silver grey. We took what we thought were the values from the customers on the train side and transferred them to the built environment as well, so Warwick Parkway is unashamedly modern with the main feature there being the car park. There were also severe planning issues on the site, including an SSI, and the embankment is very high so any station lighting is going to be very visible from the nearby village which raised quite a few planning objections. The lift towers were introduced to avoid disabled persons having to climb up quarter of a mile ramps, the galvanised finishes reduce maintenance to a minimum, so our knowledge of the customer all feeds in.

The first 168s were effectively prototype trains and there were enormous teething problems with them. But in retrospect, everyone now realises that you can't make a train that quickly and make it work straight out of the box. I remember when I first went up to Derby to Adtranz, we found ourselves standing in a derelict shed! We were assured that it would very quickly be a train production line, and so it was. Sir Richard Morris was correct when he said we paid the price of being first. That applies to the design perspective as well, being first is expensive. Being second probably loses you some market share but it is the more pragmatic approach. Thank God Mr Brunel didn't think like that!

There were times when things got a bit tense. Once we had got this design specification together and the contract was awarded to Bombardier, or Adtranz as they then were, we had to manage the design process. The design guys at Adtranz do a very difficult job well but don't have the freedom or the customer knowledge we have. They are controlled by their engineers who are designing these trains to a price. When we started, we were not exactly made to feel welcome, but together with Andy Hamilton, Chiltern's train fleet manager at the time, and the research groups, we picked our way through it. The best maxim I gave to Hamilton was 'Don't sign off anything individually, we will sign off lumps instead', in other words, don't sign off a carpet or a seat, we will sign off a whole seat bay as a piece. Then we will sign off the ceiling and the rest of it. We don't sign off the passenger information systems until we can be assured everyone can see them. So, it was a mixture of design, ergonomics, common sense and train engineering and I think we worked well alongside Hamilton. We were also the interface between the commercial and marketing side of Chiltern and their engineering side so we moved between the depot at Aylesbury and the marketing team which then was basically Turner and Proctor and colleagues. Sometimes there were issues but at the end you have to come to a good workmanlike conclusion for the benefit of getting the thing built.

Design is very much like a stepping stone process, crossing a wet patch. You are trying to get from A to B by the most direct approach but sometimes you have to know when to stop and go back and start again. Examples of this are often simple things such as the trolleys on this train. The floor falls at the inter-car connections so the trolleys bump and fall down. The people pushing them find it very difficult and they jam perfectly so they have to have a run at it and it smashes into the vehicle; a lot of damage is inflicted by the trolleys, mainly because the engineers at Adtranz/Bombardier did not appreciate the need for a level floor. Details like this are very important so the next generation of vehicles have a level floor throughout.

Trains also have to look purposeful. Remember some of those earlier comments? Part of the motivation of trying to get people out of a car and onto a train is that it's got to look purposeful and it has to look reassuring. If it's supposed to be fast, why does it look like a house brick? In the overall scheme of things of course it means absolutely nothing, but to the customer it is an emotional driver.

We were taught to think laterally like this when I did my original design course and we were encouraged to be almost anarchic in our thinking. My tutor, Stuart Osborne, would play all twenty of us at chess at the same time – twenty chess sets – and we never beat him! Another tutor, Peter Burden, really taught us to think: we never talked about design, we talked about politics and philosophy, amongst other things and he really taught us to think about design in the sense that it is not at all about drawing, it's about harnessing the raw emotion from the customer, and that is what we do now.

Neil Bates

(Creative Design continue to work with Chiltern and its sister companies.)

CHAPTER 23

WARWICK PARKWAY:THE TRANSPORT PLANNER'S STORY

Peter Barnett

My birthplace, Ross-on-Wye, lost its trains well before the Beeching era and before being given the brief for railways in Warwickshire in 1991 I had no direct experience of them. I had trained and worked as a lawyer (buying a bus company) before joining Warwickshire County Council in 1989. I became a member of the Chartered Institute of Transport and with rail privatisation on the horizons, I was given the railway brief. In the event, it proved fortuitous. Warwick Parkway turned out to be the highlight of my transport planning career; I was lucky to front a council team whose commitment was crucial to its success.

Warwick Parkway originated in the early 1990s as a result of meetings between Midlands shire counties and Centro (the West Midlands PTE) to look at various strategic park and ride schemes. One location, the Budbrooke area, close to the A46 and M40, was looked at in more detail in the Stratford-upon-Avon area rail study. With the great unknown of the upcoming privatisation things went quiet until a series of meetings in 1994/95 chaired by Warwick District Council involving us, Central Trains, Railtrack and Chiltern Railways on the shortage of car parking space at Leamington Spa and Warwick stations. Gradually the earlier idea of relieving the pressures at the existing stations by building a new station – by then known as Warwick Parkway – became an option. Chiltern were usually represented at these meetings by Adrian Shooter or Alex Turner or sometimes both of them – a powerful combination indeed! I remember Alex Turner at one of these sessions, with all the impatience of someone from the private sector trying to work through the Byzantine nature of public sector decision-making saying: 'Instead of talking, why can't we just do something?' People who know Alex will realise it was actually much more explicit!

After another of these meetings, Adrian Shooter came up to me and said, 'Let's build Warwick Parkway!' The following morning at 9 a.m., Adrian telephoned me from the proposed site which he'd been to inspect for himself. 'Peter, I'm getting very excited about this!' He really was 'up for it.' That was December 1996. I had already discussed it with my boss, John Deegan, Director of Planning, Transport & Economic Strategy and his deputy, Dave Scott, and they were very positive. John canvassed a number of the leading county councillors and they were also supportive. Now things really got going. We started detailed work with our consultants Steer Davies Gleave and received a lot of help from Chiltern on a bid which was submitted to the Department of Environment, Transport and the Regions in July 1997.

At this point we started to appreciate one of the key factors in getting Warwick Parkway built was the very special culture that Adrian had created at Chiltern. Early on, Chiltern had embraced the new world of privatisation and made very real efforts to engage business outside the rail industry. Adrian realised that if the railways were to grow, in the process reversing their long decline, then they needed to demonstrate clearly how valuable they were and could no longer assume their mere existence was justification enough. To support this he has an uncanny skill in positioning Chiltern in exactly the right place, at exactly the right time, doing exactly the right things.

A good example is Warwick Parkway, which had just opened when the Chiltern franchise renewal was starting to be reviewed. It would be a very strange SRA that would subsequently have said: 'Well, we know you've just invested in a new station, you achieved a huge increase in rail passengers, you've broken the mould and you've made real progress, but sorry, no franchise for you!'

This willingness to engage on other people's terms and agendas has now become second nature to Chiltern. For example, at their Passenger Board meetings, the company puts forward its proposals (particularly timetables) for scrutiny by approximately twenty-five–thirty representatives of user groups, local authorities and statutory consultees, along with three people from Chiltern. There are a lot of organisations in the rail industry that would still have cultural difficulties with this approach.

This culture made working with Chiltern people very easy and early on we realised that the secret of getting things done was for each party to get on with what they did best. As the different phases of the project progressed, the lead roles swapped back and forth between Warwickshire County Council people and the Chiltern/Laing team represented largely by Mark Beckett, Alan Coakley and Andy Harmer. The Chiltern perspective is told by Andy Harmer in 'The Project Manager's Story'.

The rail industry can be a bit of a 'closed shop' and slightly wary of outsiders. But like the US cavalry when going to deal with the Apaches, we needed native scouts who knew the lay of the land! Chiltern's role in this respect, as insiders, was crucial at a number of stages in the project. A good example, although quite minor, was an occasion when I phoned Adrian on the afternoon before a committee meeting saying I needed written confirmation, preferably from Railtrack, of a technical issue that was going to be raised at the meeting. Within an hour there was a fax on my desk from the Railtrack Midlands Zone director which 'boxed-off' the issue unequivocally. If I ever need proof of the adage that, 'It's not what you know, but who you know' I had it that afternoon!

Before Christmas 1997 we had an encouraging response from the Department of Transport to our initial bid for Warwick Parkway, suggesting we re-submit the following year. Then in the spring of 1998 the Government announced that, in future, funding for rail schemes would come from the Strategic Rail Authority. To this day, I still wonder if anyone had told the SRA because one had the sense that this was a ball that had been pitched but no one had caught it! However, being a resubmission, we thought it might be judged under the old rules, so we continued. More encouragement followed in December, but we were then told we should really be asking the SRA. It always reminded me of the children's story 'The Billy Goats Gruff'! At the time we felt we'd been shunted into a siding – you should judge for yourselves whether a pun is intended. Then Chiltern Railways took the lead and submitted a bid to the SRA. Much of the work for this was done by Mark Beckett. This was then refused on the basis that the scheme was too commercial, which seemed a very odd decision. Things then went quiet for a while until Adrian Shooter decided Warwick Parkway was going to happen after all and proposed a commercial venture by Chiltern/M40 Trains and Warwickshire County Council. We were able to pull together £1.15 million of funding to purchase the land on which the car parks and station building are built and M40 Trains now has a forty-year lease. The rest of our funds went towards bus services, cycle and walking routes, traffic calming and other access improvements.

At the same time as the bids to the DETR, the regulations required Warwickshire County Council, as an interested party, to submit a planning application for the scheme. In view of this, we found it helpful early on to make the officers who were undertaking the planning authority role discrete from me and my colleagues acting as scheme promoters. I think this worked out quite well because at meetings I was able to say, 'Look, I'm the developer. My instructions are to get the station built. I'll tell you all about it and consider changes, but if you want advice on the planning issues you will need to speak to the Planning Officer.' It seemed to work well because people were clear about the responsibilities and it allowed me to be more consistent, rather than combining two roles at once.

The opposition to Warwick Parkway mainly came from the nearby villages of Hampton Magna and Budbrooke. It was a slightly unfortunate coincidence – at least from the developer's perspective – that we went public on the plans just as a District Council election was announced in that particular ward. We knew local people would be understandably concerned as they were the most likely to be affected, but the local election created a series of opportunities for the opposition. So it reached a greater crescendo than it might have done otherwise, but that's the way a healthy democracy works! There were a number of public meetings and a running debate in the press and radio and television coverage. Our approach to the opposition was that there were a lot of benefits in the scheme but we had an open mind on making changes, as long as the essential elements of the scheme remained. I lost count of the times I said, 'I know you don't like the scheme, but help me make you as happy with it as you can be.' Throughout, the opposition was well organised, robust and unceasing, but never personal and I'm sure we responded more sympathetically to that approach. At the same time, we were getting a lot of support from the wider area, including members of the public, rail user groups, many of our own county councillors, the local MP, the Rail Passengers Committee for the Midlands, regional bodies, business interests, Centro, Birmingham City Council and even some residents of Hampton Magna and Budbrooke!

Shortly after the election, Warwick District Council asked the Government Office to 'call in' the application for determination by the Secretary of State for Transport, as the site was in the green belt. The District Council was perfectly entitled to do this, but it did surprise us, as we thought what we were proposing to do clearly matched the criteria for new rail stations in the Warwick District Local Plan.

At the public enquiry, our role changed and we became an equal party with the other participants. This is because the inspector and, through him, the Secretary of State decides whether planning permission is granted. When we got to the public inquiry, we had a very good turnout from the scheme supporters who were at least equal in number to those against the scheme. Adrian Shooter had also brought on board the CBI and Birmingham Chamber of Commerce. Amongst the very active opponents of the scheme at the inquiry was the county councillor representing Budbrooke and Hampton Magna at that time, and local district councillors and parish councillors supported by a substantial body of nearby residents.

We had a good, confident and robust case to put to the inspector. That's not to say we were entirely right and the opponents entirely wrong, but we had a good strategy in transport planning terms with Warwick Parkway accommodating growth and reducing car use. Not just as a strategic station for long-distance travellers, or as a local station for Hampton Magna, but also in relation to Warwick and Leamington Spa. Warwick station has limited capacity to increase car parking. Leamington Spa also has limited capacity and what capacity there was, we felt, would be linked to growth on cross-country services which would not be calling at Warwick Parkway. We therefore saw Warwick Parkway as a station for northbound passengers arriving by car. We felt we needed to be very clear about the balance between spare car park capacity, where more was needed, who would be using it and how much it would cost. We also needed to balance additional urban traffic resulting from larger car parks at town centre stations with the increased traffic on country roads if we extended the car parks at existing rural stations.

I recall that the opposition mainly focussed on the effect of the new station on the local landscape and environment, the increase in traffic on nearby roads, whether there was a demand for the new station and a possible threat to Warwick station if current users transferred to Warwick Parkway. These were all very reasonable points which we clearly couldn't deny, but the real debate was about the degree to which these things might happen. At one point, we did have the arguments coming at us that, on the one hand we shouldn't be building the station because there was no demand, but equally it would create traffic chaos! There has been much demand but there hasn't been traffic chaos. We did undertake some major changes to the local highway network – traffic signals and junction improvements – which have made them more efficient. Any perceived threat to Warwick station has to be viewed in the context of the phenomenal growth in demand, generally, at all three stations. Warwick station attracts large numbers of 'green' travellers (i.e. cyclists and pedestrians) and I was surprised that passenger counts in 2004 showed that on a weekday Warwick attracts a similar number of passengers to Warwick Parkway.

Six months after the enquiry, the Secretary of State granted planning permission. Transport policy issues and need for strategic park and rides appear to have been the biggest influences on the decision. Clearly, it is strategic but when stations cost £4–5 million you can't afford to be too selective and purist. It was always our approach that if there is demand, we don't turn it away. So Warwick Parkway has created a local facility for Hampton Magna and parts of Warwick a walk away on the other side of the A46 – roughly 50 per cent of users are from this catchment area. It's also playing a key role in the district-wide rail strategy by easing car park pressures at Leamington Spa and Warwick stations. It's near the M40 and is used by Warwickshire residents to go to London and Birmingham – about 80 per cent of weekday passengers come from Warwickshire. It's also functioning as a destination for a small number of commuters and, from my own observation, as a meeting point to travel on for business or family visiting. It has encouraged people to use the train instead of the car – about 30 per cent of passengers were new to rail – and contributed to reducing traffic on the roads by an average annual figure of 2.5 million vehicle kilometres.

Throughout the whole history of the scheme, Warwickshire County Council had felt supported by Chiltern's total commitment and their willingness, in terms of financial investment, not only 'to talk the talk', but also to 'walk the walk'! Three things about the story which stand out most are the culture of Chiltern Railways to get things done, the very practical relationship that developed between the County Council and Chiltern through their 'people' and, overall, the phenomenal success of the scheme.

Peter Barnett

CHAPTER 24

WARWICK PARKWAY: THE PROJECT MANAGER'S STORY

Andy Harmer

Warwick Parkway opened on 8 October 2000. Soon after, the Hatfield crash on 17 October 2000 – the third serious crash in three years – imposed the biggest strain to date on Britain's newly privatised railways. Unlike many other operators, Chiltern made the brave decision not to impose an emergency timetable and Warwick Parkway began to fill up with people from the start and one could see from early on that it was going to be a success. That was the key test.

Winding back to 1998 my first memory was meeting with Adrian Shooter in his office. You could tell he was huge even though he was seated. He met me for about fifteen seconds and I turned to go out of the door he said 'Andy.' I turned around again and all he said, looking over the top of his rather intimidating half-moon glasses was 'You must deliver!'

All I could think to reply with at the time was 'OK!', but I was thinking 'Help!' The lasting impression was 'I'd better get on with it!' The business side of things was well developed but the physical engineering side of it was lagging behind. Also, there were seventeen reserved matters dropping out of the public enquiry process, many to do with environmental factors. This is why there is some slightly unique engineering at Warwick Parkway.

I picked up those shards and started to work really hard on two work streams, one with the County Council in getting their highway ideas married with the station ideas, as well as the reserved matters. The other work stream was dealing with Network Rail and getting them ready to help us deliver.

The whole theory of Warwick Parkway was that it would be 'third-party delivered', which basically meant that Network Rail, or Railtrack as it was then, took a backseat role. They protected their asset, the actual infrastructure, while you go on and do the actual building. The advantage to us was that we kept control of the contracts, the budget, the programme and they were left doing what they do very well which is watching and checking that we are not damaging any part of their asset. That has become the standard model for the way we deliver. The platform and new bridge at Princes Risborough were the test bed for actually building Warwick Parkway. Third-party enhancement, as it is known now, is well recognised and other train operators are starting to use it. Part of the business I'm involved in is selling those skills and many other new ideas were kicked off by Warwick Parkway.

In 1998 I only had four or five months to pull the strands together, to put a specification together for the station, to get our responses to those reserved planning matters all worked out, to get contract documents sorted, and tender and carrying on, whilst ensuring the highway work was keeping up with the station work. The basic split was clever – while there was an important advantage to Warwickshire County Council in us delivering the rail element, they dealt with things that were much more within their control; that was the general idea of the split responsibilities. They procured the land through compulsory purchase order (CPO), looked after highway elements and subsidised the bus services for five years. It was a very good mix. Latterly we came to realise that it was the only real way of doing it within a joint public-private venture.

Laing Rail/Chiltern's commitment to find the balance of the investment and also to take on the railway risk was crucial. The railway industry would never have given Warwickshire County Council a fixed figure to supply them with a station and as a result they were able to get it through their committees. What we did was to take out the construction risk that leads to uncertainty with their costings; as far as the public sector was concerned, their contribution was fixed. In this model, both Warwickshire County Council and M40 Trains retain a forty-year interest – the council benefit and the ownership stays in the right place.

The site was on a six- to seven-metre-high embankment with the usual slopes, which meant they would need to be stabilised before we could put a station on it. There is quite a longitudinal gradient on the railway at the Hatton Bank site and in steam days the HMRI would probably have had a problem with the whole concept but modern train braking meant they were happy with that gradient. Although we had to play around with the track a little we didn't have to do anything major to make the station work apart from repositioning some signals.

Among those 'reserved matters' that had to be dealt with was surface water and drainage. The site is cut by a stream, which also takes the overflow from the nearby Grand Union Canal when there is flooding. The stream flows through quite a large ditch but we weren't able to discharge the surface water directly into it because of the flood problem. The solution we arrived at was to put a 2ft-thick blanket of stone directly underneath the car park area, which stores all the rain water from the surface. The water then runs through the porous blocks that are used for the actual surface of parking bays, through a membrane which wraps top and bottom around the stone, rather like a huge duvet cover, which in turn cleans the water which flows through into the stream. Even in the 'once in a hundred year' rainfall the delivery to the stream will still only be two litres per second. It works very well.

One of the most fascinating problems we faced at Warwick Parkway was the potential difficulty in gaining access over or through the embankment to get to the Birmingham-bound platform. The original concept in early 1998 was to jack a subway through the embankment at enormous cost. However, we noticed that there was a cattle creep, built by the original railway engineers in 1851. Although it looked ropey, it was only superficial so we checked the suitability by boring in with a rotary drill to check that the construction was stable and it proved to be so; the foundations were deep enough and the whole structural integrity was fine. Accordingly, we proposed to Railtrack and their consultants that we used the original. The main difficulty was that it was three inches too narrow for the regulations in the 'Group Standards', so Railtrack and the consultants said it would be impossible to use, and would have to jack the subway through!

The estimated 'back of an envelope' figure for this would have been about a million pounds. In reality, once you'd worked it out in normal rail fashion it would have spiralled up to one and a half million pounds with twenty-four-hour closure of the line and various other operations.

So we thanked Railtrack and their consultant for their help and thought, well, actually this is just nonsense! So we went to HMRI and gained their approval, we went to the Rail Regulator and gained his approval, checked with the planners and gained their approval and obtained planning permission as well. We checked with the SRA who said it was fine once we had gone through the process of explaining that this was not Euston, it was a parkway station and passengers would generally move in one direction through the cattle creep and that from a disabled point of view, the flows would be uniflow, the station was wide enough for a wheelchair, and we were supplying lifts as well – it was all DDA compliant. Then we went back to Railtrack and said 'Thanks, but the authorities who actually make the decisions have said it is fine so this is what we are going to do!' Gaining permission was pivotal for the project; otherwise all the sums would have been thrown out of kilter.

That result was the combination of us understanding the rail industry and using common sense. So the one to one and a half million pounds became £25,000, which was the cost of pointing up the brickwork and putting in under-lights.

That story is also a nice example of the modern affliction of people being disempowered and pointing at 'standards' and forgetting to think! A legacy of Hatfield, perhaps? The pressure to get approval quickly forced me to pick this up very early on because I couldn't go out to tender without being clear whether we were simply pointing brickwork or jacking up a subway; it would have been a nonsense.

Interestingly enough, at that stage and throughout the job, Peter Barnett and I had a monthly meeting with Budbrooke Parish Council and we were very lucky that the chairman was a very challenging lady, a former county councillor, who was firm but fair. Peter and I spent a great deal of time making sure they were happy with what we were doing and dealing with many of the reserve matters. We worked very hard with them and it worked really well. It was tough, as you can imagine, and the cattle creep was one example of selling an idea by explaining a problem and getting them to suggest the solution! So a lot of what happened was borne of their ideas.

When it came to talking to the extremely busy top brass at Chiltern about the actual station and what they wanted, they said 'A station!' When I asked what they wanted it to look like they replied 'detail, detail, detail, that's what your here for!'

So I had to ponder that – I had a few parameters: Adrian in particular was very useful because he gave me an idea of the way he wanted it to feel, how he saw its purpose and so on. To some extent its shape and form was dictated by the planning. But then I decided to ask the staff that actually run and manage the stations and went around into every ticket office that Chiltern had along the line, some of which were quite Dickensian. It's quite unbelievable when you get behind the scenes! All the ticket office staff and me, spread up and down the line, designed that station, including how the access should work an where the CCTV cameras should be. The station was designed around the needs of the public and staff, and that's why it works. That's why the offices are air-conditioned, that's why the mess rooms are the right size, that's why the CCTV and security room is right, and that's why the ticket windows and the seating arrangements work. We picked up every detail, even where the staff like to have the tickets to hand so they are happy. We realised it was going to act like a parkway, which meant the facilities needed to be quick and easy with coffee and papers. Most users will not use it as a destination station and will pass through, which is why we have the retail area designed the way it is.

We also used Creative Design, the firm who had designed the new Clubman trains, to help design the station. Neil Bates is an entrepreneur, an expert in ergonomics who designs everything from kitchen gadgets to the plastic shield that goes between the carriages on a tube train. Spending some time with Neil gets you into the thought process of the end user – Neil had already worked with me on the design for the shelters for the Midland Metro. At Warwick Parkway, we dealt with one of the reserved planning matters by cladding the thing in oak. You will also notice the use of galvanised steel components. Because the site is overlooked by some houses from Budbrooke, galvanised metal work disappears against a British skyline and contrasts with the bright blue of the Mediterranean – it suits winter and bright summer skies and it just disappears.

One thing that makes me laugh looking back was when we came to put up the lift house and the contractor that put it up forgot to put a little joint in the oak cladding for expansion. Obviously, wood moves and balances itself in its environment but here the planks started popping off, which wasn't the best advert when we started! Naturally, there was a big thing in the local press saying how it was falling apart before it opened!

We managed to pull all this together in four or five months, and get a contract let out. As usual, everything happened at the last possible minute. Two reputable firms, Mott MacDonald and Birse

Rail, in joint venture, won the design and build for Warwick Parkway. We explained in the tender that as much as possible of the station would be built away from the operational railway and as a result, taking price to one side, they came up with the best way of building it and much of it was delivered on a low loader like a giant Meccano set. For the platforms they came up with a very innovative system which meant you could get all the foundations in well away from the rail and then cantilever out the platforms very quickly. That idea has now been developed further and marketed to other contractors.

So come the day of the race, the signing of the construction contract and the land availability happened simultaneously. Many people have remarked on how quickly the station went up. In reality we designed it in two and a half months and built it in five months. Work started in early January and the station opened on 8 October, which was the target time to tie in with the winter timetable.

One of the reasons everything went so well was that we treated everyone as if they were part of one large team, Warwickshire County Council, Railtrack and us. I was very flattered at the end of it when Ian Scholey, the Chief Engineer for Railtrack Midland Zone phoned Adrian up to tell him it had gone very well and was particularly happy because everyone who had been involved from their side on Warwick Parkway had had a thoroughly good time and thoroughly enjoyed it as a project.

We did have our occasional fraught moments with Railtrack as happens. Hilariously, we had had a sign put up at the end of the platform because of a slight quirk in the signalling there, and this sign ended up in the critical path of the programme. This was because they, Railtrack, had decided that it needed to be approved by a signal-sighting committee. A signal-sighting committee is a collection of ten people drawn from various parts of the industry, the TOC, Railtrack themselves, drivers, etc. who come and sight the position of signals prior to them being put up. They have a really important function. The problem from our point of view was that it usually takes six to twelve months to get hold of a signal-sighting committee because only certain people are qualified to do it! Railtrack decided that with the platforms already built, the sign made and was about to be planted, we would need a sighting committee for the sign. I nearly keeled over. People I was talking to said it would take a minimum of six months. I kept thinking 'How is Adrian going to take this? A delay in the opening for six months from October to the following March all because of a sign!'

So I rang up Niamh Partridge, the project manager at Railtrack, about 4 p.m., and said we really needed to get the sign up the following day. This was very important because we were running a series of test trains to see how it worked. I impressed the urgency upon her. The reply I expected was either 'You don't need a signal-sighting committee,' or simply to work out some fudge until one could be pinned down. Niamh said she was still working on it. When I came in the following morning at 7 a.m., fifteen people headed up by a chap called Tom McNaughton, who was Railtrack's head of signal sighting, were all parked in their cars waiting to sight this sign. They'd had a cancellation late that afternoon, so rather than doing something important at Euston they were up at Warwick Parkway looking at a sign. The whole thing took about three minutes and then they went off again. It was another example of how you can work it out together but some of the restrictive practices were very funny. It's about personalities really and it worked very well.

The other thing we had to work through on the construction was the fuel strike in August 2000. After about a week and a half the contractor had run out of fuel and of course they use red diesel because they are not road vehicles. When they were down to their last barrel there was a quick phone call to the rail depot at Aylesbury and the next day eighteen barrels of diesel arrived to keep us going through that fortnight.

If you read back in the press at that time, there was an earthquake in the UK. It was 5.7 on the Richter scale, which is major-ish and certainly big for the UK. I was reading in the newspaper the other day that its epicentre was Budbrooke! What was even sillier was we realised when they gave the time of the earthquake we had all been sitting in a meeting in the site hut and we had felt it shaking. One or two of the contractors who had been out late the night before put it down to too much high jinks and lack of sleep and I'd thought it was traffic passing by on the road. However, despite fuel strikes and earthquakes we did finally triumph and it opened on 8 October. At the last minute it was largely down to Chiltern being so supportive and getting the new staff all trained up in good time to do all the things they need to do to run it.

One other thing was checking the platforms with the HMRI. There is a quirk at the platforms because of the gradient, which meant we had to be doubly sure when we were measuring the distance from the step of the train to the step of the platform. The HMRI weren't very sure about it. It's always very impressive when you can say 'I'll get a train', get on the radio and suddenly an eight-car train turns up! This is an important thing about Chiltern, they have kept the skill of operation and they have kept the piece of jigsaw that has been cut off from every other part of the industry due to the way it was split up. As a result you can do things much more quickly; the knowledge is still there. Combined with the investment knowledge of Laing it made a powerful cocktail.

Adrian Shooter was, of course, a frequent visitor. He'd turn up, march off, poke around and inspect those bits you didn't want him to see – the bits you'd hidden. Of course he's a mechanical engineer who calls us civil engineers concrete farmers. Nobody has yet had the spine to call him a grease monkey! You'd get the look over the top of the glasses occasionally, which is when he bears down on you, saying 'It will be ready!' In fact, most of the documentation, and there was quite a lot of statutory documentation, was signed off at Adrian's house. I'd drive over about 9.30 p.m. and he would sign it and question me at the table and I'd leave and come back with another lot a few months later. He was checking that I was not putting his standing within the rail industry in any sort of danger.

Final approval to open came via a fax from the HMRI who were wonderful throughout. They were understanding and practical and that's partly because we involved them from the beginning. We dealt with a chap of the old school who has probably retired now. He said he'd enjoyed the project as well and because he trusted us we got given a longer leash to some extent. Actually, in approval terms it was almost something of a world record to get from first inspection to approval and about a fortnight later be ready to open for operation. That had to be faxed to us and then faxed straight through to Adrian. The following Sunday the first trains started stopping. Since then it has gone from strength to strength. It has a huge walk in rate, Budbrooke has definitely benefited, it is managed twenty-four hours of the day and we have not imported a crime problem and now we are looking at further extending the car park in the near future.

Andy Harmer

(Warwick Parkway car park has been subsequently extended.)

CHAPTER 25

STILL GOING FORWARD!

Adrian Shooter

Since my childhood, I have always thought it would be a rather nice idea to run a railway. I didn't quite see how that was going to happen since the railways were nationalised at the time, which by the way I always thought was a big mistake. Before Chiltern, I had many years on British Rail, doing all sorts of exciting, interesting and varied jobs which I suppose really were things that gave me some of the background and training that would be useful on Chiltern. Such things, for example, as the time in the early 1970s when I was based in an office in Broad Street in Birmingham as a Carriage and Wagon inspector. The telephone would ring and the voice might say, there are ten wagons derailed in Round Oak steelworks (this doesn't exist any more, it's now the site of the Merry Hill shopping centre). So I would go out in my little yellow Morris 1000 van, drive round to Round Oak steelworks and there would be a Carriage and Wagon exam-iner and one or two people, and they would ask me what was to be done. I'd tell them and decide which wagons were safe to be moved after they had been re-railed and which weren't.

A little later on I moved to Bletchley to look after all the electric trains that worked the Euston commuter service and also to maintain all the 'first generation' diesel trains which then ran the Chiltern service. That was the first time I got to know a little about what we now call Chiltern Railways; in fact there are still some people who work for me now who worked for me in those days, about ten of them, mostly working in the maintenance depot at Aylesbury, so it is nice to have that little bit of continuity.

I discovered in those days that Chiltern was always a piece of forgotten railway. It had been the Great Central Railway but had then it had been taken over by the LNER. However, the LNER didn't really want it, they had more important railways running out of King's Cross and Liverpool Street. It then became Western Region, but the Western Region didn't really want it because they went out of Paddington. When I took it over it had become London Midland Region but the London Midland Region then, as now, was always focusssed on the West Coast Main Line and when they had a few spare minutes they would think about the Midland Main Line out of St Pancras. That left absolutely nothing for Marylebone. In fact, so much so that in those days, thirty years ago, the control office at Euston Division, which was supposed to control lines out of Marylebone, had a desk for the Marylebone section – the GC section it was called – which as often as not was unmanned. So there was no controller for it and the control was exercised by the train crew supervisor, whose office was next to my maintenance supervisor at Marylebone depot, where the flats are now on the right of the train as you go out of the station. I often used to sit with the supervisor, talk and listen to him ring up the signalman at Seer Green to ask if he would work twelve hours, please; that sort of thing. That was how the railway was run.

I then went to work in all sorts of other places but formed the view that actually the railway, in common with many other service industries, is one where often your most junior staff are working directly facing the customer with no supervision whatsoever. This is completely unlike, for example, a factory where many people would be supervised. So I am not a supporter of complicated Human Resource ideas, theories and all sorts of nonsense like that. I'm a simple engineer and it seems to me that one is only going to make a success of a railway if you've got a proper plan, but most importantly, that the people on the ground want to do a good job. If they don't, then it's not going to happen. So, accepting that you must recruit the right people in the first place, it's then about creating the right vision for them of the sort of business that you would like to see. And it's about giving them the right wherewithal to do it, the right tools, the right training, the right encouragement that they can really buy in to. The workers are the essential part of the business and you have to get them to believe in it because – it's true – they really are part of the business. For too many years on British Rail, and elsewhere, there was the attitude that the management has to have a monopoly of information – information is power – and even worse, communicating with the staff through the trade unions.

I've always taken the view that people in this industry are part of a team. As the leader of the team it's obvious that I don't have to be there all the time, I often do not work at weekends and the railway still carries on! But what is really important is that members of the team carry on and do their work, whether that is selling tickets, sweeping platforms or driving trains. The important thing is that those people know what to do because we have trained them and they actually want to do it because they identify with that business. That's what I've set out to do.

Just as an aside, a while ago I had a day on the Irish railways with Dick Fearn and Steve Murphy and what I observed there was a railway which for many years hadn't been invested in properly. The railways in the UK were not properly invested in but the Irish railways were far worse. Theirs were so bad that trains were de-railing because the track was falling to bits. They even had a train – the driver of which I met, by the way – fall through a bridge into a river. But now, some money is going into it and there is some future vision. While the railway has a long way to go, you can just see it starting to turn the corner. There was a buzz about it, an excitement, from everyone I met, which is really good and what I've wanted to encourage – to get people to see they can do things. And do you know what? You often find that they can!

As a result of all I've mentioned, I saw the privatisation of the railways as a big opportunity, an individual and local initiative to really make the railway something that is valuable to the community, because there is no point in having a railway unless it is valuable to the community and actually serves to improve the economic well being of that community.

I saw the opportunity to take a railway away from the sterile yoke of a nationalised industry. I certainly think that some of the detailed ways the railways were privatised, the very heavy legalistic framework, was wrong. I am disappointed that there are still some people who advocate that and we still have to change it. We have to make it work together with other parts of the rail industry, but what I have noted is that far too many people over the last few years assume that you cannot do things; in fact there is a large number of people, not in Chiltern I am pleased to say, whose mission seems to be to stop things getting done! By contrast, at Chiltern we have discovered that everyone has the potential for a lot of ability.

In 1994, in the beginning of the year before we took over the running of the business, we put together a vision of what this railway would be like. Fifteen years on, we have delivered much of that but we've still got plenty to do: although we had a vision of where we wanted the railway to go, I didn't have much idea of how we were going to do it! I wasn't actually sure we could do it! But I hope I didn't let anyone see that. The truth of the matter is, of course, that if you chart out the direction you want to go in and why you want to go there then you can get everybody pointing in the same direction and looking for opportunity. Sometimes you pick things up opportunistically. In fact, that was true of both of the track doubling schemes, the one that was started in 1997 doubling from Princes Risborough to Bicester and later on when we went from Bicester to Aynho. Both those were things we had planned without the faintest idea of how we were going to deliver them, but we spotted a window of opportunity in each case and leapt through it with the result that you see.

Adrian Shooter, December 2009

BIBLIOGRAPHY

Primary Sources

Personal interviews with:
Adrian Shooter, Company Chairman and first Managing Director, Chiltern Railways
Owen Edgington, Operations Director 1994–2000
Alex Turner, Director of Sales and Marketing, 1994–2000
Tony Allen, Finance Director, Chiltern Railways, 1994 onwards
Julie Abbott, Merryl Potts, Lesley Knight, PAs to Adrian Shooter 1994 onwards
Cath Proctor, Retail Manager, Director of Sales and Marketing, Managing Director 1994–2007
Steve Murphy, Specifications Manager, General Manager, Managing Director 1994–2004 and
    Managing Director, LOROL from 2007
Sir Richard Morris, the first Chairman of M40 Trains
Chris Green, Non-executive Director Network Rail, formerly Managing Director, British
    Railways Network SouthEast
Richard Fearn, Chief Operating Officer, Iarnrod Eireann, formerly Zonal Director, Railtrack
    Midlands
John Nelson, formerly Managing Director, British Railways Network SouthEast
David Newell, Driver and School Safety Officer, Chiltern Railways
Mick Benson, former Driver and School Safety Officer, Chiltern Railways
Donald Wilson, formerly Station Master, Marylebone station
Neil Bates, Director, Creative Design, Leamington Spa
Peter Barnett, Planning Officer, Warwickshire County Council
Andy Harmer, Project Manager, Laing Rail
Dan Gregory, Driver, Chiltern Railways
Rob Brighouse, Assistant Managing Director, LOROL, formerly Project Director, Chiltern
    Railways
Mark Beckett, formerly Business Development Director, Chiltern Railways
Graham Cross, Business Development Director, Chiltern Railways
Allan Dare, Strategic Development Manager, Chiltern Railways
Ian Baxter, General Manager North, Chiltern Railways
Chiltern Railways company archives, including minutes of Board meetings and documentation
    relating to company projects and franchise proposals.

'The British Government and the Railways', text of talk given by Prof. G.L. Huxley to the Irish
    Railway Record Society, Heuston station, Dublin, 28 November 2002

Secondary Sources:

For anyone wishing to follow the story of the building of this Joint Line in more depth, recommended reading would include:

Volume 3 of George Dow's *Great Central*, Ian Allen, 1959

Volume 2 of MacDermot's classic three-volume *History of the Great Western Railway*, revised by C.R. Clinker and reprinted by Ian Allan 1982

The list of excellent books on both the Great Central and Great Western Railways is too extensive to list here but a very thoroughly researched and detailed study of the GW GC Joint Line is *The Great Western and Great Central Joint Railway*, Oakwood Press, Second Revised Edition 2006, by Stanley C. Jenkins.

Another very enjoyable read is *The Final Link* by Dennis Edwards and Roy Pigram in 1982, published by Midas Books of Tunbridge Wells; a wealth of historical photographs is complemented by evocative text and captions. Sadly, it has long been out of print but copies can be borrowed through inter-library loan or occasionally purchased second-hand.

For students of Snow Hill's history, the book *Birmingham Snow Hill* by Ian Baxter and Richard Harper (both Chiltern employees) is recommended.

Derek Harrison's affectionate video production *Birmingham's Snow Hill Station*, issued by Heritage Video.

Kellett, J.R., *The Impact of Railways on Victorian Cities*, Routledge and Keegan Paul, 1969

Freiburg, Kevin and Jackie, *Nuts* (the story of South West Airlines).

Reed, Albin J., *Met & GC Joint Line; an Observers Notes 1948–1968*

INDEX